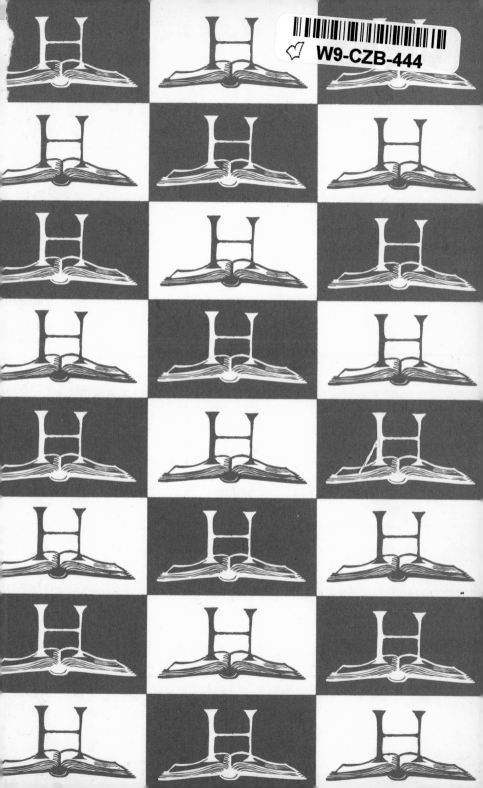
W9-CZB-444

APPROACHES TO WRITING

APPROACHES TO WRITING

by Paul Horgan

WITH A PROVISIONAL BIBLIOGRAPHY

OF THE AUTHOR'S WORK

BY JAMES KRAFT

ST. JOSEPH'S UNIVERSITY STX
PS3515.H78Z5 1973
Approaches to writing.

3 9353 00103 1515

PS
3515
.H 78
Z 5
1973

192424

FARRAR, STRAUS AND GIROUX ❧ NEW YORK

Copyright © 1968, 1973 by Paul Horgan
Bibliography copyright © 1973 by James Kraft
All rights reserved
Library of Congress catalog card number: 72-97083
ISBN 0-374-10569-3
First printing, 1973
Published simultaneously in Canada by
Doubleday Canada Ltd., Toronto
Printed in the United States of America

for
D. *and* R. *and* B.

CONTENTS

FOREWORD

A PRACTITIONER of an art and a craft who engages in theory and shop-talk takes a risk. Some readers will see him as aspiring to set down laws, to others he will seem to be telling them much of what they already know, and of still others he may invite flat contradiction. None of this can be helped, for the art of writing—a certain primary proficiency in rhetoric itself being taken for granted—embraces as many acceptable ways as there are writers who are gifted with a sense of language and an imaginative control of form.

My intention is not to make laws for anyone else in a dogmatic tone, or to be exclusive or arbitrary in my observations, but only to reflect my own view of the pursuit by which I make my living. Most of my reflections and notes were written for my own interest. If they should have broader application, of use to others, so much the better.

My book is composed of three parts of my own authorship, and one part by a valued and gifted colleague, who has done me the honor of compiling in provisional form a record of my published work which—whether youthfully inexpert or more maturely practiced—covers a period of half a century.

In Part One, I try to comment on those inquiries most commonly directed to writers. In Part Two I raid my notebooks of many years to illustrate the quantity and variety of raw materials—idea and detail—such as a writer draws on to make a finished work. In Part Three I remember the early efforts of someone who now seems to me almost a stranger, though he is, in all his eager conceit and naïve experimental energy, only my young self, whose initial attempts may hold lessons for others as they did for me. Part Four, as a supplement, consists of James Kraft's bibliography of my work.

I have made frequent reference to the writer as an "artist," and to his calling as "art." This is not meant as a pretentious flourish. I realize that such words, with repetition, might become tiresome to informally minded readers and writers of today; but if they consider that the word "art" includes reference to a technical or professional skill, as well as to high aesthetic achievement; and that the "artist" bears close relation to the "craftsman," they may accept my usage.

At the same time, I do not move from my belief that there is not much use in discussion of writing unless every claim is made for it as a fine art, calling for sustained study in every approach to it. I do not of course mean to imply any assumptions about my own status as a writer. My intention is my concern; my achievement, whatever it may be, the concern of others.

Much of what follows has been rehearsed, with gratifying response, in my work with university students. Because my exchanges with student writers were valuable to me, I give here, by way of grateful acknowledgment, the names of those whose work with me played a part in various of my formulations for this book. They were, in recent years at Wesleyan University, Jon Appleby, John Barlow, Thomas Corcoran, Melvin Dixon, Jib Fowles, Mark Fuller, Robert S. Knox, Lawrence Littell, Wallace Meissner, Francis Pawlowski, Earl G. Rhodes, and Charles Skrief; and during a semester at Saybrook College, Yale, Robert Masland and Robert Metzger.

I thank my editor, Robert Giroux, for strong guidance and advice, and I am grateful, also, for help in various forms to Peter and Henriette Wyeth Hurd (it was Mrs Hurd who once posed the general idea of note 113, page 66, while referring to her own work as a painter), F. D. Reeve, Mr Kraft, Donald Berke, Tania Senff, and to Ellen D'Oench, who read the galley proofs.

Portions of Part One appeared originally in *Reflection* (Wesleyan University), and in *Intellectual Digest*. A selection from the notes in Part Two formed the framework of a lecture I gave at the Aspen Institute for Humanistic Studies in 1971, and still another selection was published in PROSE NUMBER SEVEN. Other extracts came into lectures of mine at Southern Methodist University in 1972 and at East College, Wesleyan, and Saybrook College, Yale, in 1973.

P.H.

Middletown, Connecticut—
San Patricio, New Mexico
1968–1973

Rubens worked with things that he knew, and therefore without disquietude to his thoughts.

✷ ✷ ✷

It is probable that God alone, or a god, can say about things only what should be said about them.

✷ ✷ ✷

Method cannot govern everything; it leads everybody up to a certain point.

—*The Journal of Eugène Delacroix,* translated by Walter Pach

Experience is not what happens to a man; it is what a man does with what happens to him. It is a gift for dealing with the accidents of existence, not the accidents themselves. By a happy dispensation of nature, the poet [the writer, the maker] generally possesses the gift of experience in conjunction with that of expression. What he says so well is therefore intrinsically of value.

—Aldous Huxley, in *Texts and Pretexts*

It takes all kinds to make a world, or even to make a national literature.

—Max Beerbohm, in *Lytton Strachey* (*The Rede Lecture of 1943*)

PART ONE
TALKING SHOP

✻

i

THE ACT OF WRITING is common or special depending on what we mean to communicate by it. The very commonness sometimes makes the special purpose of writing seem too easy, too accessible, somehow too familiar in its nature, to demand particular effort. It is often said of people who "write such good letters" that they ought to write a book. But the spontaneous self is a quite different self from that of the literary maker. This is not to say that collections of letters by gifted amateurs are not valuable—but as a rule the best collections of letters are by those who have cultivated expression for its own sake in a professional context.

Regrettably, many people who want to write, without having a very clear idea of why or how, or being subject to an inner imperative which will not be denied, often think that there are a few tricks to be learned which will insure successful careers. But there are no tricks; only an abiding respect for the instrument of language, and a love for the problems of literary form for their own sakes to transform the writer of common matter

[3]

into the writer of a work of art. This respect and this love and whatever talent they may represent can become effective only if they are enclosed by the writer's discipline.

Let us look at certain of its aspects.

ii

Any writer who undertakes to make his living by writing—and most writers hope to do so—must depend first of all on discipline in the simplest details as well as in the most exalted intentions of his task. This discipline he must earn for himself, for it is he, himself, and no one else, who will have to maintain it throughout all his professional life.

The first act of the writer's discipline is to serve an apprenticeship with humility and willingness to learn. I have taught certain aspects of my craft in various universities and I have never ceased being amazed at the almost unanimous expectation of students (graduate and undergraduate alike) who look to the publication and the success of the very first works they commit to paper. You cannot help being touched at their confidence, for you observe it through the eyes of memory. It is the blithe energy of youth working in their imaginations, rehearsing fame, wealth, and position; and you wish you could let their hopes be fulfilled, you wish this until—again through a backward glance—you recall that acceptance of devoted labor at the humblest details of learning how to write, no matter how long it may have to take, will be the best thing you could wish for them.

For not only will they study the technical details of their craft in this period of apprenticeship—they will learn also the habit of work without which the writer will never be more than an amateur. It is this habit of work which will bring the writer to his work table every day at the same hour, there to do about the same amount of work according to the capacity which experience tells him is naturally his. It is this habit of work which will teach him to learn the hazardous and challenging necessity of keeping alive in his imagination a work of art which may take many months or even years to complete.

And here—since this discussion has entered the workroom— here is a parenthesis of shop-talk: a certain work of my own—a very long book—took ten years to complete. Every time I came to work on it day after day and year after year I had to draw conviction anew from the overall conception which brought me to respond to the project in the first place.

But there was more to this impulse of the initial conception than subject matter. One can be much taken by an idea, a place, a theme, and consider that it would make a fine book; but unless one's interest in the first notion is brought to projected form, it is probable that the idea itself will go the way of the hundreds of vague concepts which drift in and out of the writer's imagination without getting anywhere. There must then be two elements to insure the validity of a work about to be carried out. First, the initial impulse must have that inner sense of its plausibility which can defend itself against the myriad doubts which will assail it: those from within—the writer's own second thoughts and self-questionings; and those from without —those stray assaults upon the writer's current idea which come, all unintended in their damage, from chance remarks made by someone which can startle the writer with their applicability to his new subject, which might make it seem commonplace or unoriginal, or a line accidentally come upon in the writer's current reading which may seem to make trivial, or vulgar, or old hat, what he is nurturing in his thought. Many a potential work has been wrecked for the writer by just such idle hazards. In its inceptive stages a book is a vulnerable affair; it can be saved from extinction only if as early as possible it begins to find, in the writer's imagination, the precisely appropriate form for its fulfillment.

Once that is glimpsed, even incompletely, the subject, the idea, is safe; for in this combination of material and form, the initial energy of the work is preserved, and even through many years of composition, the writer can return daily to the next quota of his work with renewed belief in what he is doing. He is saved by the fact that the idea which first moved him is already enclosed in the design which he has found for its final presentation. If in the long haul the material momentarily seems to him to wear thin, or to have become over-familiar, he has now the beauty of his imagined form to renew him; and contemplating the whole each day as he works on the part, he is freshly empowered. Such has been my general experience. It has been this concern for a complete projection of the form, combined with the discipline of daily work, which has sustained me throughout.

Finally it is in this habit of work where the writer finds his real sense of achievement—his very content. He is really himself, at his best, only when he is observing his rhythm of work. If a day, or a week, or a month must go by when he does not work, he may think he is having a well-deserved rest; but he cannot deceive himself. He feels obscurely guilty. And if his period of inaction results from a temporary inability to work— if he is in one of those vacant phases between large productions

—then he is in a state of acute misery, and he feels that hardly anything equals his joy when the day comes that will see him at work again.

iii

Once he achieves a certain command of expression the writer must yield himself wholly to it. Illustrations are plentiful out of the lives of literary men. The yielding is not always agreeable; indeed, it is often tyrannical. Listen to Charles Dickens saying no to an importunate lady:

"I hold my inventive capacity on the stern condition that it master my whole life, often have complete possession of me, make its own demands upon me, and sometimes, for months together, put everything else away from me . . . All this I can hardly expect you to understand—or the restlessness and waywardness of an author's mind . . . it is impossible to command one's self to any stipulated and set disposal of five minutes . . . the mere consciousness of an engagement will sometimes worry a whole day. These are the penalties paid for writing books. Whoever is devoted to an art must be content to deliver himself wholly up to it. I am grieved if you suspect me of not wanting to see you, but I can't help it; I must go my way whether or no."

Some work with a stream-like fluency, some must dig every inch of the way. Flaubert wrote to George Sand,

"You don't know what it is to stay a whole day with your head in your hands trying to squeeze your unfortunate brain so as to find a word. Ideas come very easily with you, incessantly,

[7]

like a stream. With me it is a tiny thread of water. Hard labor at art is necessary for me before obtaining a waterfall. Ah! I certainly know the agonies of style."

The point is, easy or hard, the work was done, and done only by incessant application. Lord Byron found in his daily rounds —and those of the night as well—many uses for his rich temperament; but no matter how wasteful or satiating his amusements—thinking of these, one imagines him observing with a certain detachment his own acts of indulgence even at their most inventive and extreme—early morning usually found him with a clear head and a dashing pen producing fluent stretches of his current canto. Even so, he once wrote in a letter, "I think composition a great pain."

Our prime expositor of the writer's workshop is, of course, Anthony Trollope, who was perhaps the first author to discuss his working habits extensively. Even he, that master of a lucidity which seems as inevitably produced as daylight itself, even Trollope knew the writer's troubling moments. Talking of the preparation of a novel, he says,

"There are some hours of agonizing doubt, almost of despair —so at least it has been with me,—or perhaps some days."

But then at full charge he must go ahead—and here is where his earned discipline came to bear. It enabled him to set forth a daily solution of his problems of composition. At moments, he seems, measured against our later tempo of communication, to explain the progressive affairs of his novel a little too fully, and to comment upon them for our benefit where we would just as soon make up our own responses. Still, his story always has forward movement, and structurally nothing is excessive. Let him tell us in his cool way how he managed:

"According to the circumstances of the time," he says, "I

have allotted myself so many pages a week. The average number has been about 40. It has been placed as low as 20, and has risen to 112. And as a page is an ambiguous term, my page has been made to contain 250 words; and as words, if not watched, will have a tendency to straggle, I have had every word counted as I went. In the bargains I have made with publishers I have—not, of course, with their knowledge, but in my own mind,—undertaken always to supply them with so many words, and I have never put a book out of hand short of the number by a single word. I may also say"—and here speaks the true literary economist—"I may also say that the excess has been very small. I have prided myself on completing my work exactly within the proposed dimensions."

Does all this sound easy? Listen to Trollope once more, as he speaks of the very texture of style which must in the end determine the quality of a literary work—"A good and lucid style," he calls it:

"Without much labour, no writer will achieve such a style. He has very much to learn: and, when he has learned that much, he has to acquire the habit of using what he has learned with ease. But all this must be learned and acquired,—not while he is writing that which shall please, but long before. . . ."

iv

These famous observations can be reinforced by the experience of many other writers. I include my own, for what it may be worth. Shop-talk has its interest in relation to any craft—H. L. Mencken once said that he found anyone interesting who was talking shop, in whatever occupation—and it seems well to begin with it here, before aspiring to reflections on some of the higher principles of the art of writing.

My own habit brings me to my work table at about the same time every day—roughly at half-past nine. But actually, the working day starts earlier. It starts on awakening, with a sort of bated breath in the thought, if I may put it so. Preparation for the morning's task gets under way in an induced and protected absent-mindedness, as if to allow the work in progress to come clear gradually, so that its daily rebirth suffers no jarring collisions with immediate reality, but establishes its own inner reality from which it will draw conviction. Absurd as it may appear to those in other vocations, any contact with a serious distraction, or obligation elsewhere, may, at this daily moment, disturb a balance already delicate. A phone call is a minor catastrophe and a knock on the door a potential disaster. Until the day's work can actually begin, a frowning selfishness protects all the ingredients of plan, design, idea, and will; and when it begins, it flows forth, if the day is a good one, or it struggles forth, if it is a poor one; but strangely, later, it is difficult to tell by the evidence which pages came from fluent work and which from halting. It is again a reflection of the discipline we have mentioned.

Not everyone counts his pages against his clock like Trollope, who said he worked to produce two hundred fifty words every fifteen minutes in his allotted work time. This was an efficiency almost unearthly, and so was the calm technical virtuosity with which, according to the legend, he immediately began another novel when he finished his current one with a quarter of an hour to spare. A similar story was told of George Sand by the Goncourts in their *Journal*. "One day she finished a novel at one o'clock in the morning . . . and immediately started another"—this quoted from Louis Kronenberger's *The Pleasure of Their Company.*

Experience tells the writer what his proper daily quota of work should be. If he exceeds it at all appreciably, he probably finds that the quality of his work falls off, and that in consequence he must rewrite more than usual to make up for it. If the form of a piece of writing has been solved beforehand, rewriting of great blocks of work does not often follow. But revision word by word and sentence does follow, for me, not once, but many times, each for different values.

These embrace precision in meaning; as between two words of equal precision, choice, then, of that one which calls up image more vividly through color or sound or association; rhythm, the great key to readability, in small units of the text, such as the phrase and the sentence, rhythm in larger developments of the text, such as the paragraph and the chapter, and finally rhythm in the work as a whole. In fiction, revision pursues each character of the story in a separate reading to feel the consistency, the living presence of each. Another complete revision is devoted to an examination to improve atmosphere and background. And so on, paying attention to each of the elements, including the humble mechanics, which combine to make a finished work—such matters as simple correctness in spelling, punctuation, grammar, syntax—the technical fabric by which the rich English language, with all its tributaries, is given its primary power of communication.

The writings of many students would lead us to think such matters too trivial to engage the personal attention of a serious author. It is the rare student, even in the graduate school of letters, who can spell, or even cares about it, or who understands the purposes of punctuation, or dissects the sentence in order to learn its anatomy, or even rereads at least once to correct typographic errors. When I have begged students to spare me their acts of simple carelessness, and have assured them that an editor will pay little attention to a typescript whose early pages reveal a sustained illiteracy, I have been told many times by them that "the editor would put in the spelling, punctuation, et cetera."

And yet such elements as I speak of are the structural fibers of writing, and not to respect them for their own sake, and to love their purposes and their powers, is to have little promise as a writer. What would we think of a music student who disdained to master the C major scale because he preferred to think only about playing whole sonatas even with a thousand wrong notes? The illustration is not too fanciful, as any instructor in advanced writing can testify.

One day a university senior whose work I'd been reading, though he was not in my seminar, assured me when I objected to his generally faulty spelling that he had "no interest in spelling." In a story he gave me a week later, about an ambush in the Vietnam War (he had never been in Vietnam), he described how Vietcong *gorillas,* heavily armed and cleverly camouflaged, broke through the jungle wall to massacre a U.S. unit. I showed him the passage and asked him what was wrong with it. He found nothing wrong with it.

"Do you want to be understood in your writing? Do you want it to say exactly what you mean?" I asked.

"Certainly," he said with patience.

"But you have no interest in spelling?"

"No."

"But you don't think there are occasions when meaning depends on spelling?"

"I don't know how there could be," he sighed, now impatiently.

"Then," I said, unable to resist a cheap luxury, "you want me to believe that a band of large anthropoid apes, wearing helmets camouflaged with leafy branches, and carrying firearms in their hands, the knuckles of which are calloused from their use as aids to self-propulsion, staged the ambush?"

"Of course not," he exclaimed with indignation. "That isn't what I wrote."

I handed him the dictionary.

"Yes, it is. Look it up."

v

Leaving the comforts of the concrete, through which we have made common connection with the art and discipline of writing, we come to other aspects of the subject. We must go beyond pencil boxes, as it were, and look beyond the page, to consider the writer's vision of life which all simple and habitual mechanics of writing exist to serve. His worth as a writer will generally rest upon several values. He will be a writer worth reading according as:

—His vision is his own.

—His vision has the power to move him to repeated revelations of it, in whatever medium—poetry, the drama, history, the novel, the story, philosophy: in other words, if his vision is the source of abundance.

—His vision has a life-giving quality by which the minds and hearts of others are moved to their own expression in thought or act.

—His vision embraces a power of design so that not only the content but also the form of his work will create a second life out of his materials.

—His vision is complete: if it goes past the fashion of his time and the bias of current social or psychological attitude to seek out and share a sense of life's unity, and to find in it that memory of creation which seems to contain and account for all things.

Where many literary workers fall short of making significant works is just here where spiritual values come into focus in a point of view.

The spiritual life of the modern world becomes increasingly fragmented. Modern writers, like everybody else, long for a nourishing explanation of life; but all too many turn to recent and fugitive systems of imposing orderly but incomplete designs upon life's teeming and elusive variety, and in doing so, seem to lose the deepest well of their inspiration, and that is, their artistic intuition. Much of our writing now seems to be propped up by a foundation of earnest observation rather than by one of intuitive identity, or all-enduring, communion, with mankind.

To put it in another way, let us say that we are living in the age of the case history. Much of this century's admired creative literature seems to arise from clinical observation and theory rather than from a stroke of knowledge in heart and soul.

Clinical understanding of behavior has value in the practice of therapy. But literature and therapy have quite distinctly separate purposes, and to confuse the two is fatal for the artist.

Behavioral patterns of society and individuals have been taken by many modern artists as their points of understanding and departure for works of writing. But these are the stuff of science, which goes after truth and demonstrates it in a way wholly different from the artist's way. Diagnosis is not the same thing as creation and systematic comprehension does not equal empathy. Many writers in our day have lost their true way by following a clinical approach to their commentaries upon life. They seem to promise verisimilitude, and to guarantee accuracy. They show us how people act—according to theoretical interpretations, which more often rob the represented figure of unique character than endow him with it. Some works emerging under such a system may have seemed to a wide public to open new ways of expression to the writer. I think it possible that the authors of such works have been intellectually seduced by psychological speculativeness where they would better have been occupied with discovering their own best capacities to enter into human nature in their own unique terms as artists.

For systems of theoretical interpretation and schools of psychology change with the generations, and so offer only means of expression without a future. The very vocabularies of these systems are subject to fugitive fashion, as you may readily recognize if you tune in on the jargon of earlier systems of the study of life which were once taken seriously and considered perdurable. That which is based on an obedient and earnest observance of fashion must change too, and there we say good-bye to the wholeness of vision which we ask of our interpreters.

When aesthetic perception approaches its fullest realization, it is akin to man's religious vision, whatever form this may take. Faith is a supernatural grace. The true poet, the true artist, is he who knows without learning. His own intuition is closer to the supernatural than to any prevailing temper of the pluralistic and pragmatic modern culture.

vi

In workaday terms, a writer does not learn much of value if he reads other writers for the sake of repeating what they did, only modifying it with his own current intention. Many apprentices, of whom one example is studied in the third section of this book, go from model to model until sure of themselves. There is no great harm in this if their imitations are performed as exercises, or flourishes of taste. But if imitations are more unconscious than aware, or worse, if meant to be commercially expedient, it is probable that little of interest will result.

Even among professionally accepted writers we see today a sort of hunger for a format tried by success, a point of view, a common target for satire or indignation or reduction to absurdity or (most profitable of commodities) ingenious violence, so that publishers may claim virtues for a given work on the basis of its similarity to another recent triumph—only, of course, the claim is made in terms of surpassing the earlier model. An anxious vulgarity is here revealed.

What is gained from reading other writers comes indirectly, especially those of the past whose work has added to the body of the world's enduring culture. Nobody today seriously wants to write a Dickensian novel, or one like those of Balzac, or the Russians, or the Edwardians; but in reading them, and countless others, the writer enters into a climate where he feels accounted for; a stream of imagined life in which his own efforts of inventing a reality can seem to be worthwhile; and a realm of expression where his own ventures into language whose style he partly inherits and partly refreshes seem to him justifiable for their own sakes. He recognizes that literacy does not descend upon him spontaneously. It must be earned. In addition to reading, habitually literate conversation plays a great part in the process.

The matter of reading, not to imitate, but to gain stimulus for one's own work, was beautifully hit off by Maurice Baring. In his *An Outline of Russian Literature* he said, "It frequently happens that when a poet is deeply struck by the work of another poet he feels a desire to write something himself, but something different." Reading as experience joins the outward events of his life in a natural union which is productive. Those outward events which seem to come to him indirectly may be the most nourishing of all. Certainly an energetic search for experience as literary material has its pitfalls, and even its comic side. It is always droll to see on jacket flaps of first novels a description of the young author's "experience." As though to endow him with authority "on many levels" the publishers take care to list everything he has done—"dropped out of high school to work on a Great Lakes steamer as an oiler, hitchhiked to Hollywood where he became an assistant director, spent two years prospecting for gold in Arizona, accompanied a Brazilian jungle expedition as cameraman, taught night classes at the New School for Social Research, underwent psychoanalysis while singing with a rock group in England, wrote film criticism in *The East Village Other* for a year, and is presently living with his second wife and her three children in a converted lighthouse at Point St Albans, Ontario, where he is at work on his second novel."

To go in search of experience is often confused with going in search of ideas to write about. This is to see the matter in reverse. Ideas come in search of the true writer. They throng upon him, and most of the time he does not know where they come from. The best thing he can do about them as they appear is to make notes. He never knows at the moment what may come of them.

vii

Having touched briefly on two general aspects of writing—those concerned with simple mechanics and those approaching the vision of the writer—we might consider for a moment how these matters can be taught or transmitted to students, or indeed, whether they can be.

It is a reward to see a student's style and character begin to show signs of talent. Part of this—and its proportion to the whole—is the student's gradual development of a willingness to stand away and look at himself and his work as critically as though he were framing a judgment of someone else. The first time he can say, and mean it, "That thing I have written is not as good as I'd like," and tell why, he has taken his first step toward independence. It is more or less painful, but if he has other signs of talent, he will admit that the advantages of that condition outweigh the pains of gaining it.

The teacher has to temper his response to the student's offered fragments of himself with recollections of those things he cannot do for the emerging talent, as well as those things he can do.

He cannot decide or affect its essential nature. He cannot change the pace at which it will proceed to its realization. He cannot transmit his own insights as a writer, nor can he supply a set of formulas which will insure success. He cannot condone carelessness or incorrect workmanship in order to encourage originality, which in seeking freshness the student invokes at the expense of one of the two most demanding aspects of prose, which is precision (the other being unimpeded individuality of the imagination). The teacher must tactfully recognize the difference between a vague youthful desire to write and the presence of a genuinely literary sensibility, which will show itself in an awareness of the problems of form—phrase, sentence, paragraph, chapter, the whole work. He will have to risk seeming out of touch with "life" by challenging the power of prevalent influences in thought, style, and point of view. He will take the cautionary position that even the most seriously admired in the new is often the most fugitive in the end—a real danger in the teaching exchange, for it might lose him the student's confidence in the preceptorial authority of the moment, since the immediately contemporary is all the student knows by himself.

Those who in the best spirit of dedication and honest inquiry hope to learn the varied aspects of writing ask, "What, then, can be taught us by those who have made their way in these matters? Where can we look if not to those teachers who have given a lifetime to revealing the nature of literature in the classroom, or to others who have made careers in writing?"

The answer here is twofold.

Primo: The technical mechanics of writing can be taught, and in a pathetically deficient sort of way are taught, from the very first day when the new pencil boxes in school begin to figure in our lives. The way to recognize words, the structure of language, the order of written thought, the expansion of vocabulary, the rhetorical values—these, theoretically, come along grade by grade throughout the primary and secondary

[19]

school years, in degrees of complexity increasing with the gradual development of the pupil. But by the time the student reaches college, and even graduate school, his earlier schooling, and often enough his experience of conversation at home, have failed him—have thrown formidable obstacles across the path which he would follow. By the time he aspires to what is too easily called "creative writing" (it is a phrase we are stuck with through wide and indulgent usage) he should have become so proficient in the mechanics of prose that his teacher is at liberty to devote all attention to the larger, the visionary aspects, if you will, of the student's ability. In sum, the mechanics of writing can be taught, but should be mastered before the young writer aspires to create anything.

Secundo: How about "creative writing," then? Can this be taught? Here we must go carefully in order not to be discouraging, and yet be truthful.

But it must be said that "creative writing," the essential act of literary art, cannot be taught entire. You cannot teach anyone to be an artist. He either is or is not an artist by nature and endowment. You cannot insert talent into anyone else. You can point out infelicities and failures to him, and indicate how he might search for his own way to correct these; but becoming a writer is mostly a matter of continuous work to be done alone throughout whatever apprenticeship may be needed.

But, the student may ask, is this the end for me as I reach for help toward realizing the vocation of writing?

Luckily, to this there is a hopeful reply.

First, your teacher can take you seriously, if you are serious about your work. This answer is more important than it may seem at first glance. All artists, at every stage, but at none more than the first stage, need the confidence which comes from response to their work.

Next—and this is the most sensible justification to be cited in trying at all to teach the writer's art—by intimately studying your work with you, in as great profusion and over as long a time as possible, the committed teacher can help you to discover your unique quality of feeling, your own discernment of life. Once you both find this together, and have it brought clearly before your own eye and into your own ear, it must be left to you to develop for yourself the vision which animates your own particular talent, and the way of expressing it which will be yourself articulate.

viii

I can illustrate this with a satisfying little story.*

For some weeks an obviously gifted young man came to me for regular tutorial sessions to discuss the work he was giving me week by week. He was writing stories, not a novel. There was great intensity about him, he had a mind as interesting as any I had yet known among students, he was deeply serious— he found it difficult for a while to be at ease with me for fear of not seeming serious—and faithfully, week after week, I read all his authors in turn. By this I mean that one week he would give me a story he had prepared after the taciturn manliness of Ernest Hemingway, and the next we would be discussing an-other story, this time so darkly tortuous in involuted rhetoric and construction that William Faulkner was brooding in the

* In this anecdote of actual situations, I present a composite student.

background. Again, I would receive a story so laden with symbolism, narrated in an assumed voice, that it was only a matter of pages until some equivalent or other of a white whale would make its fatal appearance. A week later, and we would seriously talk about newly submitted pages in which someone with a great burden of guilt would relate an elaborately dangerous adventure in which he was found morally wanting, and we would both think of Joseph Conrad (who had a revival in English departments at about the time of which I speak).

I would, of course, point out the crippling reminders and resemblances, but I hope with respect and delicacy, such as must be due to any serious student, but in particular to this one, who was as truculent as he was sensitive, and as talented as he was baffled by what seemed to be admired by those of his generation who read books and talked about them. He did not seem to know that he was the very victim of his models. I knew that he was searching for someone in all his byways along the careers of writers discussed in his earlier college courses, but I felt that no direct reference to this search was yet possible. He would have to confront the fact of it for himself.

One day this student, whom I shall call Jeffrey, slipped a large manila envelope under my door a couple of days ahead of our next appointment. I began to read its contents almost before his footsteps were gone from the stairs of my entryway. I rejoiced. Hemingway, Faulkner, Melville, Conrad, and all the others, were gone. It was a short piece, beautifully observed, of a single incident in an old man's life—the last one, in fact—and everything in it evoked life beyond the limits of the story by detail so well seen and so purely captured that I was happy to see my belief in Jeffrey's talent sustained.

When he came for his next tutorial, I greeted him, we settled into our easy chairs, and I handed him his new manuscript, saying,

"Jeff, will you please read this aloud to me?"

He had good manners, but could not conceal a flare of suspicious irritation.

"Why?" he asked. "Haven't you read it?"

"Oh, yes," I replied, "several times, in fact, but I want to hear you read it."

"Very well, sir"—he took up the pages and began to read, more or less without inflection, but with increasing interest as he went on. When he was done, he put the story down on a little table nearby and lighted a cigarette.

"Thank you," I said. "Now whom does that sound like?"

"I don't understand, sir."

"All right. Does it sound like Mr Hemingway?"

"No . . ."

Or like any of the others, I asked, naming them, and to each he replied, "No."

"Then who?" I insisted, for I believed that I must not make the discovery for him. He must hear himself make it. He looked scowlingly at me for a brief and intense silence, and then with a winning sort of hopeful tentativeness, he smiled, turned his head a trifle away and looked at me sidewise, and said, reluctant to take the risk,

"Well, then, perhaps it sounds like me."

"Exactly like you," I said. There was still a question in his face. I answered it. "And that is very good indeed, and in fact, I have little more to teach you if you now recognize your real literary self. From now on, if you are interested enough, it is up to you to develop further the qualities in this beautiful story, which you are able to identify as your very own. Let me hear you tell me what these are, now—" and we spent an hour at the task. His apprenticeship was entering its last phase. One of my final words of advice to him, as to other students, was to form the habit of keeping notebooks where random observations and reflections, otherwise fugitive, might be stored until those notes whose original vitality survived might be developed, no matter how long afterward.

PART TWO
NOTEBOOK PAGES

I have grouped these excerpts from my notebooks under four headings:

    I. Process
   II. Of the Mode
  III. Glimpses of the Actual
  IV. Behind the Word

Though within each category there is no strict continuity, the nature of the entries seems to me to bring them comfortably together under their respective headings, and to make considerations of a given aspect of writing more coherent.

    Each note has been numbered to make reference more immediate.

I ❦ PROCESS

The notes gathered here generally refer to aspects of writing which relate to technical approaches, and to ideas concerning the elements with which the writer first concerns himself in both the plan and the criticism of his own work—texture, design, the formalities of his craft and the source and treatment of ideas.

§1

Every imaginative production must contain some element of risk.

§2

The great lack in most modern fiction is any sense of inner life and meaning in the characters, apart from the motions they are put through. Numbed by behavior-

[27]

ism in its various forms, we are expert in catching the externals—dialect, accent, exact descriptions of technical actions including the sexual—but a cumulation of these, no matter how copious, all too often adds up to one immense triviality. Imagine Tolstoy without his thought of God, or Maurice Baring without his culture—that sense of a life above and beyond our lives which is the clue to our inmost natures. In life, it is so strong that much of our nobler part is given to an effort to find others with whom to share it. It is the interior life where the real clues to humanity are to be found. The greatest artists, no matter how strongly given to activist energy, have always captured a sense of this in their works of the imagination.

§3

If a writer learns to take measure of his daily capacity for effective work, he will the more readily come to a sense of what is worth putting on paper.

§4

The key to readability is rhythm. The variation of rhythm depends on the urgency of feeling behind the syntax.

§5

The whole meaning of a work can remain inexplicit, while its parts and details are as explicit as daylight. The meaning of the whole remains an open secret.

§6

The popular speech is now vastly influenced by show-business style, exposed on TV, radio, and film, and the off-stage idiom of the public "personalities" associated with them. Hardly anyone can tell of anything without incessant recourse to the stand-up comedian's expression "you know?" The effect on written style will soon follow. The new vulgate will make U.S. obsolete slang seem classical and pure.

§7

Some masterpieces are born of observation; others of intuition. The first will ordinarily tell about the author; the second, about everyone else.

§8

Among critics, teachers, and even writers, there has long been an unresolved quarrel over the question as to which is better, the bare-boned style or the style with a rich and various surface. How can there be a flat rule when the choice must lie between, say, Shakespeare and Racine? Proust and Flaubert? Henry James and Maurice Baring? The power of a particular temperament, fulfilling its expression according to its natural vision, is what determines which style in each case. We should be thankful for great artists of both manners.

§9

Writers often say, truthfully, that they are as much at work away from their desks as in the act of writing itself.

§10

The greatest challenge in writing a long work is to sustain or renew daily, through years, if necessary, the act of imagination with which it began.

§11

The artist should look for form in everything—nature's forms, those of all the arts, those of the performing athlete, in which energy precisely meets need. The bodily tension we see in a great athletic act, even in its brevity, is a good analogy for the need of utmost co-ordination of all the faculties available to the writer when he is at work.

§12

Any act of art undertaken by the artist as a measure of therapy for himself may in the end help him in his difficulties; but it is doubtful that it will result in a work of general value.

§13

I am everyone in my novel. If this were not so, no one in my novel would have a chance to ring true, even as I work to make each character an individual, different from the rest.

§14

All notes, as you jot them down, seem equally exciting and full of potentialities; but—mysteriously—some die, while others live for years, growing organically, with new and beautiful aspects to be added every time you revisit them; and from these, finished works eventually come.

§15

The best literary critic is the one who understands what the author was unable, for one or another reason, to write; and, understanding this, is able the more appreciatively to evaluate what the author was able to achieve.

§16

Systematic psychology is a destructive principle for the writer to proceed from as he works to create character. The artist teaches the psychologist, not the other way round. The writer must be conscious of the danger of the case history.

§17

The writer may "see" internally, but it's no use unless he can also observe as the reader does—that is, on the page.

§18

One should never, before the completion of a work, indulge in spoken synopsis of it. Too much may be lost in the preliminary telling which should go into the writing of it.

§19

The writer should pay attention to what may be seen out of the corner of the eye. The briefest glimpse so seen may become as important in his imagination as a scene or situation or a person long and earnestly regarded full face. The most passing glance at persons, objects, animals, places, may contain abundance of beauty perceived.

§20

No matter how much or how little he may do about it in his actions, an artist falls in love every day—or several times a day—with some person or other aspect of life. The seizure may be a matter only of minutes—but it can be as profound as though it were to mark a lifetime's commitment.

§21

Write as clearly as possible; and in doing so, enclose mystery which is never explained, but which gives life to the whole.

§22

As the painter must love the mineral from which his color is ground, so the writer must love even the separate letters of the alphabet and their many styles of representation in type.

§23

Students struggle to give justification in current intellectual jargon to their emotional discoveries.

§24

Good writing says two things: one, which can be explained; the other, which cannot.

§25

Everything has been said; but not everything has been said superbly, and even if it had been, everything must be said freshly over and over again.

§26

One of the greatest acts of friendship is to lend a book in which you have written your own notes—that harvest which may later be of inestimable value to your own work.

§27

If a writer is honest, he need never worry about "expressing himself." It will happen inevitably. If he sets out to "express himself" at the expense of other values, he will end up writing dishonestly.

§28

Concerning the vocabulary of obscenity—the present lack of reticence in society will impose on the artist the necessity of creating a new fastidiousness and a love of new metaphor. The sexually explicit will early wear itself into a dullness so jaded that the market for even the most permissive styles will disappear. Then the writer will once again turn to what has always been mysterious—not human action in, say, lust, or the view of sex endemic to those such as actors who earn their wages by imitating its gestures and who often end by loosely living these, but those concerns which lie behind actions and often live only in the mind or heart.

§29

No matter what his influences, the writer must release his thoughts in his own vocabulary—not in that of any systematic jargon, e.g., the Marxist vocabulary, which has not enough to do with human nature in its totality, or the Freudian, which has too much to do with only a single human being—Freud himself.

§30

Even in most elementary examples, errors in writing often seem to have a perverse life of their own, and escape the writer time and again as he revises his text.

§31

The writer should be an insatiable reader—not because he may be educated or improved by what he reads, but because something he might read may suggest even by opposites a theme, a detail, a tone, natively his but hitherto lost in the profusions of his more conscious notions.

§32

Not yet knowing that a true book is like no one else's, the young writer hopes that what he has written is like what someone famous has written.

§33

A person without the gift of empathy will never be a true novelist, no matter what other gifts he may possess.

§34

There is a poet in every young novelist who must be transformed before his valid prose work is possible of achievement.

§35

As a literary resource, real suspense has more to do with understanding character than with facility in devising action for its own sake.

§36

An eminent editor of my acquaintance published through another publisher a book of his own. It amused me to note that he behaved exactly like the authors he dealt with in his executive capacity in matters of publicity, reviews, advertising, and the rest. Just as they had done, to his superior impatience, so he now complained, inquired, sulked at the treatment his book was receiving. Actually, it was very well received, with lead reviews full of praise. But it was the one or two adverse notices he talked about, and could not let alone, and he thought his publishers remiss in matters of arranged interviews and sustained advertising of his book.

§37

Ignorance and fakery are not the same, but both can have unhappy effect upon artistic statement. It is well to know as much as possible, but never to pretend to knowledge or experience which does not belong to you. Ignorance may be unfortunate, but it is never vulgar. Fakery always is.

§38

Literature can play host to all the other arts and grow by them. The obverse is not true of any of the others.

§39

How can the negative ever create?

§40

How important for the novelist is a highly developed sense of place, and how rarely is it richly realized. When well done, it compels the reader to supply details in his imagination which are not actually described by the writer.

§41

After long habit, to begin the act of writing is to invite the very flow of ideas, which, until the words are visibly in order, may have seemed stubbornly elusive.

§42

Self-consciousness while planning or writing is fatal. It destroys the natural flow of expression. Here is another prime reason for loving, seeing, using, the objective rather than the subjective world exclusively.

§43

Every true novel is a historical novel.

§44

It is not possible to create the moderately good work without imagining the utmost great.

§45

For the writer, his truth must be present, but remain subliminal. It is the gifted critic who is free to mine the meanings which impelled the artist to create his forms without having planned their symbolic or allegorical significance.

§46

The characteristic of a work of fine art is its capability of development in form. It thus remains an analogy of life. The work of popular art is incapable of this, and is thus merely a note of fugitive comment or mood.

§47

In fiction, the fine meshes of plausible action need constant attention, in the smallest details. It is astonishing how, when absorbed in other values of a story—character, atmosphere, prose style, inner significance—some of the small actualities escape attention. But one must always keep in mind how "if this, then that" must happen. Every detail must mean more than itself. The smallest error in plausibility threatens the credibility of the whole.

§48

A remark by Dorothea Straus about a work by Tolstoy:
A book so great that you never think of how it was
written. And yet, as we know, Tolstoy rewrote his work
many times, and was probably never satisfied with his
final drafts.

§49

The novelist's certainty of knowledge about his characters must be like the biographer's structure of factual
evidence.

§50

No matter how great may be a writer's intellectual perception, its expression (and thus possibly his whole
work) will be worth little unless he perceives also
through the emotions. Stark intellectuality is as un-
acceptable as stark sentimentality.

§51

Every fictional character is the writer beside himself
. . . *hors de soi.*

§52

We begin to "create" when we see everyone else in ourselves.

§53

Much modern fiction is first of all socially or scientifi-
cally conceptual, with the story and characters fitted to
an intellectualistic view. Generally, therefore, the only
valid thing about such is the original idea, which were
better stated in non-fictional terms.

§54

It is not advisable, or even possible, to use the other arts as direct models for writing; but every one of them abounds in analogies by which the writer can profit. How can anyone listen to the Eroica symphony without learning something about form? Part of the aesthetic pleasure of structured and understood form is the pleasure of anticipation answered—the surprise which confirms itself after the fashion of an open secret. Random example: Beethoven's *ritornelli*.

§55

If characters in fiction are truly created by the author, they bear relationship to each other which may not be wholly understood by him until later.

§56

A detailed and comprehensive design for a story or a novel, to be extended in text day by day, is a releasing, not a confining, instrument.

§57

Some writers present themselves as performers on their own pages. They usually have second-rate perceptions, if often first-rate wit.

§58

A familiar rhetorical difficulty for the inexperienced writer is to discover the difference between writing and talking, and then to bring them into focus together, in a style peculiarly his own.

§59

Tolstoy's power to show the commonplace as marvellous permits him to give us the extraordinary as stupendous. The first is a prerequisite to the second.

§60

"All things whisper in the blood"—the writer should never avoid through shame or niceness any idea or theme which may come into his mind. He must simply know how to use it.

§61

A writer who seems to watch himself in his pages may never create a character which seems to exist in its own illumination.

§62

When a book has an organic life, the writer at work on it sees everything about him in the book's terms. Even all the conventions of life become original for him. Everything seems relevant to the artistic problem of the moment.

§63

Every great fictional character is like life—but must seem larger.

§64

There is a difference between dramatizing your sensibility and your personality. The literary works which we think of as classics did the former. Much modern writing does the latter, and so has an affinity with, say, night-club acts in all their shoddy immediacy.

§65

One can learn much about the "grown-up" world by listening to children at play.

§66

Why is it now considered the highest literacy and the ultimate in critical verbiage by many an editor, publisher, writer, teacher, and indeed host or hostess, to limit oneself in writing or social speech to the vocabulary of the naturally prurient adolescent? It takes a singularly impoverished collection of minds to confuse appropriate freedom of expression with a sensibility open only to an argot which seems to be uttered by an anus which has learned to talk, and can talk only about its own, and adjacent, functions.

§67

The ear must always be satisfied by what the pen has silently written. Always read aloud. The ear will often correct what the eye misses.

§68

A test of characters in fiction: can you imagine how they would write letters?

§69

All events—the stuff of stories—contain the seeds of banality. It is only those to whom they happen—the characters—who can make stories fresh, interesting, and significant.

§70

The writer, by working to master his craft, must *earn the right* to represent his own experience in his work.

§71

Perhaps the most important and most difficult part of the writer's task is to revive his imagination every day during his working hours.

§72

With one part of his mind, many a writer works against setting forth any symbolism; while at the same time with another he holds the hope and intention to write so truly of anything that it can assume a universality which will be seen by others as symbolic, quite possibly in current terms undefined by, or unknown to, the writer himself.

§73

If it is to be any good, a writer must positively inhabit his book as he writes it.

§74

A serious technical problem for the novelist is how to combine richness, even diffuseness, of texture, with sustained forward movement in the narrative.

§75

The novelist's first exercise is to conjugate the verb "to see." The next is to conjugate "to feel." The next is to conjugate "to form."

§76

Every good novel—not to mention the great—takes us forward until we seem to leave the author's tempo and proceed with one created in our own impatient and enthralled interest.

§77

It is a delicate decision to make—when to cease elaborating in notes a design for a work. There is always a danger of going too far, which is almost as unlucky as not going far enough, in projecting a design. Much must be saved for spontaneity in the fulfillment of the text day by day.

§78

A constant temptation to the novelist: to stretch his novel out beyond the tensile strength of its events and design.

§79

Which is better: the first person narrative or the third person? Neither, in absolute terms. Some stories require the one, some the other.

§80

We can often believe what people say in fictional scenes—but how often do we have a sense of how they actually sound? This is not a plea for sustained dialect—that often becomes a bore. But tone of voice can be suggested by other means.

§81

A drawing can come alive in a single line if the subject is seen wholly. Thus with a few words also.

§82

To seem truly alive, every character in fiction should seem to the author capable of amorous desire, whether or not it is ever expressed or enacted.

§83

"There is so much of you in the leading character," she said.

"I am in all the characters," I replied.

"Yes, but the leading one," she insisted.

"He was drawn from someone else directly, for the most part," I said, "and so were all the others."

But she knew me so long ago, and has known me so well ever since, that she can only see me as in life, not as in writing.

§84

The journey of a fictional character: from actual life observation, into the subconscious, to re-emergence in the memory, to dramatization as if in one's own experience, to modification by addition from other observed persons, to animation from within its own limits, to the advancement of the events and substantiation of the relationships, in the fiction.

§85

The writer must find and release the significance behind even the most flat of statements if he is to give a second life to his idea of humanity.

§86

A sketch for a work should be beautiful in itself, no matter how much more it will be elaborated as part of a finished work. The sketchbooks of masters (in all arts) are in themselves works of art, wonderful to study.

§87

The ideas which "come from nowhere" have a better chance to assume a beautiful form when developed and elaborated than those derived from immediately identifiable sources. "Nowhere," of course, is one's own center.

§88

Like clear air changed into falling snow crystals, clear thought, for an act of art, changes its form by using its regular elements in another way.

§89

One should never show an unfinished manuscript to anyone. You are sure to receive opinions contrary to some aspect of what you have written and such opinions no matter how strong you are may have a weakening effect upon that conviction you must sustain until your work is done. A book cannot be written by a committee. One must obey oneself alone and take one's chances. (We are of course not talking of student work, the very object of which, as it advances week by week, is to earn criticism.)

§90

The hardest thing for even a gifted student in writing to do is to convey the significance he feels in what he writes.

§91

The most important sentence in a good book is the first one: it will contain the organic seed from which all that follows will grow.

§92

The value of an outline or précis for a projected work is this—that if the design organically leads toward a culmination and resolution, this is in the back of the mind as the writer works toward it day by day; and thus a strong tension builds up; and when the resolution is

reached, it should have the effect of an eruption, a release, so meaningful that all the writer's best resources
are called into play to convey it. Lacking a plan, then,
how can this value be present? An improvisation can
have value—but hardly in the great episodes or
moments.

§93

On the eve of beginning a large new work, one's spiritual and intellectual polarizations are highly energetic
and troubling: the subject vs. one's own temperament;
the profusion of material vs. the search for a design, a
form; the importance of "hearing" the absolutely suitable key in which to sound the first, and determining,
note. The greater the polarities, perhaps the greater the
chances of a living work. But the imaginative pre-solu-
tions of such problems can be wearing—almost, it would
seem, self-frustrating. Concentration seems at moments
impossible. But nothing is to be forced alive. One must
listen, listen, for the natural systole/diastole of the heart
of the work until one's thought lifts and falls in harmony with them. And when it does, one may proceed
with confidence, with breath half-held, and prayer in-
voked. Therefore one must always be alert to the recep-
tion of this harmony, which is proof enough that the
spirit of the work has been alive in one's under-thought

for a long time, and has at last found the moment, and the tone, in which to declare itself.

Meanwhile, until that happens, the other, the "real," world all about, seems painful, strange, and hostile in trivial ways, so that one feels a stranger in his visible ambience, whose terms he must earnestly and elaborately try to appease, even as he is inwardly concerned with another reality as it struggles to find release in satisfying form.

§94

If I should write a play with a drunken character in it, I would advise the actor in the part to observe very small babies in order to learn how to give a convincing performance.

§95

The novelist must be protean. If his characters are to live, he must exist within some vital aspect of each of them, no matter what their sex, moral stance, or significance as motes of life.

§96

The reader of a novel should be given essential information without his being aware of the process.

§97

Thoughts which come late in wakeful nights often demand to be written down. They do not always look useful, or even sensible, by daylight. But for the sake of those which do, they must be seized at the time.

§98

Many writers confess to observing certain professional superstitions which the non-writer would find absurd. Some break off a day's writing in mid-sentence, sure of how the sentence is to continue, so that the next day they can complete it, and thus find themselves in an already forward-moving phase of work. Others make a great fuss over having their materials arranged on their desks in exactly the same way throughout the writing of a work: the completed pages, the notes for those to come, the position of the dictionaries, the very direction of the lie of the bundle of pencils beside the typewriter, or the way the pen is pointing in its rack, the shading of the windows against sights outside too interesting to ignore, the shutting off of the telephone and the adjustment of the sense of barricade against interruption, the same sort of paper as yesterday's, the precisely repeated placing of the lamp if one has been used regularly, the condition of the fire in the fireplace, the position of an object on the chimney-piece, the reestablished placing of stapler, Scotch tape, and paper clips—all these are more than matters of simple convenience or efficiency. They signify continuity. They seem like a promise that what has gone well so far will continue to do so if the proper acts of propitiation are made, and they release, in their small but powerful way, through established habit, the action of the mind which, sure of not having to arrange necessary trifles, can safely enter upon the hard but invisible work of concentration. Many people would smile indulgently at what seems to them nonsensical practices; but they do not know that to the writer every pursuit of his day's work is precarious, and cannot be hedged about with too many precautions.

§99

N. C. Wyeth once said to me that a born writer, encountering a squall in a rowboat, could there derive all the imaginative essentials of being in a ship beset by a great storm at sea.

§100

How difficult it is to write a sentence according to what someone else needs—a recommendation, a bit of information, and the like; and how divinely easy (it seems) when one writes it solely for oneself.

§101

Every time one begins to brood about writing a new novel, one must forget every professional or technical solution one has learned in previous works. It is starting all over every time. What does survive is the discipline of work, and the ability to measure oneself against the dimensions of the task to be done.

§102

I saw her merely turn her head, in a throng, at a party; and I knew her whole life—for my purposes, that is, as a novelist.

§103

Even under the most intense and well-focused concentration, ideas, forms, are not clear to the writer until he puts them down on paper. Then they become objects—fabrications—which he can consciously examine, judge, and improve.

§104

In answer to a reader's quizzing letter: "I feel quite sure you will recognize that, in the most general literary and personal sense, and quite apart from the book presently under inquiry, it is impossible for the author to enter into discussions of identities of his characters and whatever instance from actual life he may have drawn upon for his story. Every act of art is an act of alteration. The degree will seem great or small, depending on the readers—and there are many varieties of readers."

§105

So long as characterization remains a leading element in fiction, the true novelist must have to a significant degree the gifts of an actor.

[63]

§106

Rouben Mamoulian in the dramatic action classes he once held could cast a spell of complete reality by sheer concentration on the imaginative ingredients of a pantomimed event. In his handling of invisible "props" he made you see them. By his response to invisible persons, he created them before your eye. By the precise control of his body's reaction to surroundings, he evoked atmosphere which enclosed you. So intently did he see and so surely did he project the human truth of a situation that he evoked out of thin air effects which the writer works to bring to page by other means. The lesson for the writer: he can cultivate the essential power behind expression with such total concentration on the materials he uses that his illusion cannot strike a false note.

§107

The successful aesthetic experiment is that which proceeds from the particular to the general—not the other way round.

§108

The inexperienced or insensitive novelist will always make his characters sound alike—and all like himself.

§109

A key question: For the most part, throughout, is the style precisely equal to the need?

§110

Most contemporary writing is content to present raw material, without recourse to the process of refining it, in the sense of extracting for survival only the non-base elements. It goes without saying that we are here not making a moralistic estimate—only a criticism of a technical process and an indictment of laziness on the part of insensitive craftsmen.

§111

How many writers take as much care over their observation of an incidental detail as Albrecht Dürer took over drawing with exactitude a tiny lump of turf? It is not realism as such we refer to here—it is the respect for, and the delight in, life at its most prosaic and incidental.

§112

Thronging within us are all whom we have known, and indeed, seen, however casually. Each has his individual resonance in memory or the subconscious, and if this is like enough to what we can recover of ourselves, it will bring back, when we write, those who will *enact* for us our *own* good or evil, as the story may require.

§113

When I read a great book, or even a good one, I am exalted and confirmed in my own work, feeling not that I am equal to its author but that I am engaged in an honorable art; and when I read a poor book, I am depressed, and see all my own failings in it, and I feel I belong to a miserable trade.

II ❧ OF THE MODE

Contemporary taste—the sum of the successes of a period—has great energy and much power to influence the writer and other workers in the arts. By this very fact it should be viewed with caution, and its elements should be examined one by one by the writer to determine whether they tempt him with more than fugitive conformity and the finally vulgar pleasures of being "with-it," to use a current expression generally bestowed as a compliment.

The following section of notes reflects my interest in the artist's own vision, the inexhaustible legacy of the past, and the perils of fashion.

§114

No one can say which of the productions of his own time are certain to survive as verities in future history and which, even those once widely admired, will vanish. What one can do, and the artist is wise to do, is to find for his own purposes the conjunction of those elements of the past which have formed him with those of the present which seem to express his nature, while he gives no thought to direct imitation of either. Contemporary subject matter is not in question; only the manner of treating it.

§115

Only by knowing a tradition well can one meaningfully rebel against it; and even then, more of it will survive than what has been added to it in the way of counter-statement.

§116

What never works: the novel which is more at the mercy of a social thesis than an impulse of art. Tolstoy was great enough as an artist to survive in his work the social theories he came to think so important.

§117

Nobody can imagine tomorrow; but anyone can be faithful to all that he truly knows of today through his own uninfluenced discoveries, no matter what organized attitudes may be brought to bear on everything around him.

§118

Important problem: how to be truly of one's time as a writer without following its fashions. A solution: to be true first of all to one's own vision, which to know requires much meditation, and then to resist the current cant, and the imperative, and often profitable, chic, of any controlling, if short-lived, theory.

§119

There is no essential difference between running after fashionable persons and running after fashionable ideas. Both are harmless diversions, and either may even feed satire.

§120

It may be dangerous to echo only the accents of the past
—but even more so to replace them with only those of
the present.

§121

Existentialism imprisons its followers in an eternity of
the present tense. For them the past is lost or wasted,
the vision of the future is blinded.

§122

To be self-conscious about conforming to the "modern"
is to be oblivious to the timeless, i.e., the sense of the self
and its perceptions, no matter what these may keep alive
of the past.

Memorandum to a colleague whose manuscript I
read: I must note the mistake of falling into the argot of
the genre you are criticizing, such as the modish permissiveness which is a present imperative. Vulgar neolo-
gisms are certain to lose their meaning, precision, and
edge in a very short time, and the more currency given
to the hitherto unprintable expressions of obscenity, the
less historical respect we can grant to them. We are now
in a moment of taste which sanctions—no, requires in
the dubious mode—the use of low slang or the vocabulary of latrine graffiti in "serious" writing. The trouble
with all such "chic" is that it can never achieve any continuing vitality because the "timely" in expression is
never fixed in meaning, style, or relevance. Your work
is essentially serious. Your intention is elegant, but too
often your manner is raw, and so your thought appears
raw also. Its texture, therefore, seems to shrink away
from importance and seriousness the more it is made to
conform to the highly doubtful modishness of popular
mannerism or references derived from the latest vulgate.
Everything you mean to say is worth meaning and
saying; I would plead for it that it be relieved of the
built-in disadvantages of style and idiom more appropriate to the impoverished, sticky self-indulgences of
pop-obscenity authors than to the rich, inherited speculative style of your own true thought and concern. In
other words, your thinking, so far as I can discern it
through its present beclouding texture, deserves better

vesture than the cheap pop-folk style which renders it trivial and ephemeral. You are too important a critic and philosopher to have to be nervous about being "with-it." I do not speak out of merely sniffish fastidiousness, but hope to make a case for the aesthetically appropriate. Language and occasion must meet in harmony, or all deeper meanings are dissipated. All "trade" words are useless in the end, and as damaging as the jargon of the academy to anything but commercial communication.

§124

In any art, in any style, there can be only one great innovator at a time. Imitations thereafter merely contribute to a body of journalism, or period reference.

§125

Those who think only of destroying the present imagine they are creating a future, when all they are doing is repeating the cage rattlings of the past. In this case, motive is all.

§126

It is now considered clever to say that the "man of letters" is no more. What we have instead are journeyman specialists in the various separate forms of literature. Many are gifted at single purpose; but how much more gifted they would be if they wrote in many genres, and evoked the several sensibilities necessary to do so, so that each would benefit all.

§127

Any art which sets out to be in fashion is sure to end up like yesterday's newspaper.

§128

The mass age, with its mechanized commodities, including its visions, has forced many an artist—most individual of creatures—to turn to the wholly subjective to find his expression. What he finds is often intelligible to no one else. Art, then, seems in danger of abandoning its search to communicate in common terms illuminated by an individual vision.

§129

The novel, for the moment, is a social statement before it is a work of art. It must "have something to say" to satisfy critics who are scholars of systems—Marxist, Freudian, Existentialist, Black, Absurdist, Sexist, or whatever—before they are responsive to the aesthetic. If a novel fulfills its natural genius to give an effect of life in large traits and intimate details, there will be plenty left over to discuss in terms of "systems"—but "systems" will never motivate a real work of imaginative literature. Let the reader supply his own "statement" in response.

§130

Originality for its own sake is always dishonest and thus irrelevant.

§131

Every generation does battle for its own enthusiasms; but there are always a few who rise above these in the vision of their own separate sensibilities, which need not necessarily have anything to do with the contemporary vision.

§132

The true artist is never afraid of anything—including the glories of the past.

§133

To be self-conscious about the "modern" is to be oblivious to the timeless, i.e., the sense of the self and its perceptions, no matter how these may relate to either the past or the present.

§134

A reason that the past is so hated by the young is that there is no way to be entirely free of it.

§135

A true innovator in the arts cannot be imitated, nor will he have any significant artistic influence. He is useful only to himself—and the public.

§136

Fashion makes cowards of second-rate artists. Stylish conformity is their vice.

§137

It is a curious critical tendency which judges books of the past generation according, not to their intrinsic literary value, but to their "relevance" or "non-likeness" to the social conditions and the tone of writing which prevail today. Recently a compendium of work by a brilliant English writer of the Edwardian and subsequent Georgian periods was dismissed by many reviewers as hopelessly old-fashioned and therefore meaningless in its moral and social values. It was as if Jane Austen, say, were to be dismissed for similar reasons. The work was not weighed for its literary achievements.

§138

He who fears to be out of the mode does not deserve to belong to himself.

§139

It is not always of significance whether an artist derives from a tradition or invents his own; all that matters is that he be an artist. Critics and teachers almost always pay attention to the peripheral matters of external "placement" and miss the essential core.

§140

The public hazard, but private gain, when one's new book is most unlike one's last previous one.

§141

Those who would now dismiss the *story* as a useful element of the novel are the victims of a critical "chic" which turns up every ten years, only to disappear. There is hardly a person alive who does not want to know "what happened next," in any context.

§142

To be deliberately contemporary is as fatuous as to be deliberately old-fashioned.

§143

For the drug-afflicted social behavior of many young people today, dreams have disastrously escaped from their proper domain, which is the unconscious. Freud offered certain postulates which resulted in confusion—none more than his attempt to identify recognizable reality through dreams. This has too often resulted in efforts to create systematic interpretations of essentially inconsistent subject matter. If there should be clinical usefulness in this process, it has nothing to contribute to an artist's realization of his aesthetic impulse. Was Freud himself more of an artist than therapist? Were his insights more like those of poetry than of science?

§144

A reason that the avant-garde never lasts is that it is self-conscious, and another is that time does not stand still, and still another is that the avant-garde's gestures were all agitated two generations before and, being forgotten by those who despise history, are presented once again as new.

§145

There are two kinds of artist. One says, "I am greater than art." The other says, "Art is greater than I."

§146

It cannot be said often enough: language is the writer's beginning and end, obvious as this must seem. *In principio erat verbum.* Yet present reputations in literature are more often made by notions, fads, current and mindless vulgarisms, what is said, than by how these are expressed. The public speech has declined into indifference to nicety, precision, and structural form. Show business has more effect on expression than the academy, or even the news media. Rhetoric is abominably taught if at all. Young writers grow up to echo what they hear—at the moment the vocabulary is limited largely to "wow" and its popular synonyms—and not to what they read, if they read anything but the work of their styleless near-contemporaries. The *ear* is the good writer's best guide to good style. A writer with no ear is hopelessly disadvantaged. Style is first of all clear and explicit, and then, because there are many choices among ways of expression, fastidious. There are many synonyms for "wow," most of them more durable and exploratory.

§147

In many joyfully admired recent novels, love appears as little more than sex-manual instruction, even to the commercial identification of coital lubricants.

§148

"Black humor" is a sophomoric attempt to disguise self-hatred.

§149

Let a professor of English, history, or social studies invent a striking paradox in his theory of any aspect of his subject, and he can make an entire career out of this single pedagogic commodity. If he can think of a catchword to express it which enters the jargon of the academy, he will attract a generation of disciples.

§150

Modishness as against style all too often prevails in academic literature and discourse. There is an always-changing recognition code for persons who can accept the word "intellectual" as a noun. In their jargon they take comfort from such words, recalled at random, as archetype, apocalypse, extrapolate, charisma, *élan vital* (now old-fashioned), paradigm, "black" (as in humor), "absurd" (in relation to a systematic view of life), viable, "radical," explicate, and the rest.

§151

We live in the age of the put-on. All periods have had put-ons—but when have they ever become models for success?

§152

The absurdity of teaching contemporary literature to its contemporaries.

§153

It takes only one great man to create a renaissance.

§154

The novelist who sets out consciously to be "of his period" will die with it. If he sets out to be himself, his own times will inevitably be present, and survive with him, if he survives.

§155

The present is only the cumulated past, with moment by moment additions.

§156

It is difficult if not impossible to find analogies between the virtues of technology and the values of the originating (as against the performing) artist. Our contemporary respect for "systems" seems to urge the artist toward technological (i.e., material) values, yet that which inspires him relates to the life within.

§157

Every period has its predominant popular tone, widely influential and pervasive. The writer must select from within this—his contemporaneous tone—as fastidiously as he selects from among those long-established conventions of the past which hold validity for his work.

§158

The unquestioned present is of no more value than the unquestioned past.

§159

In writing, there are two levels of professionalism: one —the lower—is based on ambition driven by competitiveness; the other is based solely on fulfilling a vision in word and overall design, without regard to what anyone else is writing or publishing.

§160

Taste has many conditions and elements. The one certain to be ruinous is that which tries to please others rather than the writer.

§161

An editorial or critical cult is usually the extension of the temperament and the bias of one person, or at most, of a very few. In such resides the power to make or break reputations—and all on the basis of necessarily limited views. How, then, can they be taken seriously? But they are, because the energy of the egos behind them is strong enough to require public expression. It is one of the most essentially frivolous and wasting forms of power in culture; and of course as it is subject to fashion or fad, it is eventually superseded by a new critical cult with perhaps directly opposing views. How then can the artist hope for discussion of his work in *his* terms, not theirs?

§162

The writer who keeps one eye on the public is sure to be blind in the other.

§163

A tiresome current tendency: the deliberate, bad-boy illiteracy which one encounters in novels by youngish persons or others who think all manners of expression equally good. The way for the novelist to refresh the language is not to revert to its worst habits, but to expand temperamentally upon its best.

§164

It is one thing to create a fashion; it is another to conform to one; and still another to have no interest in doing either.

§165

This may sound fatuous, but in the present climate of the arts, it is pertinent: in themselves, all words are not literature, all sounds are not music, all drops of paint are not painting, all shapes are not sculpture.

§166

There is coarseness which passes for vitality in the tone of assumptive knowingness in the writing of certain novelists of the present, who must seem at all costs to be "with-it" in all comment, styles, theories, cult beliefs.

§167

The public taste in the United States is frequently so offensive (Muzak, commercial architecture, comic strips-and-books, rock "music," most TV, radio, movies, all pop-pornography, and the rest) that it is enough to raise serious doubts about the stylistic trustworthiness of democracy, which had led to the ascendancy of such expressions. The tyranny of it all is what is off-putting. There is no escape for the individuals who detest these invasions. Worse, there is an inverted snobbery of acceptance of these by some people of cultivated taste, so that it is a disillusioning spectacle to see them go on sprees of aesthetic slumming into the climate of the prevalent cultural pollution. The popular taste will usually seek its comforts in the lowest common aesthetic denominator.

§168

For the moment [1969] communication is not regarded in certain influential circles as a principal purpose of the arts. We are to be amazed not at what the artist tells us, or how he tells it, and not even at what he seems to be telling himself, but at the mere fact that he agitates the raw materials or flourishes the instruments of the communicative process.

§169

The true artist of the contemporary is not the one who merely tries to fix the scene around him but he who finds in his own sensibility the evidences of the world which made him. If he is true, this is an inescapable process, and as a record it tells us the essentials, while the other vision ends as journalism.

§170

Experiments in form, new vessels for each generation, renewed insights, must always be hoped for. The novel at its best is no more static and fixed in a mold than any expressive procedure. But what must never be mistaken for true discovery and new illumination is the formless indulgence of an individual ego, throwing itself about in exhibition of an arrogant self-exploitation, which is rarely more than a public purgation by personal excesses of behavior. A performer with no more of a model than his own anatomy and its often exclusively dubious exercises very soon becomes a bore like a drunk at a party who is self-persuaded that he and his views are the most interesting elements of the gathering.

§171

Every period has its projections of ideal figures. This alone is enough to insure the continuing life of the novel, for it is the adventures—mental or physical—of such ideal figures which everyone craves to see objectively in order to feel experience subjectively.

§172

The most valuable writers are those in whom we find not themselves, or ourselves, or the fugitive era of their lifetimes, but the common vision of all times.

[89]

§173

In subtly influenced ways, the novel changes with each generation, even when based on traditional models of earlier times. Nobody in the twentieth century can possibly write a Victorian novel which will be a work of art. It may be a fair imitation, or a hilarious pastiche— but never if the intention of the novelist is serious will it bear stylistic relation to any time but his own.

§174

For historical glimpses of the insensitive collectivity of the *populus,* the popular arts are valuable. They rarely carry aesthetic value. It is therefore to a degree maddening that there is a cult which champions them as of artistic importance. If taken seriously at all, the cult really proclaims only an inverted snobbery.

§175

The true artist is his own contemporary only.

III ❧ GLIMPSES OF THE ACTUAL

The following entries, chosen for variety from my notebooks, consist of transcribed glimpses of life or single phrases each of which at the moment of recording held for me an impulse or fraction of meaning, with a certain resonance which seemed to promise later development. They are intimate specimens of the imagination's environment.

Many such proved to be useful, others may yet be. It is well to have an abundance of them to live with and re-examine from time to time.

Working outlines for stories or longer works belong in another category, and are of their nature not suited to publication.

§176

"We are *simple* people," he said, but saying it made them infinitely complicated.

§177

Dingy tugboat moored at Bridgeport bears the name *Ocean Prince*.

§178

The mouth motors of little boys at play with toy machines.

§179

Comedy females, grotesquely formed, who have no recourse but to make sport of being women.

§180

Autumn leaves falling like tongues of fire.

§181

Strange vacancy just above the surface of the river.

§182

Painted shadows; color within shadows.

§183

The touching—and perhaps, in cases, horrifying—differences of people in their social, public, polite situations, and in their personal, private, happy, or agonized situations. . . . In public, the habitual power of the little amenities, the flourishes of tried and proved "charm," the sage, or the witty, or the arranged style—all project self-images which are important not only to the order of society but to the public government of an individual temperament. Then, in private, the same individuals, subject to storms of desire, grief, self-doubt, disappointment, jealousy, offer what a piercing contrast, what hints of complexity in the separate person even at his most commonplace. . . . No one is wholly what he seems, and no one is only and essentially what he is in private.

§184

My neighbor's very small boy, not quite four years old, came charging across my garden where I was working on a very hot summer morning. He was pursuing an imaginary enemy. He wore only a cowboy hat and the briefest of under-trunks, and he carried a toy shotgun. Suddenly, on becoming aware of me, he was abashed by his near-nakedness and his imaginary game. He paused in his chase and said angrily to me, "I am really a United States Marshal, but sometimes I go around like this." I nodded seriously, and, reassured, he ran on.

§185

The far setting sun exactly the color of the near bonfire.

§186

The concentration between the cat's ears.

§187

When he saw his father die, he felt nothing because he was appalled by losing the sum of a lifetime's love; and his mind was busy noting objective details never to be forgotten. The hideous details, impassively noted, were what saved him from collapsing.

§188

Leaf smoke filling the hollows and valleys in autumn. I think of the hours after battle in the Civil War.

§189

A dog, listening with his nose.

§190

The reluctance to spend a newly minted coin.

§191

A love—utterly consuming—that lasts ten seconds.

§192

Stillness after victory.

§193

The man paralyzed from the waist down being wheeled on a winter afternoon in a small neat compact chromium wheelchair to his Rolls Royce limousine parked at the curb in 54th Street. On his lap is balanced an attaché case. There is a young woman waiting at the car—a nurse?—in a winter overcoat. The man wheeling him turns him to the open front door of the car. The nurse takes away the left armrest of the chair and attempts to remove the attaché case. He slaps her away from it. With his right hand and arm he arranges his inert legs to a slanting position for moving. She sets a smooth board from the car's front seat to the raised footrest of the wheelchair. He turns himself to sit on the board. He then hunches and grubs himself along into the car. His movements are like those of a seal out of water. Finally he is in, the board is removed, the chair is folded and stowed in the rear of the car, the attendants get into the car, she driving, and all doors are shut. During the maneuver the slim, shiny, black attaché case has remained on his lap, and as they drive away, he clutches it to his breast.

§194

The passing bell.

§195

How sometimes in a public room a particular man's voice will sound through and across a whole crowd, forcing us to hear him and his most banal confidences, until we long to have him led away.

§196

Evidence of tenderness from long ago.

§197

The blind man's elevated smile.

§198

Human beauty that vanishes with the smallest change of position.

§199

She sat there with the watering eyes and the rueful self-possession of a small dog.

§200

A stained and wrinkled piece of school notebook paper picked up in the street near a grade school carried large pencilled printed words as follows: NO I WOULD NOT LIKE IT & I WOULD MIND YOU WOULD HAVE TO SEE MY MOTHER & YOU WOULD GET YOUR FACE SLAPPED SO HARD YOU WOULD NOT FORGET IT SO DON'T TRY OR YOU'LL BE

SORRY. It had been folded over as a private note. On the outside was printed: TO JOHN ONLY, and above this: YOU BETTER NOT TRY.

§201

Leaf-broken light.

§202

Young sailor—really like a newly hatched chick—walking along the train aisle doleful and lost, and yet wearing a cocked eyebrow. To prove his ease and worldliness, he is whistling *Anchors Aweigh,* putting in all the trombone slides between remembered held notes—a brass band all by himself.

§203

Pullman car overhearings—man and woman—married and slackly middle-aged, commonized for each other by the presence of others. Their public voices are gravelly and loud, in the accent of the Bronx New Yorker.

In the evening, they retire in their room next to mine. Late at night I awake. The train has halted for a long stay in a station. The metal walls of the train rooms conduct all sounds. I hear my neighbors speak.

He is in the top bunk, she in the lower. Drowsy talk. "Come on up?" as if cajoling a sweet child.

Pause, then, "You come *down.*" Her voice is one entirely new—it becomes that of a tiny girl, suggesting a slight sore throat, and also a bird-like marsh sound, a playful seductiveness, a baby-doll unreal piping deep in her throat with hardly formed words. It is her *love voice.* It turns *love* into something done by someone *else,* and thus permissible, as though in her ordinary person, sagging and hard-eyed by day, love were disreputable and worthy only of corner-store gossip.

In a moment he scrambles down to lie with her. In the silence of the train and the strange atmosphere of the station with its far-off echoes of unplaceable sounds, they innocently forget that they can be heard. Endearments now between a baby doll with a squeaky mechanical voice if tipped just right, and a man, a father, pretending to speak for a toy bear to entice a smile from a shy child.

Presently the train moves out and I fall asleep, blurring all.

In the morning, he is up before her and is standing in the corridor, all dressed and waiting with public irritation. Their loud brutal voices have returned.

"Hurry-yup."

Within: "I'm packing."

"I know, I know," he bawls through the evidently

locked door. "So hurry-yup. We're gonna be late and we can't eat awwready. The train gets in in haffan hour, oh Christ, why does she have to—Listen, hurry, wiyya?"

Within: "So go and have your lousy breakfast!"

"You know I can't eat without ya."

§204

The perversity of the exquisite girl who must show indifference to the young man whom she wants to attract; and how this actually attracts him.

§205

The glory of highlights on prosaic or ugly objects.

§206

Indirect cats.

§207

A lake so still that it obliges us to break its surface.

§208

Light *within* an eye—not reflected from without.

§209

The oldening man, retired from a notable career and now forgotten, deeply tanned, white-haired, smooth as caramel, who harbors a smoldering inner heap of hot slag in hatred, self-defense, and self-sorrow. He expostulates on outgoing breath, full of decades of cigarettes and whiskey, and on the last gasp of each breath delivers his utmost words of scandal, mixed with self-reassurance; and the syllables cough into jumbled sound as they die, taking on added emphasis. "My dignity," he says, "it's all I have left, and I am going to keep it if I have to d——" and the rest is lost incoherently, and what reaches us is the last passion of a life.

§210

On the open deck of an Atlantic liner: the gale hollowed the breath out of my mouth.

§211

Light behind a leaf.

§212

Landscape on china.

§213

The woman with a painful chronic disease (such as arthritis) whose smile has been determinedly sweet for so long that it has become as habitual as the pain. An exact sweetness of line, like that of a cat's mouth; but behind it, who knows what heart-eating rage and consuming desire to punish others less unfortunate than she? She wears glasses with extra-thick lenses which suggest a vision penetrating relentlessly into the secrets about themselves which people hope to keep. Her hair is glossy black. She is proud of it and, without ever quite touching it, makes graceful gestures outlining, and commenting upon, its luster.

§214

Any lamp at dusk seen from afar.

§215

In contempt of death, the old genius therefore survives.

§216

Youthful faces in autumnal sunlight.

§217

THE CHANGELING SON. A gentle, reasonably successful couple have a son who is presently recognized as an unchallenged genius in science or the arts. They cannot account for this in his heritage. Their bewildered efforts to "understand" him make him impatient, and guilty for this, in his natural love for them.

§218

The man who when looking at me turns his head away but keeps his gaze fixed on me. A habit of suspicion? Of reluctance to let go? Of hope to detect an involuntary revelation?

§219

The first mark of age in the face of the beloved. Even yesterday it was not there. The observer feels a surge of love, to abolish fear and pity.

§220

Waiting for snow.

§221

Silver streak downstream from the red moon in the river.

§222

The river and the immovable boulder.

§223

At a crossroads highway bar in the ranch country of New Mexico, the bar girl addressed a young man seated at the bar as "Sweet Pea." He was dressed in the ordinary rough work clothes of the ranch hand. He was very small. His eyes looked like dark purple and white sweet peas—mixed with a blossom blue—yet sharp. There was a bridling challenge about his neat little nose, with its child-nostrils, his small ears, clear jaws, and lean cheeks.

He had a little but perfectly proportioned body, suggestive of latent power. The title "Sweet Pea" he could afford to let stand because he was so incontestably male. It was the perfection of his hard good looks on their small scale that got it for him. The sweetness toward him which it sought out and exposed in others was sanctioned by him and all. Women had a stir, a pang, when they looked at him. He was both their child and (in hazy mind) their lover.

§224

White horse in the dusk.

§225

Slow decision preceding an infant's smile.

§226

Oxford. The British Air Force soldier with the toughest face I ever saw—crisscrossed by deep scars which might have been knife scars or service wounds. Fixed expression of aggressive hostility. Muggishly handsome. Between the lapels of his battle jacket, the exquisite, inquiring, contented, coquette face of a small kitten whom he had buttoned inside.

§227

The disciple of the Marquis de Sade whose ecstasy was incomplete unless it was accompanied by sincere pity for his victim.

§228

Ache of absurdity after love.

§229

What called into being an enduring love: the courage of an inherently weak person in continually striving after fulfillment.

§230

The pathos of spent appetite.

§231

At Mass in the Old Cathedral at Saint Louis.

A man three pews ahead of me, with no one between. He has hair the color of dirty snow. He wears a wind-jammer jacket. He seems between sixty and seventy years old. In his seat he lurches and gazes about. His face has a strongly Irish cast—blue eyes, which are pink-rimmed and watery, cheeks ruddy with broken veins, ruined good looks about him. He is indignant about the world.

When the priest reads the Gospel, this man echoes successive phrases in mockery, out loud. The great majesty of the language induces in him a scorning doubtfulness. The priest ignores him, though his antiphonal voice echoes through the church. He joins in the sacred occasion, now changing its character. People exchange glances, expecting him to be ejected as drunken or crazy.

After the timeless Gospel, the priest starts a banal sermon, saying, "Today is Mother's Day."

The antiphon rises to a new pitch in a whiskey voice, and in an odd, stylish way of speech, the man says, mincing in mimicry,

"Mother's Day! Mother's Day! I'll mother's-day *her*. *Mother!* What kind of a mother is *she!* She was back-biting and kicking all night long." His "she" is evidently his wife.

Priest: We venerate today the idea of Motherhood.

Ant.: Venerate! I'll show her! I'll venerate her with my belt!

Priest: The Holy Mother of God is the pattern for all mothers.

Ant.: The Holy Mother of God, that's a good one, the holy mother, well, nobody ever made such a holy mess of being a mother as *she* has. Look at them. Look what she has done to them. And to me.

Priest: Just as the infant Jesus drew His life on earth from—

Ant.: I suppose she thinks she gets all the credit. What about me? Heh. If I didn't give it to her, where would they be now, them poor boys?

People stare, hardly hearing the sermon, and the man goes on, driven in sacred public to present himself and his sorrows and his grudges. The effect was terrifying as well as pitiful. He was not ejected—nothing happened to him, and when the Mass was resumed, he subsided, and when the Communion was distributed, he knelt, striking his breast, bent over as though trying to hide himself.

§232

"How did you sleep?"
    "I was awake a long time," he said.
    "What did you do?"
    "I began at the beginning and made a census of every woman I ever made love to. It seemed to take hours."

§233

Gold and silver winter afternoon.

§234

A black dog rounded the corner like a gust of wind.

§235

When he finally saw her walking toward him in the busy street through the large flakes of the falling snow, he was shaken with love for her. It was the snow which did it.

§236

The British habit of saying "Th'n-q" ("thank you"): today a woman [in Oxford] dropped her newspaper on the walk, stopped, picked it up, and said "Th'n-q" to no one.

§237

Halations of thought.

§238

False virtue of love's excuse for ending.

§239

Snow clouds before snow.

§240

Being steadily looked at, the dog looks the other way.

§241

A snake-faced woman—almost horizontal brow, high nostrils, wide jaws.

§242

In the intimate dining room of a small hotel in Oxford, a middle-aged man talking to an old woman at his table sounded like a *Lucia* character out of E. F. Benson:

"Why do I have such difficulty over names? A frightful time remembering.—I suppose if it was *Lady* Someone, I'd remember."

"—Stayed with the ——'s, most marvellous house. Upstairs nothing but four-poster beds. I slept in the bed used there once by King James I."

"She says my letters sound like the Court Circular."

"Tuesday evening I'm going to meet the Queen Mother, and the problem is, what to do with the *hat* afterwards when I dine in Soho"—presumably a top hat, and presumably raffish company in Soho.

§243

The little boy three years old who sings to himself, "Doodn doodn deedn dood," over and over. His birth of poetry.

§244

German shepherd dog—the fur-marked worried look like that of an old aristocrat long impoverished.

§245

The sad, the almost somber, formality enacted, but not really believed in, between two persons ages apart in years who feel affinity for each other but cannot acknowledge it. They will really meet only in reveries, separately.

§246

There are some beauties which only the poor can afford.
I think of excessive profusions of lilac and magnolia,
ill-placed, against a rickety shack.

§247

One symbol upon a single page.

§248

What ruined the career of an actor: early in life someone told him that he had a remarkably compelling
smile.

§249

Before darkness lifts, the first bird of day knows what is
coming and says so.

§250

Snow light in winter night.

§251

The bite of type upon a page.

§252

In remote ranch country in northern New Mexico I was spending the day with a painter friend making water-color notes of the landscape. At noon we found a little map of its shade under a sizable piñon tree and sat down to eat and drink our picnic lunch.

In a few minutes a cloud of dust came furiously along the dirt track of a road we had followed and an old pickup truck rankled to a halt near us. Two men left the car and came toward us and then stood about ten feet away. The younger of the two became the spokesman. He was swollen with anger, a young man in work-whitened blue jeans and sweated shirt, with a .45 pistol against his right thigh. He shouted,

"What are you doing here! Didn't you see the sign? This land is posted!"

His right hand moved to grasp his pistol, while his left, swiftly, exhortingly, stroked in a single gesture his genital parts where they bulked under his worn jeans.

"No," I said. "We saw only a sign way back pointing the other way. We are just having a sandwich here."

His hand made its single flashing touch again at the groin as if to take further prowess there.

"That sign covers all this land!" he yelled.

His virility swelled and again he made his almost serpent-like flicking touch upon it as his talisman. He looked ready to commit violence.

"Sorry," I said. "We'll pull out, if you say so."

"I say so? You bet I say so! Get going!" he shouted, now holding on to his engorged member. The other man, much older, was motionless and silent throughout. We left. It was an unconsciously clinical demonstration of the obscure link between sex and violence.

§253

In a smile, teeth like an irregular row of corn on the cob.

§254

The high-strung person who, in speaking in public or in meeting strangers, has a sudden rise of scarlet welts on the side of the neck. They itch and are pinched—and gradually they subside as the occasion becomes familiar or reassuring.

§255

Some women, talking, sound like small, grey, middle-aged men. It is always astonishing to turn and see who speaks.

§256

After ecstasy: body thanks head.

§257

Put two couples—married pairs—at a dinner table. At first, general conversation, all false, but homage to amenity. But soon, without awkward transition, the two women will be talking to each other, and the two sirs, relieved, will explore their common trite and vital interests, apart from their dames. Society first makes its formal bow, and then gets on at once with what is really interesting, which is what interests the sexes separately, carnality apart.

§258

An onlooker is more quick to be aware of unreturned love than of any other kind. Indeed, he often sees it before it is plain to the one who cannot return it to someone else. Of all kinds of revelation, it is the one we could wish were private. And yet that would deny it its only poor reality.

§259

All the colors in the grey of England came out under the rain—like the colors in a rock when you put it in water.

§260

A phrase spoken by Henriette Wyeth Hurd about an adolescent boy—he had "a blurred look about the muzzle." I thought it must lead to a story—everything was blurred about him, enlarging, taking form, not final shape. His swollen thoughts.

§261

The drunk sings and staggers along held up by his bicycle which he calls "Georgie." "Georgie, you get me home now. I'm counting on you." He then falls and bitterly reviles Georgie for letting him down.

§262

A youth with the effect of a maimed smile.

§263

Married couple dining mutely in public.

§264

Twilight and nightfall over the seashore—or at sea—
seem more melancholy than the same hours of the day
over land. Is it because there is in that ceaseless motion
of the waters—"thalassa, thalassa"—our subconscious
recognition of our primal element of life on earth? A
return to our beginnings, which remind us of our even
far-impending ends?

§265

The young woman, removed to New York from some
inland place a few years ago, who overreacts in public
restaurants. Her "vividness" is a signal that the evening
will deteriorate with each drink.

§266

Arm in arm they came briskly along the sidewalk on
Park Avenue. They both must have been almost eighty
years old. Both were extremely chic in an old-fashioned
way—he with slightly tilted fedora, up-brushed short
mustache, overcoat trimly tailored to his cadaverous
figure, yellow chamois gloves, a malacca stick; she with

a flaring off-the-face hat, furs on her shoulders, gauntlet-length white gloves, a severe suit clinging to her equally bony figure. Their faces were animated with the gossip they seemed to be exchanging. They laughed with voracious malice at each other's remarks. Their cheeks were high in color—his buffed by the autumn wind, hers by art. They were like visitants from another time, and the best houses here and abroad, jerkily striding like the closest of friends who far past marriage could afford to say anything to each other. By accident I saw them an hour later lunching across the room from me. Their appetites for food were as voracious as for communication. With the fixed hilarity of skulls, they were like skeletons feeding.

§267

North Atlantic waves in storm—the colors and surfaces of chipped obsidian.

§268

Voices carry on summer nights.

§269

The prelate who after a lifetime's austerity has come to resemble a fleshy, pallid Mother Superior.

§270

ANNISQUAM, JUNE. Sundown at a small, crescent-shaped beach. Every glory of light on cloud, air, sea, as the sun went past the horizon. In the foreground, silhouetted, yet still "back-lit" from the fading general light, two young people—teen-aged—a boy and a girl. They sat on a low rock, their backs toward me. Space between them. Her hair was flat, full, almost below her shoulders. His head was classic, hair long but molded to his skull. As the sun vanished turning the ocean to fire, he made cosmic gestures, evidently explaining something to her of this vast splendor. She sat immobile. His arms made superb arcs of abstract possession, and then returned to their fixed position, hugging his own ribs. She remained motionless, seeming unresponsive. The after-glow lingered. He was transfigured by it. He would take deep staggering breathings which seemed almost to double his size; and then he would slump again, abstracted. She sat, lovely and impassive. The water began to lose its fire as evening blue took its place, but moving, always moving, like the breathing of the earth. When soon enough the abstract ecstasy was finally gone, she embraced him.

§271

The ache of a love that used to ache and cannot ache any more.

§272

Change of color in reflections.

§273

A heart, not a mind, full of God.

§274

STRAWBERRIES ALL YEAR. The woman at the table for four in the Verandah Grill of the R.M.S. *Queen Mary* who brays and wrangles along at the top of her voice, laying devastation by decibels about her for thirty feet in every direction. What she talks about are only the most maddening trivia, all to do with appetite and money. A whore's temperament and perhaps her calling. She makes grand-lady proclamations about hotels, etc., around the world. Ordering food, she says she has to have strawberries.

"But they're not in season," exclaims a table mate.

"Oh yes," she replied, "always on the Queens. Strawberries, fresh strawberries, all year. Marvlus. But of course I put no sugar on anything. I like it plain," and we think of her other appetites, including those of sex, and perhaps not irrelevantly conclude that she prefers those without love. She has a Yorkshire terrier called "Pudding—get it?" She paid £70 for it—"*her,* actually, she's a bitch," and we reflect, A perfect affinity. She drives me to elaborate precautions for my mealtimes, for fear of being seated within her range.

With her is a hard-voiced German woman who has a brutal Continental accent in English. Two men sit with them, both resembling movie extras who could be cast as waiters. They, too, have Continental accents. The whole lot together are so underbred and animal and swindling that they make you shudder for your human kinship, and—the worst of it—the necessity of *consciously* invoking the charity of God.

§275

Bird falling.

§276

Rays of blue eyes.

§277

A light on the mountain at night.

§278

An old professor emeritus, feebler by the year, grows more garrulous. Can he talk death to a standstill for a few more hours—days—months—years? But talk was the very medium of his effective years: he must prove, yet, that he is effective. Listening, one hopes for wisdom in his words. If it fails to appear, one is all the more eager to respond as if it had.

§279

There is a love which fears everything but its own resolution in prayer.

§280

The brief and overwhelming sense of weakening in the thews which is the first sensation of lustful desire.

§281

She was beautiful. Her husband was handsome. They came to the party together. It was clear that she had recently been weeping. He was unmarked, charming. His smiles were a bore. Hers were deeply touching. But one preferred to talk to him than to her, under the circumstances.

§282

Two types: those who believe love is and should be eternal, and those who do not. Both are in any given moment sincere. It is a pity when the two types become involved with each other.

§283

In a furious rage over a sense of injury, she can't help
blurting a lip-blown laugh at something he says which
is not meant to be funny or clever. In that moment, he
knows that she is unable to take refuge in anger any
longer. It is only a matter of moments until she is help-
less, then responsive, in his arms.

§284

Two fat women who bear every sign of accepted re-
spectability are having noon cocktails in the "elegant,"
carpeted, empty bar of the hotel. They get carried away,
laughing at their own exchanges. They try to suppress
their own wheezy sounds, putting their plump hands to
their lips to cover their words. But all escape anyway,
and presently they forget to look about to discover if
anyone is overhearing them. Their enriched gaiety in-
sists on shattering the atmosphere, even when one leans
to the other confidentially and, hardly able to speak for
boozy laughter which threatens to strangle her so that
certain syllables emerge as little breathy screams, says to
her friend, "I've never told this to anyone before, and
Harry would kill me, but you know? I'd like to be a
whore. . . ."

Cognate: the Air Force sergeant with a wife and

small child who said, in my hearing, while squinting into a vision beyond his thin, rumpled face, "If I was t'be born again, I'd like to be a woman and a whore."

§285

In a Penn Central dining-car corridor, standing alone, an elderly Negro waiter, in his starched jacket and apron, reading a page in a small, well-worn Bible, while the train clanked and shivered along.

§286

It is only late in life that we can believe in the passions which moved our parents.

§287

A man or woman has an ever-present desire which is fulfilled only after half a lifetime. Until then, nothing of it will ever have been seen by anyone else.

§288

The visceral pang of noticing an object once given by, or associated with, someone whose love we felt long ago.

§289

They came in great numbers to the funeral service to pay tribute to the friend who had died; but each one could not help thinking more about himself, and his inevitable end, than of the death which drew them all there. In their faces I saw the mortality they did not know they revealed.

§290

There are some people whose high spirits make you groan.

§291

A confession made to me by an intellectual and highly placed elderly priest at a house party. "And then Queen Mab rode through my mind like a whirlwind. In an instant from me to someone else (i.e., *I was instantly changed*). You will hardly believe it, but in that instant I fell wildly in love with my curate. How will I ever recover? What will I ever do?" He looked at me with the eyes of a basset hound, dragged down and haggard. His face was grey, flesh rolled over his starched Roman collar, his teeth had wide spaces between them and were set forward so that his lips closed over them with difficulty. Even in his youth he must have felt damned by lack of external beauty. Now he had lost his ideal of internal beauty of soul.

§292

If a woman was once beautiful, she will always feel so, and behave accordingly, no matter how long she lives. If a man was once successful, and then becomes a failure, he will behave according to his failure, no matter how long he lives.

§293

Young men today are consciously beautiful, but resent being looked at—except by themselves. What flower will they die to inseminate?

§294

Leaving Cherbourg by sea, 9:45 P.M., June 10, 1972: the last lights of France.

§295

A COUPLE OBSERVED:

He loved her so much that he must suffer her repeated sins of infidelity rather than lose her. The strongest power in his life was the terror he felt every time she had a new affair, for fear that she would leave him. In hers, the strongest was the fear that he might force her, out of tolerance exhausted, into a freedom where she knew she would be lost to a life of vicious promiscuity. Their bond was, luckily for them, of a tensile strength equal to both their fears. In the end, they were both saved by a surcease of struggle which came with age. Their last years together were almost what they had hoped for as bride and groom—except for the ecstasy of bodily joy, which she had seemed to look for, but never find, in others. When, suddenly, she died before him, he was, even in his grief, at peace for the first time in his adult life. He presently began to seem years younger; but when well-intentioned people wondered why he did not marry again, he smiled and said that nothing he could imagine would ever equal the happiness of his long married life.

§296

The exquisite girl, eleven years old, who without an inkling of conscious meanings, was absolute mistress of all feminine gestures of sexual attraction, strategy, and false beguilement.

§297

A soldier I knew saved himself in combat instead of trying to save his comrade, who was, as he saw, already beyond saving. But because he did not try even so to save him, he lived the rest of his life as a betrayer, and escaped it only when drunk. His wife and children never knew why he was a capricious, sometimes charming, sometimes threatening, drunkard; but they eventually felt that they must leave him or lose the futures they desired. The effect on him was to increase his self-hatred, until he found a bearable compromise in a life of vice which supported his need for alcohol until he died—not of these, but of his old act of treason to a fellow man in surroundings of mortal peril. If he could have spoken soberly of the event to anyone whom he respected, he might have been freed by logical argument from his ruinous self-judgment. He never knew that the crux of the matter was love.

§298

In college, he committed a dishonest act in regard to his academic record. Ever after, in his career, he tried to live it down; but his awareness of it was enough to keep him from feeling the confidence on which success is built.

§299

One day she discovered that she looked like a kitten—adorable, exquisite, and eternally inquiring. From that moment on, through an adjustment of style, her fortune was made.

§300

Her virtue was as evident as her beauty. Together, they invited a lifetime of indecision, and in the end, regret, which cost her both beauty and virtue.

§301

The ten-year-old boy's mother died. Everyone was amazed and then troubled because he showed no grief. He seemed to feel nothing of the sorrow all about him, though he clearly understood death. But many weeks later, he said to his governess, "Missy dear, ever since Mummy died, I have had this big lump inside here"— the base of his throat. "Will it ever go away?"

§302

CREATURES OF MYTH. Lying near the corral fence, the large, black bull calf; his forelegs tucked under him, his eyes like wet polished knobs shining sidewise, his jaws moving in foodless rumination, his draped velvety dewlaps waving slowly. And before his moist and pebbled muzzle, the white and grey young cat flows to and fro with her back arched, her tail raised, her legs stiffened, her hinder-parts twisted seductively toward him; and as she passes his dripping mouth which she so frankly invites with her archings and her tiny steps, he lets forth his lingual member and licks her flank. It is an enactment of desire and consummation—no matter how disproportionate—which refers in every gesture to timeless animal union, whether of gods in creature guise, or of humans, or of a mixture of both orders of life, as in myth.

§303

Yellow storm light.

§304

The river on fire.

§305

The man trundling his little iron sphere, about the size of a bowling ball, which moved on casters, who let everyone on the station platform at La Junta, Colorado, know that it contained a concentration of radioactive substance. He pulled it along by a long leash of woven leather. People following him marvelling. They looked at the sphere as if it might communicate with them. He took it into the station waiting room, and out into the light again, like a man walking a dog for an airing. He was pleased to be notoriously the custodian of the most terrible power of the century. Though it was doing nothing demonstrative, the sphere was doing things inside the minds of those who watched its little outing while the train waited. You could see that they were in awe of the inscrutably powerful and perilous device, as though it were a baited monster momentarily at rest, but balefully on its guard, and unpredictable. Someone asked its custodian if "they" were on the way to Los Alamos. In reply, he merely raised his head a little higher and looked mysterious.

§306

The elegantly crossed forelegs of a sleeping dog.

§307

The deliberately slow stride of mountain youths—life is uphill work.

§308

Sunlight behind pollen in air.

§309

WHAT KILLED FUDGE. He died of his home town. Because of his pliant nature and doleful prettiness as a baby, someone in the family said he was "sweet as fudge." His lifelong nickname was born. In the end, nobody thought of the actual meaning of the word. The sound of it simply came to represent him. His great success came early, as leading man in a high school play. Everyone said he should go on the stage and, with longing fantasies, he believed them. But when his father died, Fudge had to stay home to support his mother and sister as a clerk in the men's clothing store. His sister eventually married. Perhaps in time he would be free for his supposed destiny. But his mother lived long enough to see his youth pass by. When she died, he went to live with his sister and her husband. Fudge was now fat, from moodily drinking beer after work. Presently he took to hard liquor. People, at first kindly, "forgot" his early promise, and then gradually became impatient with the morose drunkard who lost his job. The town tightened its hold on him. There was nowhere else for him to go. His brother-in-law gave him just enough money to buy whisky and go to the movies several times a week. By the time he died in bloated middle age, Fudge had become a local figure of fun, and knew it.

§310

On the train. Very small girl child in next stateroom, speaking to her mother, who is bored, a "glamorous" type:

"I hurt myself."

No reply.

"I *hurt* myself."

No reply.

Child: "Does it still hurt?"

§311

She: Now let me tell you about X and Y.

He: You told me last year.

She: I couldn't have. This happened only this year.

He: Oh.

She: What does *that* mean?

He: It means "oh."

§312

A child seriously waving as I go by.

§313

"I have my pride," she said, looking earnestly to see if you think she has something worth protecting.

§314

A character in a bar-restaurant, a drunken blonde with short-cropped hair, is supping with a young man who is narrowly attentive to her increasing looseness of thought and talk. Attacking a salad of raw vegetables, she says, between bites and drinks, "I'm of rabbit descent. Irish, German, and rabbit." Eating: "My choppers are in good shape." A drink. "Ought to be, price I paid my dentist." Exaggerated demonstration in a dazzle of smile to show off teeth, which she then slowly and lasciviously tastes with a sweep of her tongue. In all this, the young man sees the acquiescence which he can expect of her later, when they will be alone. Sure of what is to come, he has to shift in his chair, widening his thighs.

§315

The mother's sparkling strikes of intuition in her love for the others. Her imagination took the form of finding ways to make the world into what they desired, to the full extent of her powers.

§316

A young man setting masonry.

IV ✼ BEHIND
THE WORD

The entries in this section try to capture notions which may lie behind the actual text of a writer's work—those broader concerns, attitudes, speculations, which sustain but perhaps do not dictate to him in matters of technique or contemporary view. Breathing through every aspect of his work, the writer's general response to life, while it may remain inexplicit, shapes and declares the very anatomy of his nature.

Such notes sometimes have little to do directly with the technical act of writing.

§317

Knowing beyond thought.

§318

Why is there no philosophy of pain incidental to love?
We are prepared for it in all other human undertakings,
but not in love.

§319

Is the beloved always pre-imaged by the one who would
love? Is everyone born with a type of beauty in mind
and heart which overcomes reason and restraint once it
is recognized in life? Once loved, then, only one ideal
being, one beauty, all one's life—even though in different persons, bodies, spirits. We must pursue our own
outline of beauty and love. Perhaps man is merely trying to recover his lost rib, to reconstitute himself, to be
Adam whole again, in his quest for Eve.

§320

Literary scholarship in the United States suffers under
a fixation upon apparatus, and within the apparatus,
upon fads. It tends to take life instead of give it. It
brings our national culture into derisive disrepute
abroad, especially in England.

§321

Many writers naïvely think their lives have to be exciting before their work can be.

§322

Everyone is obsessed by something, which is often concealed. It is often as innocent as it is guilty. It may be the central fact about any individual, from which all actions radiate. The novelist must know what it is, in each case. He may not always state it.

§323

The word "creative" has, through enthusiastic and often misapplied tolerance, lost much of its primal dignity. It was once reserved for acts of high achievement. Now, rather, it reflects, in its connotation relating to the arts and sciences, a naïve respect for any individual's longing for fulfillment through self-expression. This has made its effect in our educational system, from the pre-kindergarten through the graduate school. A wobbling line leads from the earliest finger-painting and free-word exercises to the swarming activities in "creative writing" courses in high school, college, summer "writers' conferences," graduate schools, and, by a pathetic stretch, to alliance with the masterpieces of the great. Out of a kindly conviction that self-expression is good, indeed, therapeutic, in itself, we have fostered in today's young a condition of cultural aspiration and confidence which brings the opportunity to "create" within the reach of anyone with the smallest impulse toward original expression, whether the result be smudge or beauty. My favorite exhibit in result of this process is a pair of earrings which a dentist, skilled professionally in working with gold, fashioned for his wife from the baby teeth of their adored daughter.

Thus, because the act of art is necessarily an individual matter, the reassurance of the artist, however modestly gifted, is indeed an affirmation by his democratic society that what he tries to do is worthwhile, if only to honor his vision, cranky or inspired, of happy fulfillment; and that it may in some cases—who ever knows?—lead to a career in his chosen field which will be appealing to the public.

§324

If sincerity ever *sees* itself, it is lost.

[145]

§325

The pervasive U.S. fictional theme: leaving boyhood. Why?

§326

Sometimes we have the sense that even the best current American fiction is not quite adult in its perceptions and styles. Why do many of our accepted novelists write like truculent adolescents? Can our national boyhood have lasted *this* long?

§327

Every person with a fairly well developed body of knowledge—which will generally consist of education of his own interests—has a special feeling for a particular period in history.

There he finds affinities of character and style which have much to do with how he sees himself, how he relates to his own times, and how, if he is an artist, he will present both in his work.

§328

The worst pornography is that which promises more than it delivers.

§329

A deliberate search for broadening experience often results in a levelling of the unfamiliar to the commonplace. The writer who needs to go far afield for his essential subject is not by true vocation a writer.

§330

If one were to write a lecture or essay on the reality of the artist's imagination, one might call it "Balzac's Physician," after Dr. Bianchon, whom Balzac invented for his *Comédie,* for on his deathbed Balzac said, "Only Bianchon can save me. . . ."

§331

If all art (I paraphrase Pater) aspires to the condition of music, perhaps all perception aspires to the condition of disembodiment. The abstract as analogy for the mystical.

§332

It is not necessary to be an original thinker to be a great novelist—that is to say, an artist—for it is not his purpose to contribute to systematic knowledge. Moreover, as any creative scientist will tell you, science is fugitive, while art is long.

§333

Every act of art is an act of love.

§334

Every act of growth in an artist is painful; always to the grower; often to his observers.

§335

Among man's irresponsible impulses is that which would destroy history and all its evidences. Why is respect for "what really happened" left to the concern of specialists, for the most part?

§336

In general, the artist is a more trustworthy critic of literature than the most intellectualistic analyst or annotator whose culture is bounded by the prevailing cults for social, historical, or psychological theories. Theories are fugitive. The intuitive response of the artist is enduring, for it is of the very nature of the thing it discusses.

§337

What treachery any change in an individual character appears to be to its familiars! This is no less true of valid and beautiful change, with its inevitable withdrawals and substitutions in relationships, than of disheartening change in disease, impropriety, or decline.

§338

A philosopher without the ability to command a clear rhetorical style is like a swimmer trying to breathe water.

§339

If Byron's life had been less profligate, would his poetry have been more profound? Was there too much practice and too little intuition in his work? Or did he know that he did not possess the gift of profundity, and so gave himself to the cynical languors of the sensual amateur in both life and work?

§340

The true writer is always at work, even when he does not know it.

§341

The vast popularization of "psychology" is the writer's chief hazard in our period.

§342

The boy's wish is ampler than the man's success.

§343

Like Antaeus, the artist must touch earth to gain strength. Each artist must define "earth" for himself. It will be the image of his hidden needs.

§344

To love, and experience, beyond himself, is the writer's most rewarding obligation.

§345

Perfect elegance represents justice to material or occasion—the arc of style between all culture and even its most humble materials.

§346

The object of our satire is the other face of our love.

§347

Suffering is generic. Joy is particular. That is why it is easier to depict the first than the second.

§348

What one will always sorrow over is determined in childhood.

§349

Memory invents more than it remembers. Hence the art of fiction.

§350

There is no writer, from the early student to the great public figure, who can with entire equanimity receive the smallest adverse criticism of his work.

§351

Nowadays, one's students turn in their new writings with the remark, "I like it. I think you will." I have never in my life said to anyone, of my own work, "I like it." Nothing I have set down fulfilled entirely what I meant it to do.

§352

Innovation may, or may not, be attached to a particular talent, of which it is only a single element. It is the talent which matters, not the innovation.

§353

The idea of competitiveness between artists is infantile and finally destructive to good work, as it distracts attention and dissipates energy in the wrong direction, for an ultimately trivial reason.

§354

Everyone can endure fame, worldly rewards, recognition of merit; but if to achieve these is the reason why one writes, his work will not finally be worth much in itself.

§355

§355

Banality and Heroism. Why do we expect heroes—
such as the moon-landing astronauts—to be heroic in all
their thought, their rhetoric, their style, as well as in
their triumphs of technique and character? It is always
a shock to hear, from the mouths and spirits of such
men as space conquerors or geniuses of surgery or en-
gineering, the sounds and sentiments of peppy under-
graduates, and see them chew gum, and watch their
happy firesides in their game rooms, and feel their un-
critical contentment in the milieu of the mechanized
banality and mindless style of life as advertised today.

§356

Movies as against reading: one reason movies are so
often exhausting: the medium because of the nature of
photography is of the highest momentary plausibility,
and when it indulges in movement for its own sake—
which is its greatest danger and temptation—we are
dragged along by a sort of dynamic negativeness. Our
effort to comply, and agree, as partners to a spurious
performance, simply exhausts us.

§357

The artist's performance rests each time on a conquest of himself.

§358

The difference between myth and fiction: one is culturally collective, the other an individual creation.

§359

We now exist in the Age of the Loss of Choice.

§360

The writer who thinks himself larger than life will never have any secrets to discover.

§361

Profoundly to understand one art is to be able to articulate principles—though not necessarily techniques—applicable to all arts. "Form" in one art can never convincingly be imitated in another; but analogies are possible—and not only from one art to another, but from science to art, and *vice versa.*

§362

Stravinsky once said—apropos critics *et al.*—that the real point about not paying any attention to their views, whether pro or con, is that nothing they say can in any way at all affect the inherent quality of a work—make it better or worse than it actually is. One should therefore pay attention only to one's own vision, desire, and practice in one's efforts to make (his word for create) a work of art. This made explicit for me what I had long but vaguely felt to be true; and it fortified my own view that vanity and a spirit of competitiveness in the arts are not even childish—they are simply idiotic.

§363

To tell, because he knows, is the artist's passion. What he knows is that all things are new every day.

§364

Myth: the collective dream of the deep past recovered.

§365

Art is a body of revelations about life, and the artist's genius is the power to make plausible to others that which has been revealed to him.

§366

To "teach writing" is to help a student to recognize his own true voice, and then let him go.

§367

One can like another writer's work without in the least desiring to be influenced by it.

§368

To be possessed, and at the same time self-critical—this is the writer's intimate challenge at work.

§369

Whatever the degree of his talent or genius, the artist never feels superior to his subject or the material of life. If he possess every gift and lack humility, the writer will never speak with a whole spirit.

§370

The true writer feels humility not before the greater aspects of life, but the lesser—even the smallest.

After re-reading *Anna Karenina:* The first lesson is humility before all objective life. This must be learned before any true right exists to focus upon and express the self. The meeting of these two callings may make an artist. Both are needed, in the order I have indicated. The fact that we are in an age of the subjective and abstractionism or non-objectivism does not change the principle. The meaning of everything may be *felt* from within; but not everything can be *learned* from within. The paradox: the self is eloquent only as it loves beyond itself.

§372

A writer may be as arrogant as you please in his personal life, but if he is not humble in respect to his work, all is lost. A true writer is as humble under his successes as under his failures.

§373

Art: where wisdom and feeling converge, in an act of aesthetic value.

§374

A true work of literature exists, above all, between the lines.

§375

The young writer is often more effective with style than with substance. The older, experienced writer commands substance—and mourns the time when style was all.

§376

For the writer, suffering is seen and endured in two fashions—one, in personal pain; the other, in active and detached observation.

§377

The book which seems to write itself, as the saying goes, is—if it is a good book—almost always the outcome of years of development, enrichment, and the forming of design, whether in notes or in the unconscious.

§378

A given piece of flattery is good for once only.

§379

In the beginning was the word: and so also at the end.

§380

God latent in us.

§381

Any truth, wholly perceived and precisely conveyed, contains an abundance of symbolic meaning. Truth always contains symbolism, which is for others to recognize, not for the author to contrive as such.

§382

A writer who loves his art more than his own work as part of it will never begrudge a fellow writer the praise due to him.

§383

How painful it is not to love the work of persons you love.

§384

Motto for teachers: The debt one cannot pay to the dead must be paid to the living.

§385

To release the anonymous human beauty within the banality of daily life—this is a novelist's challenge which even Flaubert did not meet with entire success.

§386

It is a delicate thing—that fabric of plausibility upon which a work of the imagination rests. One implausible detail, and we distrust the whole fabric.

§387

There is a kind of glib, expedient inventiveness in fiction which can give a novel a tired air of running for fear of falling.

§388

To share his enigma without explaining it—this is one of the artist's natural purposes.

§389

An inverted prudery is at work downgrading writers who do not adopt the new permissiveness in the vocabulary of obscenity.

§390

Art is an analogy of life by example and parallel: *I* will be *felt* and *known,* that *you* may *feel* and *know.*

§391

The artist's *real* hardship: daily communication with others, in *their* terms.

§392

The artist's completion is in art, rather than in "life," however much he may fancy the opposite to be true and —God knows—desirable for happiness. *All* the ordinary completions of "life" would not enlighten or satisfy him whose channels to reality are by way of art. This, unluckily, it is almost impossible to remember in the midst of pain or passionate solitude, whether these last for an hour or for years.

§393

The greatest artists are those who fuse, in their own natures, the most antithetical anomalies in character. This fusion they have used as very part of their genius, suffered it, and fostered it. By aesthetic means, the artist strives to reconcile opposites. The more extreme the opposites, and the more central the reconciliation, the more aesthetically satisfying.

§394

Some writers continue to the end the vulgar process of inventing themselves in public.

§395

His own experience resonating against the world of others—this is the writer's reference.

§396

What gives us pleasure in reading? Cast of mind? Profundity of thought? Technical excellence? Ingenuity of invention? Pulse of life? Any or all of these, at any level of writing, from the most serious to the lightest—provided the author believes wholly in what he is doing.

§397

Cynicism provides the easiest and cheapest way in the world to be sure of everything.

§398

Irony differentiates. Cynicism never does.

How many all about us live desperately on memories which life—but not love—has transcended? We should pray for every human creature we pass in the street. Each has his own internal history so complicated that only God the Creator can sort out its elements and make judgments. Am I being told that charity is nothing if it is not entire? That above all it is those who helplessly move to destroy my hope, my happiness, my love, and myself, who must *first* have my prayer and absolution? Time enough, after that, for me to try to forgive myself through the anonymous, vast companionship of the human world.

§400

Across time and distance.

§401

Fiction and biography are related arts.

§402

We need a word somewhere between "talent" and "genius."

§403

In values of art, which is more important: that which is said, or how it is said? The first relates to the short view, the second to the long. How far are the two separable? Questions to meditate upon before beginning a work.

§404

The spirit that can imagine God is inexhaustible.

§405

The writer and the necessity of a spiritual conviction: not necessarily that within formalized religion, but a view which allows—demands—of him a sense of kinship with all creation. The ego may have to be the vehicle for any statement of this kinship, but must never take precedence over it. It is a signal of spiritual decay in our day that the most received (read notorious) authors are those whose work is merely a howling pretext for the exploitation of their infantile appetite for attention and feeding.

§406

In my fiction I hope to enclose in a precisely appropriate and thus beautiful form a story which rises from the interaction of characters brought alive through empathy for human life, in settings which are evocative in atmosphere, set forth in language interesting for its own sake as well as for its suitability to the subject matter.

In my non-fiction—history, biography, other forms—I hope to keep the truth of actual events while retelling them in such a manner that the resources of the novelist in presenting episode and person allow the reader a sense of experiencing the past rather than simply hearing about it.

§407

Generally speaking, abundance of works is an essential mark of the true writer, who is open to a multiplicity of themes, and thus to multiple choices of appropriate forms.

§408

Once again, art is form. Without form—order, design, felicity in related ideas—raw material remains raw; nature remains wild; life buries its own meanings. Form is for the writer as for all artists the great inclusive problem. Solve this, with all its parts, and you will enter into the mystery of the maker.

PART THREE

MEMOIR OF AN APPRENTICE

i

THE SENSIBLE THING to do about a literary apprenticeship is to accept it as a necessary experience of growth rather than as a period of repeated disappointment and frustrated ambition. The aspirant always hopes that his first efforts will be publishable works—I hoped so myself. Having always been a devouring reader, I was in my late adolescence certain that the literary arts were already at my command, and I was given encouragement by my elders and betters to believe that my vocation as a writer was a true one. At the present stage of my life and work I can only conclude that in general they were right; but I was wrong in thinking that all one had to do to be published and hailed was to deliver one's first book to any eminent publisher, as though high ambition in extreme youth presupposed the possession of mature talent.

The actuality is almost invariably otherwise, except in the case of extraordinary genius, and that usually a poet's, not a novelist's. Poets of genius, like creative scientists of the first and very spare rank, have sometimes made their essential discoveries, if not statements, early in life; and if they lived long, it was to factor out, as it were, the equations, poetic or scientific, which they early discovered as illuminative truth about life, whether aesthetic in nature or systematically intellectual.

Other "makers"—once again I use Igor Stravinsky's designation for the artist, which, with his etymological awareness, he habitually preferred to the word "creators"—other makers have generally found that they must in a certain passage of their earliest adult years allow for time in which to learn the structure of their art.

This was true in my own case. From years of working with students of varying degrees of talent I suppose many other cases to be similar, though not identical even in essential aspects. Here I tell the story of my own apprenticeship, effort by effort, in the assumption that the chronicle may be helpful, perhaps even amusing, since many of its events may justifiably be treated in a facetious tone, though my underlying purpose was entirely serious; and in some instances my experience may approximately confirm that of younger artists who if gifted may still feel trapped in a period of failure and obscurity, while they long for immediate achievement and acclaim.

ii

The apprentice's early work will usually reflect the influence upon him of writers in whose works he is currently living. I put it this way because there are few experiences more intense that those of the young reader whose sense of reality is captured by the vision of someone else's books. The outlook of whole generations is sometimes colored by a prominent contemporary writer's persuasive view of the world. The first responses in writing by novices are likely to be reminders of one, then another, author, whom they read. The imitation is not helpful if it is an unconscious one, for the young writer, not ready with any formed vision of his own, or with a style which reflects his own quality of mind and the measure of his physical energy, will tend to reproduce that which seems to him excellent in the work of others, and in doing so, he will fabricate something untrue to his own being.

Seeking, sometimes almost with desperation, for ways of self-expression does not often lead directly to finding one's own authority in the matter. The apprentice writer is usually more concerned with the act of writing than with its innate meaning. He learns earlier how to say something rather than what to say, paradoxical as this may sound. He has not yet lived long enough to know a bountiful life, whether in thought or act, and thus has less to write about than his technical abilities might already be able to set forth.

My own earliest imitations took form as verse. These were first devoted to echoes of the sentiments of Anglo-American immigrants from the East about the folk practices of upper New Mexico, where some of my boyhood years were spent. Later I proceeded to manneristic exercises after the early poems of T. S. Eliot, notably *Portrait of a Lady*. Derivative as they were, a few such pieces were published by Harriet Monroe in POETRY: *A Magazine of Verse* before I was twenty. Some of the "little magazines" and fugitive anthologies used others of my poems, then and later.

It was, then, as a poet, among other roles, at the age of twenty that I arrived in Rochester, New York, from Albuquerque, New Mexico, to enter the Eastman School of Music, where I was to study singing in a full curriculum of musical training. I was also a painter, stage designer, and actor. At that time, this variety of purposes seemed to me no great burden to carry. I was blithe in the face of the judgment of solicitous family members and friends who enjoyed saying that I was so versatile that I would never amount to anything. What they observed was a lack of continued concentration on my part in any one field, which was naturally upsetting. Even more so must have been my refusal to consider any other purpose in life but to be an artist of one or another sort. I exhibited this with less than becoming modesty.

A young man of extraordinary talents converged upon Rochester as I did. He had recently served as musical assistant to Serge Koussevitzky in Paris. This was Nicolas Slonimsky, a Russian musical virtuoso—pianist, composer, conductor—who possessed also astonishing capacities for scholarly undertakings, particularly in matters of language and literature. (He became the famous musical lexicographer of today.) When we met he could use only two expressions in English, "Please" and "Thank you." He learned that I was, however obscurely, already a published author, and he asked me to teach him English. Thinking this quite natural, I assented, and gave him *Pickwick Papers* to read, asking him first to learn the English alphabet and then to read the Dickens without the aid of a dictionary. He had some difficulties for perhaps two weeks, but not long afterward he was with startling effect speaking Pickwickian English in a dense Russian accent, and asking for more books to absorb. I kept him supplied, and when he asked to see my meager writings, I let him have them.

Not yet critically literate in English, he concluded that I was an important writer. He urged me to publish a book of poems, and to continue with my writing of short stories—for I had shown him one called "The Baptists" which described the terrifying experience of attending a week of revival meetings in Albuquerque when I was sixteeen. It was the final venture of an exercise undertaken with a close friend of my own age. Together we spent many evenings attending the services of a great variety of denominations in pursuit of what, with mock pedantry, we called "An Investigation into Religion in the Interior of America." On the last day of that week, when I went alone to the meeting, no more converts remained who could be urged down to the mourners' bench to "confess Jesus." Absorbed in making surreptitious notes, I suddenly heard the sweating revivalist pleading directly with me, where I crouched at the rear of the hall, to come forward. All eyes in the emotional congregation were at once turned upon me with awesome hypnotic power. I tried to feel invisible, but I felt myself slowly becoming subject, under a mindless impulse, to move forward down the aisle to join the bellowing and wailing mob of the inspired. I came to stand, and seemed to sway dizzily in the direction of the evangelist, who held his arms out to receive me while the congregation began to raise their voices in a sort of bleating incantation to overcome me. At the last minute I rescued myself by running blindly into the vestibule, seeking safe exit. But there I found my access to the door barred by muscular Baptist youths who were convinced they must save me. They tried to detain me with soothing words and stout arms. I heard myself shout, "For Christ's sake, let me alone! I am a pagan!" at which in their shock they fell back, I escaped, ran ten blocks, and then fell upon a curbstone of South Broadway in Albuquerque, and sobbed with exhaustion and relief. My own shouted words echoed in my ears and I could not think where they could have come from, for I was a Roman Catholic —a fact, in those pre-ecumenical days, which might have been even more effective if I had shouted it against my captors.

This story, declared Slonimsky, was a masterpiece, and should have recognition as such. Asking permission to have it translated into Russian, which I granted with affected indifference, he sent it to Paris, where after many months it appeared in the June 29, 1926 issue of the Russian refugist newspaper *The Link* —Звено, as the masthead said. My story was announced on the first page and printed on the second. The translation, which I could not read, as I have never known Russian, was by one K.M., unidentified. My title read Баптисты ("The Baptists"), and my name appeared at the end as Поль Хорганъ. I stared at my text with swollen satisfaction. Nothing more was ever heard of it, but to have my first story published in Russian, in Paris, was not only exotic—it seemed a career in itself.

As for poems, I gathered a volume under the title *The Burnished Caravel*, which Slonimsky, in his initial stage of admiring English which was ornamented and excessive, thought nobly fine, perhaps making vague connections between my title and *Le Bateau Ivre,* and Arnold Böcklin's painting *The Isle of the Dead,* with its mortuary ship, about which Rachmaninoff had written a tone poem; and I set about finding a publisher.

How, I do not recall, but I selected all unknowing one of those houses which make their way by printing books at the author's expense. The editor wrote enthusiastically about my book, making one or two suggestions which I thought proved a high degree of professionalism on my part and his. I returned my revisions to him and announced to Slonimsky that *The Burnished Caravel* would presently appear.

[180]

I was wrong, for in a return mail came not only the editor's firm acceptance of my book, but a request for the "usual" payment of nine hundred dollars by the author, who would retain all rights, while the publisher would manage distribution of review and bookstore copies. My career collapsed. I coldly asked for the return of the poems, declaring that even if I had the money, I would refuse to pay for the publication of my own work. Several letters followed offering to reduce the charge, but I was fixed in my principles and my dignity, and eventually the manuscript was returned to me, while I received the condolences of Slonimsky, who had made rapid progress in English, and could see that it was just as well—as I now could— that the book would not, after all, appear.

On the whole, it seemed that I would do better to give what time I had for it to the writing of fiction—something sizable; a fresh view; a major effort; in fact, a novel.

iii

Through my need for a job, which came upon me suddenly, my work as a singing student had merged with the duties of scene designer and painter to the Rochester American Opera Company, and I had little time in an unreasonable schedule to find the discipline and the energy for writing a novel in addition to performing my paid services. But it was a time of life when a reasonable schedule was an absurdity, and by a simple scattering of energy alone, I suppose, I made myself into a figure of the arts whom others took seriously—or at any rate indulgently. I was made a member of the Corner Club near the Eastman School and Theatre where I worked, and there at lunch every day and at parties after concerts in the evening I was allowed to be a peer of notables in the world of the arts as Rochester then drew them together—such as Rouben Mamoulian, Eugene Goossens and his wife, Vladimir Rosing, Ernst Bacon, Otto Luening, Martha Graham, and other members of the school faculty. Along with these, certain artists identified with Rochester, such as the painter Kathleen McEnery Cunningham, and the architect Herbert Stern, and various local people who supported the arts, were also members of the Corner Club. It was a gratification when the Club committee decided to hang a large oil painting of mine of the Sangre de Cristo range near Santa Fe, painted in impasto as thick as cake icing, and in colors as joyously contrary to nature as befitted any Fauve, as I thought of myself.

Wondering all that winter what to do about invoking my desired novel, I was given my central character when the Peruvian prima donna contralto Marguerite D'Alvarez came to town for a concert. I was exactly ready for her.

She was already a cult with me through her remarkable phonograph records, which despite the early shortcomings of acoustical recording technique caught a surprising plenty of her vocal opulence and emotional style. Her legend as a fatal woman off-stage was known to music lovers, and I could place her prophetically in the world of the criticism and the fiction of Carl Van Vechten. His characters were persons of extravagant styles and pliable morals, all set forth in unconventional prose in which characters spoke without quotation marks, gratifyingly like those in French novels, and what they did was described in a beckoning mixture of common frankness and richly obscure polysyllables. Nothing could be more to my taste at the time, and when, first, I heard D'Alvarez in her concert, and, afterward at the Corner Club, when I met and talked at length with her, the encounter was like a confirmation.

Madame D'Alvarez was like a sculpture of overflowing womanhood by Gaston Lachaise, whose work I admired. Despite her great depth of bosom, width of arm, breadth of hip and thigh, she was beautiful; and when she spoke it was with a deep throaty voluptuousness rapidly expressed in English of the utmost theatrical elegance in pronunciation. As for what she said—nothing could have been more satisfactorily outrageous. It was an epoch reaching from Theda Bara to Nita Naldi in the films, but D'Alvarez made them seem like convent girls instead of vamps to distraction.

As I came into the upstairs drawing room of the Club after her concert, I saw her seated in the center of a yellow silk sofa, occupying it all but totally. She was addressing a fifth of a pound of *Port du Salut* cheese on a piece of French bread which she held above eye level. Her heavy black eyebrows, converged in a lofty angle of suffering and ecstasy as though in a moment of sex, drew her huge black eyes into a focus of deathless beauty, I thought, as I heard her say to the cheese,

"My God, cheese like angels' lips—divine, damp, and thrilling." In one great swallow, it was gone.

This was how a leading character in a novel must sound, I was certain. On being presented to her, and speaking ardent compliments on her magnificent singing, I accepted her invitation to take the last edge of her sofa, while she continued with her consumption of a trayful of post-concert solids which had been set on a small table before her wide, shining knees.

"What was my best?" she asked in a speaking voice enriched by the crumbs and pastes, the sauces and dressings, the meats of

[183]

sea and pasture, which in a continuous stream of nourishment invited and enlarged her appetite. She seemed, in fact, all appetites personified, and I was enlivened by the seductive aura of her presence.

"Oh," I said instantly, "the Debussy—*La Chevelure.*"

"How clever of you. You are right." (An inch-thick spread of *pâté de foie gras* between triangles of toast went down.) "I always sing it in honor of my darling. He never knows it."

She had sung it with such heavily breathed carnality and at the same time such beauty of tone and inflection—had acted the insatiate endurance of love's coupling with such elegance of gesture which her body enlarged—that she had made the belly go hollow with desire. The performance had been as frankly sexual as it was wonderfully lyric. She had made me imagine explicitly the scene of which Pierre Louÿs had written, and to which Debussy had composed his song. In translation, then, something like this:

He told me: "I dreamed last night. I had your hair about my neck. I had strands of your hair like a black necklace around my nape and across my breast. I caressed them and they were mine. And we were bound mouth to mouth forever by the same hair, like two laurels, which often have but one root. And little by little, our limbs were so mingled that I became yourself, or that you entered into me like my very dream." When he had done, he gently laid his hands upon my shoulders and he looked at me with a gaze so tender that I lowered my eyes, quivering.

In the last lines, her impersonation of maidenly modesty had been so implausible that by its very artifice she managed somehow to increase the voluptuous intimacy of her effect.

With a solemnity which must have excused its cheekiness I asked her my question, which she received as naturally as though youths of twenty asked it of her every day,

"You are in love, Madame?"

"My dear boy, insanely." (A forkful of five shrimps dipped in *rémoulade* sauce.) "He lives in New York. When I am home between tours I send for him and when I hear his steps coming up my *escalier* I break into flame within myself, I become an awakening volcano, and then, as he comes nearer, I freeze, I become a goddess of frigidity whom he must reduce to her native fire, and when he at last enters my *boudoir,* I am like the moon—visible, glowing, but untouchable." (Four narrow, sliced chicken sandwiches held together, garnished with water cress and dressed with escaping mayonnaise.) "He has a waist like a wasp and shoulders like a grand piano." (A clutch of Spanish olives stuffed with peeled Moroccan almonds.) Her great restless eyes, black as smoky topaz with gold lights, roved the room and kept returning to me, and I must have breathed like the visitant in *La Chevelure,* for, looking at me now, she said, reading my thought,

"Yes, yes, isn't it?"

I shivered and she laughed gorgeously, pleased at having made her effect, and laying her hand, with its huge rings encrusted like sea deposits, on my tingling thigh, she said,

"You must come and see me when you are in New York. I scream with loneliness."

"Oh, no, Madame!"

"Oh, yes. No one is constant, I am so simple, all I ask is to be understood, perhaps you understand me. I feel that in you. I am never wrong when I feel, only when I think.—What is your life to be?" she asked. "You will be an artist." She managed to convey in that word an essential nature using it so broadly as to allow of my existence in any of the arts. Before I could go beyond the word "aspirations," she said, "Let me tell you about mine. How wonderful that someone will listen."

"I have listened to you for years, Madame," I said, "through your wonderful phonograph records."

"Yes, they tell me something about my voice is suited to the machine.—But let me tell you:" and she went on to say, in a monologue with hardly a pause even when she dealt with her swiftly selected snacks, how she was the daughter of an ancient royal Inca house of Peru, how her father had been ambassador to Belgium, where the King after hearing her sing at a soirée— she was still a girl—had tried every imaginable method of seducing her, how she had run away secretly one night because she was virtuous and he was loathsome, how her family had finally consented to allow her to become a stage person, how Oscar Hammerstein had built his London opera house for her despite which she had never taken him in sin, how he had pursued her to America where he had created his New York seasons for her even while she still resisted him, how she had gone to the Chicago Opera there to endure ingenious snubs from the star of the company, Mary Garden, who was also the manageress, who seemed to sing through a narrow rubber tube, and then, how she herself had had public triumphs in Chicago despite the accident at her debut as Delilah in the opera of Saint-Saëns, for at the top of a long flight of stairs where she had made her first entrance her heel had caught on a loose board and she had fallen and rolled the entire length of the staircase to the stage floor, only to rise as if nothing had happened, and had entered upon her first notes with such magnificence that the audience had gone mad, halting the performance in a demonstration of love. Why, she asked, was public love her fate, when God had made her for love in private?

She sadly swallowed a draught of champagne and held her empty glass forth without looking at it to a waiter who was passing with a wrapped bottle. He filled it while she gazed at me, working her circumflex brow up and down dreamily. Her lips darkly rouged almost to blackness made silently tasting motions. When I began to speak again it was in a shaken voice which I tried to control by asking a desperately trivial question.

"Madame, have you ever sung with Goossens—" pointing to him where across the room he was conversing in abstracted charm with a worshipping group.

"Oh my God yes," she replied. "He is such a total musician, and so *soigné* besides. Not," she added with luxurious scorn, "like the man now conducting the New York orchestra, with whom I have sung. When that one conducts, he spreads his legs behind him like a Percheron stallion relieving itself in a great yellow stream splashing into a layer of straw in a byre on a farm in Brittany! How can one sing next to that?"

I had never heard a woman refer to such natural functions at all, much less in her extravagant particularity. I was momentarily muted, if fascinated, and in that moment, someone else came to absorb her attention which, turning to him with an enlarged grace and tumbling all her jewels and brocades, she distributed in the impartiality of celebrated persons. I must give way.

George Houston, the singer, was across the room. A tall young man of splendid presence, he had a constant air of detachment except where young women were concerned, and, I thought, a strangely original way of talking which I tried to adopt when with him. We were close friends. Older than I, he had served as part of an ambulance unit in France during the war which I had missed by several years. Now he was observing everyone at the party and he was ready for me when I joined him and began to repeat Madame's most extreme remarks. He listened gravely, taking air into his nostrils in little inward gusts, in an effect of comment. I relayed the scene of D'Alvarez awaiting her lover. Houston said,

"The poor bastard."

"It isn't his fault," I said.

"No, it isn't his fault. He's not a poor bastard," he said.

"She's an experience, all right," I said.

"A very foreign experience. All foreigners are experiences. Have a drink."

"No thanks," I said.

"We're all poor bastards," he said, "when we think of it. Let's not think of it."

"All right, we won't think of it. Have a drink," I said.

"All right." He raised his glass. *"Vivent les vulves,"* he said.

"Do you think he knows he's a poor bastard?" I asked over my glass.

"He knows. They always know. He pretends nobody else knows."

"You have to pretend sometimes," I said.

"That's right. Sometimes you have to. Don't ever pretend," he said.

"What am I to do about D'Alvarez?" I asked.

"Go up to her and fall on one knee and say, Madam, when can I sleep with you?"

"I've only just met her. She would think I wasn't showing respect," I said.

"All right. If you said, Madam when can I sleep with you, that wouldn't be showing respect. But it would be very fine and full of respect if you put it the other way."

[188]

"What way?"

"Put it any other way you like, so long as you put it. Putting it is the important part. It's very fine, too.—It's time we had another," he said.

"All right," I said.

"This is fine Canadian rye. *Vive le bootlegger,*" he said. "You must drink it truly and well. Never with soda, though."

"Why?"

"Bubbles," he said. "Bad for the aim."

Throughout countless such dialogues—the one I give is of course not remembered verbatim but the style and attitude are really how he talked and how through practice I fell in with his convention—we always preserved blank faces. I had never heard anyone talk like him; and when two years or so later I read *The Sun Also Rises* on its first appearance, I was astonished to hear Houston on every page, and I concluded that the author's generation and Houston's, returning from the War, echoed a system of expression common to alienated ambulance drivers whether they served in France or Italy. But at the time, I had no idea that Houston was prophetically voicing an artificial style which later found its popular master.

As for Madame D'Alvarez, in a little while I said a decorous good night and left her—but not forever, for I saw her a few times in after years, and we had friends in common, one of whom—he was very handsome—had mailed her his photograph asking for hers in return. She sent it with the inscription, "To Mr Hunt, whom I should like to bite." She used to answer my letters in her huge handwriting—eight or ten words to a page—in purple ink on gray paper. Carl Van Vechten once told me that she had a fine technique for maintaining a correspondence: whenever she had a free moment she wrote a letter on a few pages, without salutation or signature, and filed it in her desk. It was composed of extravagant generalities in her most lavish manner. She had dozens of such pre-written letters available, and whenever she received a letter which required an answer, she would at random select one of her own stock, add a florid salutation and a passionate signature, and send it off. Readers who may feel that I have exaggerated her style should consult her autobiography (*Forsaken Altars,* 1954) whose tone more than confirms my own impressions.

She later figured in novels by Van Vechten under the name Claire Madrilena—in *Firecrackers* (1925) singing *La Chevelure* with "shameless effrontery," and in *Parties* (1930), eating "so much that one wondered how she found time to be witty." Even as late as 1972, Alfred Knopf told me at luncheon a story about her which had the unmistakable tone. He reported how she had told Van Vechten that Vicente Blasco-Ibañez, taking her home one night in a taxi, bit her in the shoulder and left a gold tooth there.

In 1920 Van Vechten published a broadsheet about D'Alvarez in the *Musical Courier* which her manager used. It said, "I have never heard her sing any song in which she did not exhibit everything inherent in the music and sometimes a great deal more. For Debussy she has an almost mystic understanding . . . She has one of the most noble voices of our time," and "on the platform she becomes imbued with an ecstatic spirit, the contagion of which easily slips across the footlights into the vast spaces of any auditorium; her noble presence, her beauty, her eloquence, her passion, her intensity, her unconventional method of approaching her task (for she does not entirely forego the privilege of acting even on the concert stage) will reach the heart. . . ."

To resolve not my own earlier reaction to her but a renewed

connection with this memorable woman, I will recall that during the Second World War, when I was stationed briefly in Hollywood, I lived at a lavish billet called the Château Elysée. The air was languorous and fine to breathe, and I kept all windows open high amidst palm trees, and above jacaranda trees, plumbago and bougainvillea and scented groves, and so, evidently, did everyone else; for diagonally across from my place was another apartment hotel, from whose open windows I kept hearing unsettling sounds. They were loud, despairing shrieks, vocalizing on the scale, rising a half-tone with each repetition, and forcing me to shut my windows to avoid the most unmusical noises I had ever heard from a human voice.

My friend Houston was then living in Hollywood, directing productions of opera for a local company and also—so various was life in Hollywood—starring in low-budget films about cowboys and horses, both of whom he detested. One day while we were playing tennis I told him about the depressing screams from across the street. He said,

"Yes, of course, that is where Marguerite lives. That is whom you are hearing." In fact, he meant D'Alvarez. "She has Sunday soirées when people come to play and sing for her and she keeps promising to sing for them but never does. I'll take you."

We went the next Sunday evening. Houston told her I was her neighbor. With much grace of manner she swore she remembered me and our exchanges of letters, and she told me a new chapter of her sorrowful story.

A disastrous love affair in Paris had destroyed her voice, though she had not given up, but vocalized every day to recover it. She read my face.

"You have heard me?" I admitted it. "Then you know." I said nothing—she said it for me. "Alas."

[191]

She was in poverty, having to sell one emerald at a time to exist. Once or twice a year a film studio called her for a small role—I saw one humiliating movie in which she was made to play a shrewish, comedy keeper of a boarding house.

"But they never ask me to sing in the films," she said sadly.

She was much aged, after two decades, but still vivid and interesting in her looks. I went to her evenings a few more times before my orders returned me to the War Department in Washington. Somehow, during the war, she managed to get to London and there she died before the war was over. I had come to know affection for her where before she had supplied me only with moments of preposterous comedy.

Anyhow, after my meeting with her in my extreme youth, I felt that I must plan my first novel around her. It was to be about a young man searching for a career, experience, love, who meets and is fascinated by a great singer whom I named Madame Lolita Goepple. He is timid and unsure of how to reach a figure of such splendor and—it had to be admitted—menacing ardor.

The novice often wavers between two extremes of ineffectiveness. One is to contrive too eagerly to have things happen—to overconstruct his narrative. The other is to be caught up in the torment of wanting to make a statement without any idea of how to shape it.

My novel was invertebrate. Little "happened," and such events as I described evolved from no inner logic or connection. My straining after effect was visible in many passages, and in nothing so clearly as in my invention of the name Lolita Goepple. Like many of the young, I had a glib and crazy logic to explain my absurdities—the first name was to be Spanish to establish temperament for my prima donna, while the second name was meant to convey lusty appetite for food ("gobble") to which other appetites could be attached by implication and episode. But the total name was intended to be "funny," and so revealed that primitive use of outlandish names to which people of unassured talent often resort, hoping to cadge laughter. There were long descriptive but inert passages. Madame Lolita Goepple had many adventures in which the hero did not figure dynamically. Everybody but the hero was famous—conductors, novelists, painters, whose dialogues were full of expressions and touches derived from my daily discoveries in the kind of world of the arts where I was learning my way. I was happy to drop hints to my more accomplished seniors that I was working on a novel. Nobody seemed to think this unlikely or unsuitable, and in fact Eugene Goossens and his wife Boonie who had befriended me with genuine fondness, returning the love I felt for them both, proposed in an offhand way that they might be able to convey my manuscript to the publisher Alfred A. Knopf. Their faith was empowering. I kept working at my pages. I already had a title and in my inexperience I was pleased to repeat it to anyone who asked. It was *The Furtive Saint*.

"What does it mean?" they would then ask.

As I did not know, I would answer that they would have to wait and see. Slonimsky agreed with me that it was an excellent title—it sounded meaningless enough to seem significant, in a Dada sort of way.

In due course I had two hundred or so pages, and I decided that the novel was complete. I sent it to Goossens who was conducting in New York. Wisely he did not read it, but telegraphed me that he was handing the book to Alfred Knopf. I communicated this sign of fortune to my close friends and drew a Borzoi on the title page of my carbon copy. About three weeks later I received a note on blue paper which said, "Dear Mr Horgan, this is certainly not for us"—for my novel came with the letter—"but we should be glad to see any future work of yours," signed Blanche W. Knopf.

Actually, because of the brisk professionalism of this, I already felt like a novelist, though one without a publisher. I began to develop another long fiction about which I had been brooding even during the final stages of *The Furtive Saint*.

iv

I had already been immersed in a venture which gave me energy for the atmosphere of what would be my second novel. In Rochester, Rouben Mamoulian decided to stage a production of Maeterlinck's *Soeur Béatrice* using actors from his studio of theatre and dance at Eastman, with a new musical score by Otto Luening. He read the published English translation and found it inadequate. He asked me to make a start on a new English version, and when he saw my first installment, he told me I could do the whole play. My version was used for the production, in which he cast me in the role of the priest who torments Sister Beatrice—the nun who falls into earthly love and whose place is taken by the Madonna who comes down from her niche in the convent chapel to carry on the nun's humble duties so that the absence of the defecting sister (she has run away with a passionate suitor) will not be discovered by the other holy ladies. Mamoulian's production was wonderfully beautiful in every detail. To my regret I was unable to play in the finished performances owing to exhaustion traceable to my multiple duties.

But still under the spell of many weeks of work on the production, I was awash in symbolism, and the misty visions of Debussy, Maeterlinck, Dunsany, the early Yeats, various Pre-Raphaelites, Tennyson, James Stephens, Walter de la Mare, and I was even touched by the ironic medievalism of James Branch Cabell.

It is hardly remembered now, but in the twenties, Cabell exerted a great influence on critical opinion about what "literature" was, and he received the extravagant admiration of his leading contemporaries. Stephen Vincent Benét was "spreading his fame at Yale." Hugh Walpole was determined to find him an English publisher. Joseph Hergesheimer admitted him to the inner circle of beautiful letters. Sinclair Lewis and H. L. Mencken praised him unreservedly, and Carl Van Vechten went on "a Cabell debauch" of reading. Cabell himself maintained an ironic detachment—"It is with such fairy tales," he said of his books, "that I regale myself," but his mythical kingdom of Poictesme and its arch eroticism veiled in imitations of obsolete idiom he clearly intended as acts of literary art. Little of it had to do with its time of composition, except in the general attempt of elevated American writing to break away from its long prevalent tradition of drab gentility. It was not surprising that I felt the influence of the far away and long ago in writings which my elders and betters so fashionably admired.

So, from an elaborate burlesque of the contemporary sophisticated world, I was transported into the mystical and pale allusiveness of medieval legend, and I lived in a field of reference which included chivalrous princes, distant hunting horns, visions of the holy, forbidding castles with their brutal keeps, long journeys and feats of endurance and impossible trials—there was also a strong hint of Wagner here—and miraculous interventions, and malign counter-forces, all veiled in prose half-lighted and self-consciously archaic.

My paternal grandparents were Irish, and I summoned in myself all that I could imagine of the Irish faith in the piously ghostly. There was a fine freedom from logic in all of it, for one could arbitrarily have characters come and go, they hardly needed definition beyond names like Yseult and Maubrage and Fontlaven the Pure, and if anyone failed to understand what they might be about, one could allude in some disdain to an absence of interest on someone's part in the symbolic and the life behind life, if one made oneself clear. Much intellectual labor was saved by performance in such a genre, and further, there was intoxicating opportunity for the on-run of Gaelic garrulity in the narrative, so that if a thing were well said once, it were better said twice, or even thrice, with variations in the syntax to provide persuasive atmospheric assurance that the tale was indeed of the far away and long ago; so far away, in fact, and so long ago, that no one lived who might with authority challenge the inner truth of it—especially in New Mexico where I was again living.

My second novel, accordingly, was entitled *The Grey Swans*. They made their appearance in an ominous flight in an evening hour on the first page. The beat of their great wings was meant to be heard in the meter of the prose. The reader was to stir in some uneasiness, asking where they had come from, and whither they were going, as it was well known that when swans were grey instead of white or black, and that when they flew between twilight and dark, there must be reasons almost too terrible to relate, which would be related nonetheless, in the pages to follow, though as allusively and imprecisely as possible.

By means which had to do with the flight of the grey swans,

a prince of golden mien and radiant purity of heart in a far province came to know of a princess who was lovelier than the briar roses which twined against the cold rough stones of the tower where she was held prisoner, from which she must be delivered. Who could doubt that the prince must at whatever hazard be her deliverer?

Chapters were planned to account for his days. He was a great hunter, was much given to pricking his way through forests accompanied by richly decked retainers, all mounted not on horses but on caparisoned steeds, and when night fell upon the hunting party, bonfires on the floor of the great hall of one of his castles showed us the prince partaking of rare viands from golden salvers and not drinking but quaffing heady wines from golden cups rimmed with jewels taken from the crown of Maubrage the Maleficent, a neighboring king who of necessity had been vanquished by the prince's father and who lived but for vengeance. When he retired for the night asking the protection of Our Lady and St Hubert, the prince flung himself down on a bed of rushes covered with nun-made velvets, while at his feet slept his great hounds, who were sure to stir at the smallest suspicious sound, for no prince lived who was not at one moment or other, usually in the hours just before dawn, threatened by treachery on the part of one of his most trusted and comely companions. Often, when he dreamed, it was of a noble white hart wearing a coronet and gleaming like silver through the most impenetrable aisles of the forest, who must be hunted and captured, not killed, for this was a princely animal to whom a true prince would leave the gift of life. But there came a night when the prince stirred uneasily in his sleep and the great mastiffs lifted their huge heads and softly growled until their master was quiet again—he who had dreamed this night not of the crowned hart but now of a flight of grey swans passing like swift clouds into skies far away from his kingdom to a place toward which they seemed to beckon him where stood the prison tower of the sorrowful princess who awaited deliverance.

There she prayed seven times daily to Our Lady for freedom from the pains of immurement and the threat of an impending fate too appalling to be revealed just yet, as it had not yet been invented, but the very thought of which caused the princess and her faithful dame-in-waiting to cling to each other for hours at a time with their wakeful eyes fixed on the bloodstained oaken door with its great hinges and locks of beaten iron to detect the first sign of movement which would mean that the hour had come when the horror must begin, for the swans had gone, pray Our Lady they return some soon sunrise, for alas word of the prince's progress across plain, mountain, and sea was not yet known, a coming from which even the most fear-driven heart might take courage for just long enough to—

It was desperately hard work to make this sort of thing advance by even a page or two every day. I read all of Maeterlinck for Flemish courage, and walked back and forth in my room with a volume of Yeats, and I read aloud and acted alone the one-act plays of Lord Dunsany, and resorted to Malory for situations which if not to imitate at least to use by inversion, but none of it grew easier. How could this be, for others wrote medieval romances with much success and to serious acclaim, odd as this may now appear. I invented a sort of handwriting which was meant to look vaguely of the period, as if it belonged in an illuminated book of hours, and could be deciphered only by a saintly king or else a first cousin of Merlin who had spent a lifetime at scholarship amid cobwebs, guttering candles, and philosophical instruments in which beads of mercury were held in balance against grains of pure gold—all this in the hope that the very marks of my pen (who could possibly typewrite a book of that sort?) would kindle newly every day the necessary belief in what I was about. The swans and the forests, open hearths on castle floors were all well and good, but after all, what were the people like, and how could they do things unless I knew that? My established tone, lofty in the manner of an ancient tale, had to proceed, but toward what? There must be a passionate resolution between the prince and princess in all their naked glory and fleshly commingling, but this must not happen too soon.

Delaying vicissitudes and compelling postponements were required.

How would it be if, unbeknownst to them, they were brother and sister? One warmed to the possibility for technical reasons. What if the knowledge of this came to them from a wise old woman who lived in a hut of wattles and clay where she made her precarious living by gathering in a bee-loud glade faggots for the scullery of a nearby castle, and who had known long ago of their blood relationship but had been put under the terror by Maubrage the Maleficent to keep the secret until for his own evil designs he should choose to reveal it? And if one day toward eve, the prince, wounded in the hunt, were brought in delirium to her hut where she bathed his wound and saw how fair he was (Cabell would have let it be known also how bountifully he had been favored by the god of love) and how she must risk breaking her oath by telling him, upon his recovery, that the princess he was wooing in life after seeing her in dream, was alas his own sister? His despair. His noble resolve to free her anyway from the stone tower. Nodding by her candlelight, remembering like Yeats's lady after Ronsard when she herself had been fair, the old forest woman slowly recalled a spell taught her by her own grandmother, which said that if anyone ever saw the grey swans it meant something; and that if the swans flew toward the evening star it meant that certain lovers must never again think of love, for it would be evil, which in this case could only apply to the hunting prince and the immured lady; but that if the swans flew toward the new moon, it meant that the lovers were safe, and that their union would be blessed. Thereupon the old woman, though her poor bones ached for nothing but rest and sleep, sat before her hut evening after evening while the prince lay suffering but recovering slowly within; for she was watching anent the great flight should it come, and one evening of the new moon, it came, and the ghostly birds seemed to beat their way directly into the sickle of light which resembled a moon by William Blake or Samuel Palmer, or the one in Sir Patrick Spens—"I saw the new moon yestere'en wi' the auld moon in her arm"—and she painfully bustled into the hut where the prince lay on her tattered but clean old paillasse, and told him what she knew, which brought about his recovery as if by a miracle. He must be up and away—

But nothing helped, really, and lacking belief myself, I was done with the book before it was finished, even before having reached the scene of the lovers' consummation, which would have to owe something to James Branch Cabell, without adopting his nudging phallism which had so titillated a newly sophisticated public and engorged the righteous fury of Boston. The swans never flew back, the prince never arrived, and I was granted the knowledge that a book can be stillborn no matter how strong the pressure of that desire *to make* which is a torment until a proper form, rooted in conviction, is imagined.

v

With my first, I had undertaken exaggerated if not outrageous satire; with my second, a humorless and romantic unreality. I was resolved now to invoke my third novel from fragmentary materials which I had known early in my days, and to find in them humor combined with pathos which would, I felt, be a step ahead.

I knew the title before I did the story. It was to be called *Jupiter*. The allusion was to Jupiter Tonans, the head of the classic gallery of Roman gods, whose wrath was splendid, whose scowl was enough to induce thunder, and whose venerability was so commanding and so virile that in itself it brought lesser creatures to trembling. What circumstance would ever bring low such a god?

But my Jupiter was to be human—an oldening gentleman, superficially resembling my maternal grandfather, in fact, whom I knew as a child only to fear and feared only to defy in daydreams. He moved in a climate of dignity, which on occasion—trivial or great—could be disrupted by grandly elevated declamations of rage. He came from nineteenth-century Germany, and he bore within him, among many lyric and appealing traits, that sense of headship which years later I recognized the first time I heard Wagner's *Die Walküre,* and listened (it seems for hours) to Wotan as pointing his spear accusingly at her he berated his daughter Brünnhilde with bitterness, fury, and outraged vanity, in that Teutonic genius for carrying out an idiotic premise with splendor. *"Ha, Freche du!"* he cried, excoriating her disobedience, calling her an insolent girl. In noble tirades he demanded to know how she could rebel against him, she, who was meant to be only the blindly obedient instrument of his will (*"Frevelst du mir? Wer bist du, als meines Willens blind wählende Kür?"*). Let her be careful, that was all, if she didn't want to feel his wrath, for if ever its lightning should be thrown against her, her courage might fail her! (*"Kennst du, Kind, meinen Zorn? Verzage dein Mut, wenn je zermalmend auf dich stürtze sein Strahl!"*) The daughter bore it all like a submissive feature of landscape—a rock or a tree, as I had seen members of Jupiter's household do under the storm of his discipline. Hours later, on Wotan's mountain crag which tore the clouds as they flew past, the all-powerful father declaimed to his still immovably cowering daughter, *"aus meinem Angesicht bist du verbannt!"*, banishing her from his sight. In vain her sisters called their father *"Du schrecklicher, schrecklicher Gott!"* He was immovable and they could only retreat, wailing *"Weh! Weh!"*

I cite Wotan from my later experience to sustain my sense of the Germanic temperament at its most impregnable which I felt in my development of Jupiter as a character. His view of himself was so splendidly invulnerable to criticism or hints of his possible imperfection that I considered many a time what might be his flaw—for surely he had one; it was only a matter of discovering it. If I could discover it, or invent it, for the purposes of my novel, then I would have the sort of contrast in human nature from which a story could emerge. I stared at him in my mind to keep his likeness alive, and no doubt the more I stared the more I saw what I invented rather than the venerable reality with which I had begun—for by the time I was framing my novel, my grandfather had long since, and innocently, and most touchingly, died.

He was majestic. He reminded me of photographs I had seen in his house of Central European royalty. His beard was silvery and well trimmed. His face was rosy, his eyes were blue, he wore gold-rimmed oval glasses. An immaculate white, his hair was nicely trimmed to a well-shaped head. In his clothes, he showed a taste for elegance and formality. A fact awesome to me as a child was that the white Panama hat which he wore in summertime had cost, said the family, one hundred dollars —a sum I could hardly imagine. On formal occasions in winter he was resplendent in a high silk hat and a frock coat, and there was white piping to his waistcoat. He had grand style, serene and confident, courteous to lesser creatures so long as they did their duty, stern with those not yet disciplined, like grandsons. I never saw him without a fine walking stick when he was out of the house.

He went to Europe almost every summer, usually alone, for his wife was an invalid, though once or twice he took his youngest daughter, my most imaginative and favorite aunt. It was his habit to buy handsome rarities abroad, such as sets of extraordinary wineglasses. He made a small ceremony of drinking a glass of wine, and at his table he would give me watered-down wine to drink with him in gravity and respect. In his youth he had been an instructor at the University of Bonn, and he had published poetry in German. Emigrating to the United States to avoid military service (a citizen's then admired act for which we now persecute youths who migrate to Canada or elsewhere for the same reason), he settled in Buffalo, New York, and presently married the daughter of a German family. They had twelve children; and the *Kaiserlich* tyrannies which had driven him from his homeland he soon brought to prevail in his large family, so that he was an autocrat, a dispenser of all laws, a Wotan, a Jupiter, in his own house. His wife my grand-mother was a gentle and sweet-souled woman who suffered with clear inner grace the crippling stroke which rendered her immobile and all but speechless for the last fifteen or so years of her life.

How, I cannot remember—often enough I had heard myself called *"Schrecklicher Kerl!"*—and I am now sure that my grandfather was as virtuous as he was autocratic, but I became convinced early in my life that Jupiter had contracted an amor-ous alliance with a famous German opera singer (I confused her with Madame Ernestine Schumann-Heink) and I believed, again upon the basis of what hints or childhood imaginings I cannot say, that he was enormously rich, because of a secret fund of $40,000 which I thought he possessed. Perhaps he was planning to elope with the opera singer. Was he a victim of uncontrollable love? People sometimes were! Nothing in his decorous and in fact pious life, which was frequently graced by bishops and priests as guests at table, pointed to this theory, but if he were, then there was one half of a story at my disposal.

The other half must come from the existence and the circum-stances of a woman who would have power over him. I did not know any German opera singers of the *Hausfrau* variety, and clearly Madame Lolita Goepple did not suit the style of the situation, for Jupiter would never have understood a thing she said. I raked my memory for a woman to cast in the role of Jupiter's vision and—so it must come about—his downfall.

I found her. She was a teacher of music and stage subjects I had known in a high school I attended far away from Buffalo, and I could see her in my literary eye as the proper agent of complication, climax, and terminal irony for my new novel. She was one of those women who in middle age—Jupiter would never succumb to a frivolous young thing—look top-heavy because their hairdress, shoulders, bust, and hips are large, while their thighs, calves, ankles, and feet are delicate and small. Such a woman can often move, even dance, with captivating lightness and grace. She had pale violet eyes with heavy, half-dropped lids whose lashes looked like thick black silk fringe. A perpetually inquiring smile played over her small mouth with a speculative and inviting pout. When she walked, her breasts, under uncorseted dark blue silk jersey, swayed like udders. I delighted in watching her conduct the school orchestra with a hooked forefinger which served as her baton, while her whole body slowly rippled and ebbed with flesh in the rhythm of the music. Dealing with a performance of the Boccherini minuet necessarily slower than the proper tempo, she stimulated the violins to the pizzicato arrangement by singing out with them, "Plucka-plucka-plucka-pluck" for as long as necessary. Her name was Miss Melton, and it was a joy to be asked by her to address her as "Meltie." It was also superbly descriptive. She had a habit of looking into one's eyes and saying with bemused inattention, "Wha'?"—for in repeatedly saying "What?" she indicated that she was thinking of oneself as a male in high school in conjunction with herself rather than giving her ear to what one was saying to her. At the time I knew her I had because of my extreme youth only vague intimations of a sexual atmosphere about her, but now, as a man of letters, as old as twenty-two, as I set about facing her toward Jupiter in my novel, I was certain of her ruling passion.

And now my book had to have more than persons—it needed their atmosphere, and it wanted, so far, a decision concerning a suitable style. I decided that Jupiter must be an old gentleman of vague but grand powers, whose natural world would be that of high affairs in finance, politics, society. To me, at that time, the grandest symbol of such a milieu was a private railroad car, and it struck me that my opening scene could take place no more effectively than in the private car of a Mr Pennybannock, who was president of a railroad, and also a titan of finance, in search of high political office—senator or (could I pull it off?) president of the nation. I settled upon senator.

My knowledge of big business was extensive if canted in a certain direction, for I was filled to capacity with the novels of Theodore Dreiser, Frank Norris, and Upton Sinclair. Moreover, I had also, in my tenth year, made a trip to New York with my father, who went there on business, and my memories of the nation's financial capital were imaginatively heightened. I felt calmly certain that having overheard the accents of business—big business, I was sure—I was fully charged with its atmosphere, and therefore in a literary position to command all necessary substantiating details. I had already owned private cars in my childhood imagination; but more—in later school years I had been a passenger on one. This happened by grace of a fellow cadet in boarding school, whose grandfather was president of the Northern Pacific Railroad. To the jeers of other cadets, the family private car brought my classmate to school every autumn, returned to fetch him home for Christmas vacation, delivered him to the school again in January, and came to take him away when the school year was over. He once took me aboard as his guest for an overnight run to a junction near my home town. I "had" my private car. To make it a tangent to high financial environs, it was a simple leap for me to enter into grand suites of offices in the Woolworth Building, which my

father had pointed out in 1914 as the tallest in New York—
so tall, in fact, that in my children's encyclopedia, the great
steamship *Vaterland* of the Hamburg-Amerika Line when
stood on end beside it barely topped it. I knew the *Vaterland,*
too, for arriving by the Delaware and Lackawanna Railroad at
Hoboken, and before crossing to New York by ferry, we saw
the ship herself, interned at a New Jersey pier, and her astonishing size and splendor were other attributes of the world I
would try to enter with Jupiter.

Whoever knows what is going to be useful if he is a writer?
We had gone, my father and I, to a famous restaurant in Times
Square called Churchill's, which had silk lampshades of a rose
color covering small double silver lamps on every table; and at
a certain moment a vivid lady, with a frank bust consisting of
two ellipsoids evidently filled to capacity with some rolling
fluid, and with a waist so small that, as I had heard it often
said of other ladies, you could span it with your two hands, and
with blond hair so long "she could sit on it" (which I thought
an odd exercise and which long later gave rise to ribald sur-
mises), came out on a stage before a backdrop representing in
detailed painting the New York of the early steamcar era, to
sing a song which went, "Oh, the five-fifteen, I hear the whistle
blowing," whereat someone in the hidden orchestra tooted an
engine whistle; and I was sure that in such a place bank presi-
dents, owners of goldmines in Peru and private yachts like
Mr Morgan's *Corsair,* which I had seen anchored in the North
River, all black with gold figurehead and a tan funnel, would
gather to consummate deals representing hundreds of millions
in dollars. And yet at small tables ladies and gentlemen in pairs
leaned toward each other in rosy light, talking anything but
business, surely.

[207]

My father's discussions of business were carried out with a Mr Doremus in a suite at the McAlpin Hotel. Ignored, I overheard them. The details were meaningless, but the tone was the point, and I absorbed it. Mr Doremus unluckily was unwell, and for the conversations lay mountainously on his bed clad in a heavily tasselled dressing gown over oatmeal-colored long underwear. The fact that he had eyebrows and mustaches like Mr Morgan stayed with me. He was surely a captain of industry. He could speak bitterly of Theodore Roosevelt. I was pleased when a dozen years later his details merged with those of Mr Pennybannock. I could see this composite figure as he sat in the rear area of his private railroad car, his knees spread to permit his enormous belly to depend between his short thighs, jellying to the rhythmic vibration of the swaying train. A man of substance, then, with the power and acumen to recognize the superior talents of Jupiter Tonans, the Orator of Thunder, who would by his speeches elect him to the Senate of the United States.

I had, thus, the values of external observation, without knowledge of the experience which would support visible details.

As for style, I summoned one the reverse of commonplace. While serving to record, it held a mental countenance contained, reserved, in the density, richness, of the writings of Joseph Hergesheimer, who at the time ruled literary America as the heir of Henry James and Edith Wharton; and I wrote my book in a prose style at once formal, elaborate, and, I thought, gorgeously ironic behind a still face and sets of paired locutions.

The climactic scene toward which all proceeded was a public meeting at which Jupiter gives his opening oration on behalf of the candidacy of Mr Pennybannock. He makes a tremendous beginning and is moving on to a thundering climax when he is suddenly as if struck by a club made aware of the lady who says "Wha'?" with every expression of her person. She sits immediately in front of him in the first row. She is dressed for open air in something which gives opened views of her frank flesh. To his elderly eyes she is distracting, seductive fearfully and wonderfully. He tries to ignore her; but his long-smoldering sensuality comes alive and he returns his gaze to her, and in his view she is promising, maddening. He falters in his speech. She makes signs of encouragement to him which, coming from a stranger who wishes him well, only serve to torment him further with unnerving thoughts. High mindedness and low (in the morality of the period) set up great tumult in him, and the result is that his oration collapses and is a failure, and, worse, he is robbed of his sense of authority. Somewhere in my narrative there was a parable of the pathos of old age, elaborately set forth in my own form of tribute to Mr Hergesheimer. Mr Pennybannock loses the election, and Jupiter himself would have been lost to life itself if he had not by happy accident met his lady. She consoles him, complacently blaming herself, but cannot marry him for he already has a wife and family. But he begs her to use forty thousand dollars which happen to be at his disposal to establish herself in a comfortable and secret dwelling where he can call upon her. She refuses twice until, dining one night with him at Churchill's while the five-fifteen left during the nine o'clock cabaret, she accepts his offer when he appeals to her for the third time. One day in his usual habit, as he is on his way to see her, he grandly steps into traffic, holds up his gold-headed walking stick—Wotan's lance—to halt a streetcar which is bearing down upon him, but which unable to stop in time strikes him to the pavement. He is taken home to remain an invalid for the rest of his life and his loving friend can only read about him in the newspaper.

By the time I had completed this work, I was fortunate in having attracted the interest of the literary agent Miss Virginia Rice. Despite her best efforts, *Jupiter, A Novel,* failed to find a publisher. I must advance to another project. After all, Mr Hergesheimer himself had confessed that it was seventeen years before anything he had written was published, and that then it was only a food recipe.

vi

For by now I had at least come to the achievement of a professional view, if not to public attainment in general, which led me to persist in looking ahead to my next book, no matter what the fate of the last previous one. Once again I began to lose myself in intentions, settings, matters of style, all of which through accretion of sketches began to help me to frame my fourth novel, which would be shorter than all the others.

Again it was derivative from other authority than my own in all but the essential impulse. As before, I was exploring the medium, and taking soundings of myself. If all my variety of approaches had any virtue, it lay in the fact that I held my eye on matters of expression and form rather than on any popular models which might have brought me some sort of temporary recognition.

If *Jupiter* had been a comedy, it was one of somewhat ponderous irony; and my temper now was to turn to something decorative, frivolous, stylized, precious, having for its theme the light mockery of an egotism and the world which enclosed it.

Both my view and my topic owed much to recent and extended reading of the ingeniously decadent tales of Ronald Firbank. Here was literary tissue extraordinarily developed for its own sake; and the less "acceptable" my stillborn novels became the more devoted I was to that pursuit of expression which gave no thought to how to earn editorial or popular acceptance.

Firbank was *outré,* a master of the most specially allusive humor. His dialogue was woven of seeming irrelevancies and non-responses, yet on examination it quite astonishingly forwarded the fulfillment of his characters and their firefly lives. His craft fascinated me, his subject matter was presented in a fastidiousness that was often wildly comic, and his general shudder before the brute realities of the world conveyed an individual temperament so strongly that I was more taken by the fact than by what it stood for—that is, the hinting diffidence resulting from his particular sexual orientation, which I did not then identify explicitly. I read and admired him in a sort of literary innocence, which gave my admiration an abstract value for technical purposes. Later, when the theme of homosexuality was more freely acknowledged in literature, the schematic source of his special comedy came into view, which would explain all concerning his life, and much in the genre of his wit.

My new novel was to be called *The Golden Rose.* It was about a Roman noblewoman (I had never known one except an old Rochester friend who married a *marchese*) named the Princess Maimonides. This personalized construction was a caricature in the thin line and pale washes of a drawing by Max Beerbohm, to give her an equivalent in another medium. She abandoned her venerable Old Testament faith to become a Catholic convert, and thus to enter a world of fashion not hitherto open to her. She was enormously rich, eccentric in her appearance, dress, actions, and about her revolved a chic *coterie*. There were probably echoes of Thornton Wilder's first novel, *The Cabala,* in all this, for as I recall, possibly without accuracy, the Princess Maimonides was the familiar of prelates and other well-informed ornaments of the Roman scene. The Catholic milieu into which I was born had its universality not only in matters of dogma and theology but in historical and social tonalities as well, as the main vehicle of Western culture after Constantine. Of this, that mite which was my portion, and so continues to be, had much to do with whatever tension and energy *The Golden Rose* may have shown, whether in satire or reverence.

Despite a childhood distaste for sermons at Mass which for the most part remains with me, except at Farm Street in London and at the Blackfriars' in Oxford, I was always an absorbed participant in the Roman liturgy, and a lover of all the sacred objects which had to do with its ancient duty to make manifest the inner beauty and form of the hidden heart of faith. Even so, in my state of spirit at that time there seemed to me, in the styles and habits of the religious, opportunity for superficial and irreverent comedy. I had the atmosphere for it quite naturally. One of my uncles was a Jesuit who reached the dignity of sub-deacon, and then entered into emotional adventures which led him to resign and marry. I had three aunts who were creatures of beauty, like my mother and all her sisters; and these three had all become nuns, one of whom rose to the post of Mother Superior who was to be addressed as "Reverend Mother" under pain of rulered knuckles. I believe it was at this time that I wrote an elaborate short story called *Holy Orders* in which I invented an order of sisterhood styled "the Aunts of Jesus," which permitted its members to write after their names the powerful initials "A.J." The story was accepted for the first issue of *The American Caravan,* edited by Lewis Mumford, Paul Rosenfeld, and Alfred Kreymborg, but I withdrew it at the last minute, reluctant to give offense to devout members of my family, and to open myself to questions from my confessor, with his reach into my peace of mind. None of this had to do profoundly with faith—only with comment upon some of the more assumptive of religious customs and styles.

Still, at the time of which I speak, when I was writing for the most part farcically, there were deep and serious preoccupations behind all my successive roles and postures; and I was now in youthful throes of philosophical doubt, oscillating emotionally between the skeptical and the mystical. What persisted was a sense of reality within the liturgy, and of the historical validity of the pontifical descent from St Peter. This concern led directly to the Papacy, and it was a matter of interest to me that my grandfather Jupiter had had audiences with Leo XIII, who resembled a saved and genial Voltaire, and Pius X, now sainted.

With the Papacy inevitably came pomps unmatched in tradition and splendor by anything else on earth; and in due course, the Princess Maimonides conceived a passion to earn, through conspicuous good works and brilliant social leverage, that extremely rare papal award blessed by the Pontiff on Laetare Sunday, and reserved for ruling monarchs, usually queens and empresses, namely, a potted rosebush wonderfully fashioned out of pure gold. As material for satire, the princess's particular form of striving was reminiscent of the ambition of the lady in Firbank—Mrs Shamefoot, in *Vainglory*—who worked to have a stained-glass window erected to her memory in the cathedral of St Dorothy while still alive. It was a theme tenuous enough to have called forth all of Firbank's half-uttered extravagances at their most significantly trivial.

For even the trivial, when pressed by urgent meanings, muted or delayed in revelation, is enough for an artistic theme; and I was mindful of Mrs Wharton's climax in her novel, *The Custom of the Country,* a long work in whose final pages the edifice of the heroine's ambitions (is it possible that her name was Undine Spragg?) is shattered at the last minute through the fact that she has long been divorced of an earlier marriage which is enough reason under protocol to prevent her husband from receiving the appointment as ambassador which is their joint ambition, and which had seemed just within grasp.

In the end, ironic disappointment worked in my little book also, and the princess—as I recall it—received the Rose only to be shocked out of life at her joy of achievement. In both Mrs Wharton's busy and experienced novel and my own elaborate jape it was the mechanics of irony at work rather than that vein of human singularity which makes all trifles real and some fictional characters great. The serious purpose of satire under the frivolous is always more than mechanical. In my case, it was the aristocratic life which I strove to make hilarious even though its grandeurs were impressive enough to be described with admiration. I risk the guess that to almost any literate American-bred youth, an over-decorated life would have its elements of the ridiculous. What was difficult about my management of the current story was to keep the manneristic surface from usurping all interest in that which was supposed to lie concealed.

I can still see Madame Maimonides, though, whose name was intended to be exotic rather than comic (no Undine Spragg here), and that at least was a step forward. I must have come casually upon the name of the Spanish rabbinical scholar Moses Maimonides, of the twelfth century, author of the *Guide for the Perplexed,* and, through various avenues of appropriateness, have decided upon the name for my leading figure. I can describe her yet, thanks to a neighborhood prototype whom I had watched in life, and whose physical attributes I freely transferred. The princess was tall, bony, and she moved with the stylish impulsiveness of a great earthbound bird. Her head was small, like a bird's, in proportion to her body and long neck, her nose was like a finely sculptured beak, and her eyes as bright as wet coal seemed perpetually open, so fast were the frequent blinkings of her hemispheric eyelids. In now describing her I see not only the Roman princess in a pretentious pursuit of a royal honor, but the neighbor wife out of my early years in her homely frocks gently propelling herself with a skilled foot back and forth in a strictly maintained rhythm in the wooden settee-swing hung from chains on her front porch, and turning her head and using her own bird-like glare up and down the shaded street to take in what her limited but all-important world might have to show. One hand, in a gesture as awkward as it was habitual, reached across her bosom to grasp the opposite side of her neck, a gesture I see Signora Maimonides making as she too speculates on life visible but inscrutable.

Even I had small expectation that this work would have any success with publishers—it was too short to stand by itself, it was fanciful about seeming irrelevancies; but it was one which I was compelled to finish; and it must surely have revealed the familiar marks of an apprenticeship in which the writer goes to any length to stretch his imagination, or bring structure to his musings, which may amount to the same thing, even to entering subject matter, places, and personal psychologies of which he has no first-hand knowledge. All this, in any case, was true of my effort with *The Golden Rose*. It was not enough to captivate an editor.

vii

Are we the products of our subconscious traditions as much as of our genes? Both are inherited. It made some sort of pattern that in three of the four novels so far undertaken I was working in atmospheres removed from those of my native land, and my intimate home environment. For this, in whatever it contained of repudiation, there were probably reasons of family troubles which belong in another recital, and which I was not ready to face with either depth of understanding or artistic competence. As for the fact that the allusions of my social settings were for the most part European, it may have been that what I felt so strongly in my heritages—German-Alsatian on one side, Irish-English on the other—compelled me to make up places, persons, and situations which had nothing to do explicitly with the United States or even with my own century, for the most part. Add to this the voracious if unsystematic nature of my reading, and it seems clear that my imagination struck more deeply at that time into roots imaginary but strongly felt than into the realities of my own direct knowledge. I was subject to a familiar literary experience which was probably more prevalent then than now, when the nature, if not the act, of imaginative writing is so extensively taught, and often so valuably.

As I came to my fifth novel, *Death Insupportable,* such sources of impulse still held for me; and I was now lost in an eclectic fantasy drawing enthusiastically upon the styles of attitude, behavior, and idiom in a remarkable set of literary accretions. This included elements from the letters, poems, and histories of Voltaire, and his own romances of *Candide* and *Zadig;* Lytton Strachey's hilarious essays about him; the socially and sexually enlivening memoirs of Casanova in the translation of Arthur Machen; the memoirs of a whole squad of dukes—Saint Simon, Richelieu, Luynes, Lauzun; the reminiscences of the Margravine of Bayreuth and Catherine the Great; the biography and works of Mozart; albums of plates depicting the palaces of Versailles and the Louvre, the residences of prince-bishops, and details of German and Austrian churches from the time of plaster draperies, white and gold organ pipes, clouds of *putti,* and gilded curves in all places whose structures would have been sufficiently supported by vertical severities. I was mindful of the *brio* in the novels of Alexandre Dumas *père,* whose energy I still admire. From what precise adventure I do not know, I felt a great interest in travel by coach, with all its grandeurs, dangers, and discomforts. I gazed at maps of France and Germany, never yet having seen those countries, and with dream-like ease imposed upon their abstract information the scaffolding of my romance. This had to do with lovers of the period, in peruke, flared tailcoat, gold-hilted sword, satin waistcoat with jewelled buttons, muffling cloak, a pair of pistols, on the one hand; and on the other, towering, powdered wig, gown sculptured stiffly from satin weighted with bullion thread, the graces of gauze and pinned flowers and swaying loops of diamonds and pearls, and all the other human scenery I could acquire. The whole enclosed ardent love in the face of dynastic or other obstacles requiring subterfuge, intrigue, indiscreet letters, and even worse risks, flight, peril, frustration.

I have wondered whether my retreat to the eighteenth century had to do with my personal unwillingness to bend to the ideological requirements of the literary world of the early thirties, when a proletarian "realism" was in energetic charge of intellectual life, probably given its chance by the miseries of the Great Depression. Even fiction became doctrinaire, according to the canons of the Left, and "realism" was once again, as in Zola, and some of the Russians, equated with material squalor. The question is immediately proposed as to whether there are no "real lives" above what are offensively called the lower classes. The answer is too obvious to belabor—that life at any level and in any circumstance is "real" and "realism" can justly encompass it. Even the "romantic," if he is an artist, allows the "realism" of the decorative life and also readily faces moral squalor if it is present under the expensive graces of the baroque.

Anyhow, whatever story was present in my new undertaking was helped in its movement, restricted though it was within the luxurious inanimate of the setting and its conventions, by a crafty priest called Monsignor Zahn, whose sympathies were never made clear until the end—was he with the lovers, or did he spy upon them and prearrange disasters for them under orders from his master, the prince-bishop? No matter. Every risk must be taken on behalf of love, for the alternative was clear, and my title stated it. It came from a poem which Voltaire wrote to his niece Madame du Châtelet containing the stanza,

On meurt deux fois, je le vois bien:
Cesser d'aimer et d'être aimable,
C'est une mort insupportable.
Cesser de vivre, ce n'est rien.

[218]

To arrive at the title I saw so imperatively useful in this I made a mechanical translation:

> *I know this well: a man dies twice—*
> *To cease to love and lovable be,*
> *Death insupportable is to me.*
> *To cease to live, is no great price.*

But however indiscriminately I was lost in an addiction to period, drawing at will on the seventeenth and eighteenth centuries, and greedily raiding many princely realms, all was borne down in the end by the weight of the décor, like an inferior opera overproduced; and the manuscript returned from its many hopeful submittals until keeping it home was the sensible thing to do.

I found years afterward in the wonderful journals of Eugène Delacroix (here translated by Walter Pach) an entry which could serve as an epigraph for the long apprenticeship some of whose stages I have been confessing. Referring to young writers, he wrote: ". . . In their youth, when all their qualities stifle them, they give preference to puffery and wit . . . they want to shine rather than to touch; it is the author that they want to have admired through the characters he creates. . . ."

viii

There was an aspect of the literary apprenticeships of my generation upon which I used to reflect with interest, wondering whether matters might have moved faster for me if I, too, had been a member of the expatriated flock of writers who went to Paris after the 1914 war to find themselves. But in the first place, I was just too much younger than they to qualify through experience in the war, and generally, I have concluded that what they found was not so much themselves as each other and their exchanged sanctions, in a stimulating atmosphere of an updated bohemianism whose youthful affectations perhaps offset any lasting benefits of exposure to such truths as can be unearthed only upon foreign soil.

The two leading reputations which came of the movement—those of Scott Fitzgerald and Ernest Hemingway—have, it seems to me, resulted more in lively biographical materials about the two of them than in essentially literary values, which, given their authentic talent, would have come to expression no matter where.

Without doubt I missed some remarkable contacts, and to my regret it was twenty years before I saw Paris, and by then I was already the author of five unpublished and eight published books. (I discount *The Burnished Caravel*.) I should have liked to know Scott and Zelda Fitzgerald at that time, despite all their troubles, which drained the vitality of their close friends; and of the other Americans, Janet Flanner and Edwin Lanham, who was at work on his early novels. It might have been elevating, though not necessarily influential, to have been introduced if possible to Paul Valéry, Ramon Fernandez, and Charles DuBos, and to have watched the elaborate but I believe unconvinced antics of the Dadaists and Surrealists.

In the fact, after my return to New Mexico, I was lucky in finding a job and an atmosphere which allowed me independence for my own undertakings. I was able to search for my way alone, however deviously. During my earlier New Mexico period—that of late boyhood—it had been an appropriately intoxicating experience to go to Santa Fe from Albuquerque (where we lived) and encounter writers and painters in the flesh. The artistic aspirant attaches an extra, rather touching, value to mingling with his elders in the world of the arts, not always to learn anything technical—that is a different and quite strict process—but often to breathe a climate and absorb justification for his own often socially unorthodox values. I then uncritically accepted the idea of a "colony" of artists and writers at Santa Fe and Taos, but it was not long until some of the individuals who were locally called "sensitives" began to seem somewhat grotesque, self-advertising, and responsive to opportunities for envy and competition. Viewing the Paris phenomenon of the expatriates, I thought that it too could be seen in effect as a "colony," though it was set down far away in the midst of a great capital of culture and style; and I suppose, apart from the notoriety of some of the names, French, English, Irish, American, of various participants, its essential character was not remarkably different from what I had observed in northern New Mexico, where certain temperaments and habits of non-conformity were pretty much like what prevailed in the Parisian circles of American revolt against the tone of the victory-proud, Babbitt-governed, United States. I could hold my view of all that in New Mexico as well as in Paris.

During all this time of concern with long works (including an unsuccessful trial at dictating a novelette), I was scrubbing away also at lesser trials—book reviews, plays, articles for magazines such as *Theater,* little stories, a number of which appeared in *Vanity Fair* and *The New Yorker,* and some poetry. I had long since adopted the discipline of writing every morning at about the same hour to produce daily about the same amount of text. This became my lifelong habit; and one day during the slow year while *Death Insupportable* was winding down its career with editors, I went to my typewriter to do a five-page sketch to be submitted to *The New Yorker*. It was to be a neat little portrait of a lovely and implausible Russian woman I had known in Rochester, an emigrée from the Bolshevized fatherland, who brought to America the exalted Tolstoyan spirit which had always sustained her and which now, in the new country, might be put to use to enlighten the boyishly irresponsible Americans. The scene was Dorchester, New York—a composite of Buffalo and Rochester I invented and have often used since.

I worked, on that day, for the usual time, and found to my mild discontent that I was not finished—usually I wrote my modest *New Yorker* pieces at one sitting. Returning the next day, I resumed my work with my mind full of brisk resolutions which would finish the story during that second morning. Again I was thrown off schedule. My Russian lady, Nina, the persons whom she called into life all about her, the background of Dorchester, compelled me; and I found myself swept along on a current of real experience, place, and point of view which in very short order made it clear to me that what I was writing was not a brief sketch but another novel—my sixth.

Those first days on that project gave me one of my very few experiences as a day-to-day improviser. I soon saw that I must declare an intermission to forecast the direction and design of my book. From what had almost dictated itself in the beginning, I was able to project its future course, conclusion, general shapeliness, and recovered truth. What had originally called for, at most, three thousand words, proceeded until it became a novel of one hundred fifty thousand.

It was the first of my full-length works to sound like myself. It had taken years of experiment to hear my own voice, but when I did so, I was, by all the rehearsal through which I had gone, ready to speak in it. The book became *The Fault of Angels*. Its title came from a line out of Alexander Pope, in which he spoke of ambition as "the glorious fault of angels and of gods." For my Russian—Nina—had the touching ambition of setting out to bring true spiritual awareness to the United States, which had none, by bringing it first to a leading American tycoon, who with his vast wealth and calm ethical influence would surely become a model to be followed by the millionaire community of the whole country. How could anything but good come of it? It was a comedy—some said "high comedy"— and its theme led to Russian tears and futility, but in its course the story brought the reader a feeling of reality, for it was compounded of elements all of which I myself had known well, though with proper license I embellished them in the telling.

Miss Rice thought something could be done with it. The first editor to see it was himself an author. This condition sometimes held disadvantages for the writer as he submitted his work, for such an editor had a tendency to rewrite or reconceive in his own terms what was presented to him. As I recall, we retrieved the manuscript since the editor was unwilling to make any commitment until I had made considerable changes in it; and presently, in my own version, it went to Harper and Brothers, was accepted, and we were presented with a curious situation.

The biennial Harper Prize Novel competition was in progress. Manuscripts were being received daily, and the distinguished board of judges (Dorothy Canfield, Sinclair Lewis, and Harry Hansen) had been unable to approve even tentatively of any of the works so far examined. The contest still had a while to go. Under the utmost of confidential conditions, the chief editor of the house, Eugene F. Saxton, told Miss Rice that if I insisted, Harper's would publish the novel immediately; but that if I would agree to wait until the following year, when the Harper Prize was to be announced, he was, upon the advice of the judges, able to guarantee that my book would receive it. He hoped I would wait. They all seemed quite certain that no submittals subsequent to mine would endanger my chances. Amazing.

It was a dilemma. My own desire, after five novels which served only the learning process, with all its accompanying deferments and disappointments, was to publish at once. But I felt also that I owed much to Miss Rice, who had for all those years continued to represent me without any significant gain to herself, but with undiminished belief in my work. In the matter of the prize, she exerted no pressure on her own behalf, but she was quite properly, from a professional viewpoint, eager to see the book launched with all the exploitation and response which the Harper Prize would bring. Previous winners included writers of much prestige, such as Glenway Wescott, Julian Green, and Anne Parrish. I decided, mainly for the sake of Miss Rice, to agree to wait. In due course the prize came my way, for my sixth novel, on my birthday, in 1933.

Sinclair Lewis, a singularly generous man in his attitude toward other writers, wrote me a lively letter of commendation which from an author of his public position was strongly encouraging to me in my first season of book publication. Some years later when I met him in New York (the only time I ever saw him) we hit it off in the terms of his habit of impatient familiarity. He used my first name and I was to call him

"Red." I had been taken for tea to his apartment, where at the same time his ex-wife Dorothy Thompson had brought their baby son and the child's nurse on one of those court-decreed compassionate visits. Miss Thompson was large in mold and officially civil but notably silent, while the nanny and the baby made obscure additions to the background. Presently Red told a droll animal story, and I another, and we exchanged several more until he said, "Paul, you and I have to do a book together—a book of animal stories. —Do you know what the elderly flea did when he got rich?" And I, a proper Mister Bones, said, "No, what did the elderly flea do when he got rich?" and Red, slapping his thin shank in glee, replied, "He bought a dog!" The animal story book never progressed any further.

A book which becomes a sudden best seller and attracts wide attention as a result brings highly varied adventures to the author. One of the first for me was a telegram from a lady, the proprietress of a Middle Western music store, who telegraphed to announce that she would arrive in my home town of Roswell, New Mexico, within three days, with an intent which was clearly romantic and even matrimonial. A secretary who has served me well through the years, though he is fictional, replied that he regretted to have to inform her that Mr Horgan was in Mexico for an indefinite stay, and that mail was not being forwarded.

Another was of a different and most astonishing sort which resolved itself into the most ample compliment—truly Texan in size and spirit—I have ever received. Very early one morning after *The Fault of Angels* was published, I answered my telephone to hear a high, drawling voice say,

"Horgin, is that you?"

"Yes?"

"Thiz John McGinnis, over at SMU in Dallas. Are you going to be home late this evenin', five, six, o'clock?"

"Oh, Professor McGinnis"—for I knew of him and his editorship of *The Southwest Review* and his reputation as one of the great American professors of his time—"yes, I expect to be."

"All right. I'll see you."

He hung up.

All day I pondered over his message, not at all sure what he had actually meant. I was answered when a little past five o'clock on that day I heard a car draw up beneath the window of my cramped quarters on the second floor of the school building in which I lived, and a voice call out into the general air, with no precise aim,

"Horgin? Are you around here?"

I leaned out of the window. There stood Professor McGinnis, a rather stooped, grey-haired man with glasses. With him were his two small sons and a dog. All were stretching themselves after long confinement.

"I'll be right down!" I called and hurried to meet them. Mr McGinnis shook my hand in an old-fashioned pump-handle style, introduced his young sons and the dog, and then said,

"May I come up t'see you for a while?"

I led him upstairs after he instructed the boys and the dog to wait for him below. He came into my room, deliberately saw its wall of books, its low typewriter table, some paintings by Peter Hurd, and my large disorderly desk with its strata of unanswered mail. He then sat down in a chair, lighted his pipe, and talked for thirty minutes about *The Fault of Angels,* in terms so complimentary and (to my notion) so discerning that I was muted by gratification and diffidence. I wanted him to cease, and I was hungry for more. Finally, he said,

"You don't have to say anything. I've said my say, and I mean it. I just wanted you to hear it."

I took refuge in my duties as a host, and asked what arrangements I could now make for dinner and the night's lodging for him and his family. They must all be starved and thirsty after a drive of five hundred miles from Dallas to Roswell, in the desiccating plains heat of August.

"Oh, no," he said. "We can't stay. We're going right back. I have a class first thing in the morning."

"But it's dinner time already," I exclaimed, "you have to have something . . . You mean you drove a thousand miles round trip just to stay half an hour and commend my work?"

"I do. I'd do it again, under the circumstances. As for dinner, we'll get us a hamburger somewhere on the way back. Goodbye to you, young man."

With that, he was off downstairs to his car, and into the return drive of five hundred miles, which would take all night long, before a class first thing in the morning.

A few months later another response to the book came in the form of a request for its dramatization. This came from the intelligent and distinguished actress Eugénie Leontovich, who declared that she must play the role of Nina. No one, she said, had ever so wholly caught the essence of a particular kind of St Petersburg lady, with her intellect, her charm, her soul, and her nonsense, so accurately as I.

I consented to make a play from my novel, and in due time, I read it to Madame Leontovich and her female companion whom Miss Rice had invited to her apartment for the occasion. It was a long play, but I was allowed to perform all three acts without interruption. In addition to Nina and her tycoon, it contained young lovers, sage elders, a great orchestral conductor, an exiled grand duke, and others, and I gave the accent proper to each. It was a performance which quite lifted me out of myself. It was therefore deflating when at the end Madame Leontovich, looking as plaintive and lovely as Nina at her most characteristic, said to me after a long, thoughtful pause,

"No, Misser Hhorgan" (she carefully doubled the H to make it sound, since Russians had no H in their language) "I am like dog." She! like a dog, when she was so beautiful, so classically serene with her head and long neck held so erect with the grace of a ballerina! "I am like dog. When I do not like, I put away, I do not know whhy, it is not necessary to know, I simply put away." (Eloquent gesture of rejection.) A pause while I considered this negative judgment with as much plain countenance as possible. But in a moment she continued. "And, again like dog, when I like, I do not know whhy, but I like, and I simply take; and *I adore your play!*" and as she said this she turned to me and in mid-air "took" my play in pantomime into her beautiful expressive hands. "I will act your play if dthose people will produce it for me."

It developed that by "those people" she meant Guthrie McClintic and Katharine Cornell, who were friends of hers. They were sailing for Europe the next day, she said, and she would herself take a copy of the play to them on board when she went to say *bon voyage*.

"Dthey will adore it, too," she declared.

Miss Rice then gave us all cakes and wine, the play went to the ship the next day, and that was the last I ever heard of the prospect.

There were other tangents of effect ranging out from my novel, one of which had to do with attitudes in the loftier strata of Rochester society, some of whose members were offended that my tycoon had been sketched in somewhat of a likeness of George Eastman, who, as philanthropist and social figure, was Rochester's great man. I called him Henry Ganson, and I thought I made a sympathetic, if occasionally droll, figure of him. But one never knows how what one writes will affect others, and it was not until the book had been read locally for almost forty years that I was officially restored to favor in Rochester, when in 1971 I was given a public luncheon and a private cocktail party upon receiving a beautiful silver bowl signifying that the Friends of the Rochester Public Library had bestowed upon me their annual literary award.

To return to the earlier time: a notoriously successful first appearance can bring with it disadvantages in some ways, and I encountered a few of them, along with the rewards; but I was not sorry to have deferred to Eugene Saxton's wish, for until his death during the Hitler war while I was in the army, he remained my friend and my editor in the course of publishing eight of my books; and I feel the debt I owe him cannot be measured.

ix

And what of the first five novels? Surely, I was asked—though never by Mr Saxton—I could publish at least some of them after my auspicious launching? But I never considered reviving, or revising, any of them with a view to exploiting the considerable success, critical and popular, of my first published novel. I had learned something of value from writing each of the earlier books, but the overriding lesson yielded by them told me that they represented a necessary apprenticeship served without interruption, though marked by the extremes of satisfaction and disappointment. All of the five were destroyed but one, which went to a private collection, never to see the light.

It may be of interest to cite the specific lessons each of my failures taught me.

The Furtive Saint told me that even with a commanding central character, a book of fiction must have other inhabitants of interest in themselves, and that all must logically obey a premise implicit in a pattern which they make together. *The Grey Swans* told me that a vague desire to invent an atmosphere under any prevailing fashion could not by itself make a novel. *Jupiter* told me that a single climactic scene is more useful to a short story than to a novel. *The Golden Rose* told me that a literary conception rooted in a mechanical turn of irony is both unreal and too facile, and that even decadence must have its own conviction. *Death Insupportable* told me that materials better suited to history or essay cannot be animated for fiction without the presence of "living" characters. All of them together told me that second-hand insight or style acquired like someone else's old clothes, no matter how well they fitted their original owners, or however handsome they were when new, could not produce work proper to my own experience, knowledge, feeling, or voice. It took the run-away energy of *The Fault of Angels,* with its small initial purpose as the seedling out of my own direct experience and nurtured into fullness by my own altering imagination, to indicate how I must try to work in the future.

X

There were, of course, other lessons all by the way which have continued throughout my writing life. One of the earliest, again, was that I was wrong in assuming that once I had had a successful work, all my following books would be progressively more easy to write. The opposite was the case. Each succeeding book is more difficult than the last, for at least two reasons: first, one's self-critical standards grow higher with each; second, in each there is always a new problem in form to solve; and in these regards, one's novitiate never seems to end.

One also learned that even with the experience of many books behind him, a writer was not immune from planning and beginning a work which might have to be abandoned, for reasons as various as the inconstancy of human temperaments and as unpredictable as uncontrollable outward conditions. (Mark Twain's experience and anguish in this regard come to mind.)

When a book in the making aborts, the event is as difficult to explain as the way notes for projected works behave. Originally, these come out of the blue, as the saying goes. An idea for a character, a story, an event, a memory, an imaginatively exciting supposition, may come to one anywhere, at any time. In such a case I always write it down, intensely believing at the moment in its validity. A collection of such notes grows rapidly. On reviewing them later, it is astonishing how some of them have become inert, dead forever so far as the imagination is concerned, while others seem to possess an organic life of their own, putting out branch-notes, and interlocking systems of designs, like a tree, so that every time one returns to such as these, one makes fertile additions, and in the end, a story or a book results. It is a moment of delicate perception when one becomes certain that the note-system for a particular piece is ready to use; and it must be used then, or it may, again mysteriously, lose its generative power. Notes mature at different rates of growth, again unpredictably. The first key ideas for a novel of mine were noted in 1939. Until 1968 they acquired enrichments every time I re-read them. When at last they contained the whole scheme, I wrote the book in eleven weeks. If asked how long it took me to write that book, I can reply, twenty-nine years and eleven weeks.

Such a process holds true, for me, in the matter of fictional writing especially; and I have a number of times set aside other work in history or biography to fulfill the original vision for a piece of fiction, short or long, when it seemed complete, lest I lose it. As for non-fiction—such work, based on solid fact, seems able to endure interruption or postponement without loss of the imperative sense of empathy and design which led me to plan it in the first place—though one's imaginative response to the subject matter must originally have been so strong that it can be revived.

xi

At last, what seems clear about an apprenticeship is that it takes time to learn to recognize one's own truth. In works of non-fiction, this process is a matter of searching through evidence already recorded and discovering how to align one's view of the evidence with the evidence itself. In works of fiction, the truth rests upon an aesthetic fulfillment of its presentation, so that what is unquestionably true for the writer will seem true also to the reader. Many elements of the art of writing—almost too many to list and certainly too many to discuss in brief—enter into such fulfillment. Nothing is implausible in fiction provided all is seen by the author with appropriate style and belief, and presented with an energy almost beyond control—yet controlled by the formal limits of design which shape the meaning of the whole work. Within a mountain, its separate features are revealed—ridge after ridge in seemingly endless succession, canyons, streams, pinnacles and caverns, trails of animal or man, changes of weather, obstructive cliffs, lost springs, hidden lakes, sudden openings of vista and perspective. One must enter into the mountain to see them. But to contain the mountain entire, one must emerge and see it also from afar, in all its coherent form. So with the material of imaginative art in writing, whether given to fiction or fact.

PART FOUR

THE
BIBLIOGRAPHY

TO THE READER

I HAVE COMPLETED this bibliography because of my interest in the work of Paul Horgan, and it is presented here for whatever assistance it can be to his other readers. It is considered "provisional" in that any bibliography on its first outing must be so to some degree. It is only over a period of years, after the material has been made public, that all the many variations can be noted and the less conspicuous items located for a later, more mature edition. It is as the first step in this process that this work should be considered.

A brief explanation of the format is necessary, for this bibliography is directed to both the bibliographer and the general reader, and their interests will of necessity vary. The material has been arranged in six categories: (*A*) Books and Pamphlets; (*B*) Contributions to Books; (*C*) Contributions to Periodicals; (*D*) Translations; (*E*) Miscellaneous; and (*F*) Anthologies. These are largely self-explanatory: books and pamphlets are items by Paul Horgan; contributions to books are his additions, as in a foreword or an introduction, to books by others; contributions to periodicals are essays, criticism, poetry, and fiction published in journals and newspapers; translations are all known editions in foreign languages; miscellaneous is a catchall of what does not fit elsewhere but is of interest and significance; and anthologies are reprintings of Paul Horgan's works in editions not by him.

The first category contains the most descriptive material. I have not collated pages, nor given a complete page-by-page description of each item, but I have tried to give enough detail to identify the books and pamphlets. Here the works are listed by year and then by month within the year. There are three items that might have gone into other categories, but because of Paul Horgan's unusual contribution to each, and because of the nature of the book in which this bibliography appears, I have included these in category *A*. I am referring to *The Library 1–7* (1927), *A*2; *New Mexico's Own Chronicle* (1937), *A*11; and *Maurice Baring Restored* (1970), *A*40. I have been quite strict in what I included in Contributions to Books. I have allowed here only works that were especially written, or rewritten, for a specific book publication. I have not included any anthologies, even when such an anthology was the first book appearance of an article or story after its first periodical appearance. All *first* appearances are listed, wherever they may be, but if the first book appearance is in an anthology, this is listed under *F* and does not appear under *B*. For category *C,* I have held quite closely to the definition of a periodical as a work that is published with some regularity and is for general distribution. This includes journals and newspapers, but does not include irregular publications by a museum, or catalogues for a special museum show. These I would place in Miscellaneous. Perhaps this is the category that most needs explanation. Often in a bibliography it is an unimportant category that includes what does not fit elsewhere. This is true in this bibliography, but I have also considered it an *important* category to include significant items that do not fit elsewhere. Also, I have used this category to allow me to include two manuscripts that are of an unusual nature, one of which is directly related to a significant matter that is discussed in the text of this book. Here I refer to item *E1*, the manuscript of *The Golden Rose,* which plays an important part in *Approaches to Writing.* Translations I have arranged alphabetically by title, and then by date. I realize that this is not a traditional method, but it seems to me that most readers will use this section in this way. The last section, Anthologies, is arranged alphabetically by title, and then by date. I have included a reference to the exact item by title and, if a short item, a cross-reference to the book in which that item appeared. When the title of an item in an anthology is not the original title, or when the title is to a section of a book, I have listed that reference under the original full title and then given the other title.

Perhaps the way for a bibliographer and the general reader to think of what I have done is for each to consider what the other might want. I have proceeded under the assumption that, as literate men and women, their interests might not be the same but need not be mutually exclusive. Such an assumption may necessitate that each moderate his interests to some degree, but I hope this will not be, in either case, uncomfortable.

Unless otherwise noted, copies of the items in category *A* are in the author's library or in the Yale University collection of Paul Horgan's work that is in the Beinecke Rare Book and Manuscript Library. As Yale is to obtain all Paul Horgan's material related to his writing, and as some of this material is now in the process of being deposited at Yale, no attempt has been made to distinguish what is at Yale and what is still in the author's possession. Eventually, everything will be at Yale. Often more than one copy of an item has been examined, but it is true that other copies must be studied for variants. Copies have been examined at Olin Library, Wesleyan University;

Lauinger Library, Georgetown University; and the Library of Congress.

The people who have assisted me are many, and their assistance is important, and appreciated. First, Paul Horgan, who has been completely open and diligent in supplying information. It is a rare opportunity to work so closely with a writer on his bibliography, for much important information is obtained. Next, I want to thank Mr. Donald Gallup, Curator of the Collection of American Literature at the Beinecke Library at Yale. Mr. Gallup is a very fine bibliographer, and I hope he accepts this provisional effort with my thanks for his assistance and great good will. I wish to thank as well Mrs. Anne Whelpley, and the staff at the Beinecke. It is an extremely pleasant place to work. I have had excellent student assistants in Philip Lewin, Ellen Davis, and Martin Bunin, and typing assistants in Mrs. Vera K. Yancey, and especially Ms. Martha Blehm, who typed the final copy and assisted me in the proofing. Mrs. Andrea Anderson, Mr. and Mrs. William J. Maher, Mr. John Spike, and Ms. Susan Wagner also helped me in the proofing of the manuscript. I wish to thank Miss Joan Jurale and Mr. Michael Durkan at Olin Library, who helped me to get started and who assisted me throughout my work in a most generous way, and Mr. Robert Giroux, who completed the project by printing this complex manuscript. Mr. Richard M. M. McConnell and Ms. Susan A. Frey had done a partial bibliography of Paul Horgan's work for *Western American Literature* (volume VI, number 2), which helped me at the start to organize material, as did the briefer bibliography of Dr. James M. Day in his pamphlet on Paul Horgan published by Steck-Vaughn in 1967. The staffs at the Martin Luther King and Palisades libraries in Washington, D.C., were most helpful. The Library of Congress, considering the magnitude of its task, is unusually effective. I want to thank especially Mrs. Carolyn Larson of the Periodical Division, who was so helpful and pleasant, as was Mr. Wayne D. Shirley of the Music Division, and Adetokunbo Owurowa, of Nigeria, who is one of the very competent staff. The University Librarian at Georgetown's Lauinger Library, Mr. Joseph E. Jeffs, kindly gave me a library pass, and this library was a constant resource throughout my work on this bibliography.

Several people helped by supplying information by mail, or when necessary, by telephone. First, a large group from the Southwest: Mr. Robert O. Anderson and his secretary, Mrs. Suzie Wagner, Roswell, New Mexico; Mrs. Bert Ellen Camp, The Horgan Library, New Mexico Military Institute, Roswell; Dr. Arthur L. Campa at the University of Denver; Mrs. Drucilla Denney, Roswell Museum and Art Center; Mr. Roland F. Dickey, Socorro, New Mexico; Mrs. Phebe Harris, Director, Santa Fe Public Library; Mrs. Margaret L. Hartley, Editor, *Southwest Review;* Mr. Peter Hurd, Mrs. Henriette Wyeth Hurd, and Mr. Walter Robinson of San Patricio, New Mexico; Mrs. Virginia Jennings, New Mexico State Library, Santa Fe; Ms. Darla Kiker, University of Texas Press; Mr. Thom Martin, Reference Librarian, Hayden Library, Arizona State University, Tempe; Dr. T. M. Pearce and Dr. Dudley Wynn, both formerly at the University of New Mexico; Dr. Lon Tinkle of *The Dallas Morning News;* Mrs. Alice H. Whelan, Librarian, St. John's College, Santa Fe; President Ferrel Heady and the staff of the Zimmerman Library, University of New Mexico, Albuquerque.

Other people who have assisted me are: Miss Virginia Rice, Paul Horgan's agent, in New York City; Miss Enid Allwood, *Cosmopolitan;* Mr. John J. Delaney, Doubleday & Company,

Inc., Ms. Lietta Dwork, *Ladies' Home Journal;* Mrs. Elizabeth Easton and Ms. Ann Patane, Book-of-the-Month Club; Mrs. Naome Lewis and her assistant, Ms. Deborah Launer, *Good Housekeeping;* Ms. Suzanne Lord, *Senior Scholastic;* Ms. Florence Schwartz, Crown Publishers, Inc.; Mr. Russell G. D'Oench, Jr., Editor, *The Middletown Press;* Miss Janet Gonzales and Miss Nettie Herrera, The Cabinet Committee on Opportunities for Spanish-Speaking People; Father Henry J. Klocker of the Society to Aid the Missions, Cincinnati, Ohio; Miss Shannon Macioroski, Mullen Library, Reference Division, Catholic University; Sister Sylvia Rauch, Librarian, St. Paul's College, Washington, D.C.; Mr. Joseph B. Rounds and, especially, Mr. Ridgway McNallie at the Buffalo and Erie County Public Library.

I wish to thank the Chairman of the National Endowment for the Humanities, Dr. Ronald S. Berman, and especially my immediate director, Dr. John H. Barcroft, who heads the Public Programs Division. I also wish to thank my fellow staff members in that division for their good will as I pursued this project. I wish to thank as well the former Deputy Chairman, Mr. Wallace B. Edgerton, now head of the Institute of International Education, who for six years gave to the Endowment the quality of distinctive purpose that has, to this point, characterized its mission.

This work is offered to the bibliographers in our society, and to the readers of Paul Horgan, to suggest the extraordinary range and character of this American writer who is seventy in August 1973. This bibliographer has had a superb time with his task and takes pleasure in the prospect of refining and expanding this work over the years. In this last process—of refining and expanding—I look to the reader. I hope his interest is aroused enough so that he will assist me in this process by sending on any missing items, or any corrections noted.

JAMES KRAFT

January 1, 1973
National Endowment for the Humanities
Washington, D.C. 20506

A. BOOKS AND PAMPHLETS

A1. *Villanelle of Evening*   1926

[a horizontal black decorative rule] / VILLANELLE OF EVENING /
PAUL HORGAN / CHRISTMAS, 1926 / [a double horizontal black decorative rule]

21.6 x 14 cm; [4].

The pamphlet is a single sheet folded in quarto, with the top edge uncut
and the pages unnumbered. The title page described above is on page [1]; on
the inner fold, page [2], the title of the poem is repeated and the poem begins
with a capital B set within a shaded box. On pages [2] and [3], there
are three stanzas to the page. Page [4] states at the bottom: "Two hundred
copies / of this poem were / printed in December / 1926." The poem was
sent as a Christmas message by the author.

A2. *The Library 1–7*   1927

THE LIBRARY / 1–7 / Edited by / PAUL HORGAN / Myron McCormick
/ Assistant / [here follows a thunderbird design] / *ROSWELL* /
THE NEW MEXICO MILITARY INSTITUTE / MCMXXVII

30.1 x 22 cm; [i-iv] introductory pages; each issue is separately numbered:
[Page One], Page Two, Page Three, Page Four; the bound set of seven
copies is hand-stamped in red 1–28 on the top outside corner.

On page [i] is the title page described above; page [ii] states: "This edition
of the bound file of THE LIBRARY'S / first year consists of / ten copies, lettered
A to J, of which this is copy [written in black ink] A." Pages [iii] and
[iv] contain an index. The thunderbird design on the title page is by Paul
Horgan and is similar to one that appears on the bookplate he designed at
this time. The author's copy contains this bookplate on the inside front cover,
and on the front endpaper are his signature and below it the same thunderbird
emblem drawn by him. The book is bound in black cloth with a yellow
label pasted to the front with the words "THE LIBRARY / 1–7" in black.

This volume is included here because of the unusual circumstances. *The
Library* was published monthly at the New Mexico Military Institute, Roswell,
New Mexico, and the copies bound here consist of its entire publication of
seven months, from November 15, 1926, to May 15, 1927. It was designed

and edited by Paul Horgan, and the unsigned articles are largely by him; in addition, the largest number of signed contributions are by him. Certain articles in *The Library* are signed "Vincent O'Shaughnessy" and these are also by Paul Horgan. "Vincent" is a confirmation name; "O'Shaughnessy" is the maiden name of his father's mother. At this time, in the flowering of artistic youth, and for a brief period, Paul Horgan let the world know him as "Paul George Vincent O'Shaughnessy Horgan"—the first two being his baptismal names. Later the author wisely simplified to Paul Horgan, his professional name ever since. Witter Bynner and Langston Hughes were also contributors to *The Library*.

The articles by Paul Horgan from *The Library* are listed under C5–30.

A3. *Lamb of God*   1927

LAMB OF GOD / BY / PAUL HORGAN / [white thunderbird design on black rectangle] / At Roswell / MCMXXVII

22.9 x 15.1 cm; [8].

The pamphlet consists of four pages, folded once and stapled twice, with a black paper cover and purple endpapers. The title and name of author are printed in black on a purple rectangle pasted to the cover. The pasted piece contains a border of a single black rectangle and then a decorative rectangle. The title page described above is on page [1]. Page [2] states: "Sixty copies of this poem were printed in / March, 1927. This is number [stamped in red] 38." On page [3] the poem is dedicated "To Witter Bynner," the American poet, who was then living in Santa Fe. The title is repeated on page [4] where the poem begins with a capital H set within a shaded box. The poem consists of six roman-numbered sections, one on each page and the last two on page [8].

A4. *Men of Arms*   1931

MEN OF ARMS / WRITTEN AND / DRAWN BY / PAUL HORGAN / [a blue and black sketch of a soldier and a cannon, and beneath it a blue star outlined in black] / PHILADELPHIA / DAVID McKAY COMPANY / PUBLISHERS / [1931]

30.5 x 22.9 cm; [1–9], 10–62, [63–64]; $2.50.

On page [1] is an illustration and the words: *"This Book Belongs to   "*; the title page described above is on page [3]; page [5] contains a half-page illustration and states [all in caps]: "This book is for everybody who likes to look / at pictures and read about how things are, / and especially for / Peter Wyeth Hurd   Andy Wyeth / The Goossens Twins Sue and Elyse Saunders / Betty Cassidy / Peter, Joan and Michael Cunningham / [brown star in black outline]"; the contents is on page [7] and has an illustration in blue and the words "What There Is"; the text begins on page 10 and ends on page 62; on page [64] is an illustration and the words "The End / [brown star in black outline]." The book contains the author's illustrations throughout, and a full-page illustration on every odd-numbered page, pages [11]–[63]. The pictures are drawn in black outline with the effect of wash in a second color, variously brown, rust, blue, and olive. The cover is red cloth with gold lettering and decoration on the front and on the spine.

Contents: i. An Egyptian Spearman—ii. A Greek Lancer—iii. A Roman Soldier of the Emperor Trajan—iv. A Saracen Fighter—v. A French Crossbowman—vi. An English Archer—vii. A Knight in Full Ceremonial Armor—viii. A Great Chinese Warrior—ix. A Great Japanese Leader—x. An English Sailor Under Queen Elizabeth—xi. A Musketeer of King Louis XIII of France—xii. A Cavalier—xiii. An American Iroquois Indian—xiv. A Prussian Guardsman Under Frederick the Great—xv. A Pirate—xvi. A Continental—xvii. A Kentucky Rifleman—xviii. An Officer Under Napoleon—xix. An American Naval Officer, 1812—xx. An African Savage—xxi. A Union Recruit in the Civil War—xxii. A Sioux Indian Chief—xxiii. A Western Plainsman—xxiv. A Rough Rider of 1898—xxv. An English Officer in the World War—xxvi. An American Doughboy in the World War—xxvii. A War Time Aviator.

Five thousand copies were printed and 500 bound when imperfections were found in the illustrations on pages [15], [45], and [61]. The remainder of the edition was destroyed.

A5. *The Fault of Angels* 1933

a. first edition, 1933

[the following set within two borders of gold-yellow vertical rules, each composed as follows: one thin rule, two thick rules, one thin rule, and one decorative rule] THE / FAULT / OF / ANGELS / *by* / Paul / Horgan / [Publisher's device in gold-yellow] / *Harper & Brothers Publishers* / NEW YORK AND LONDON / 1933

20.5 x 13.8 cm; [i-vii], viii, [1-3], 4-349, [350-352]; $2.50.

The title page described above is on page [iii]; on page [v] the book is dedicated "TO / MY MOTHER / AND TO / THE MEMORY OF / MY FATHER"; the contents is on pages [vii]-viii; the text begins on page [3] and ends on page 349; on page [350] is the publisher's imprint; and on pages [351-352] is a statement entitled "The Harper Prize Novel Contest." This novel was the recipient of the Harper Prize for 1933. The book has endpapers in a yellow design. The cover is tan cloth with the title and author in gold on black bars on the front and on the spine. The publisher's name is in gold on the spine. For the fifth printing, the cover is dark blue rough cloth with the lettering in gold on dark blue smooth bands on the front and on the spine.

Contents: I. AUTUMN—i. Provincial Opera—ii. Vladimir and Nina—iii. Blanche—iv. Chez Schrantz—v. Imminence—vi. Nina—vii. Imperator Americanus—viii. Gemütlichkeit—ix. Landlady—x. Nina's Début—xi. An Evening with Mrs. Kane—xii. Very Simple—xiii. Intellectual Evening—xiv. Theater Moment—xv. Love—xvi. Post Concert—xvii. Scandal with Janitor—xviii. Tristesse and a Party—xix. Theater Scandals—xx. Mrs. Bliss in Tears—xxi. Reputations—xxii. First and Last Performance—xxiii. Memorandum. II. THE SUN IN WINTER—xxiv. Idyll in Winter—xxv. Descent to the Catacombs—xxvi. La Vie—xxvii. With Lydia—xxviii. A Date to Hear a Swami—xxix. A Commission—xxx. George—xxxi. Martin Bliss—xxxii. La Schrantz—xxxiii. Julia's Return in Memory—xxxiv. Little White Bird—xxxv. Mr. Schwartz—xxxvi. The Spell—xxxvii. "Boris"—xxxviii. Afterward—xxxix. Arrival of a Personage—xl. Justice—xli. Scandal—xlii. Evening Concert—xliii. Was Party—xliv. Cross Current—xlv. White Night—xlvi. Public Carnival—xlvii. Sacrifice—xlviii. Leona—xlix. Spring Rain—l. George—li. Love Again—lii. The Iconoclast. III. SPRING—liii. Walking in the Dusk—liv. Style—lv. First Farewell—lvi. "Homeric"—lvii. Hilda—lviii. Lunch Party—lix. Revelation—lx. Second Farewell Wiz Adieu.

b. English edition, 1933

There was an English edition published by Hamish Hamilton in 1933 for 7s, 6d. No copy has been examined.

c. reissue, 1935

[the following set within two borders of black vertical rules, each composed as follows: two thin rules, a space, two thin rules] THE / FAULT / OF / ANGELS / *by* / Paul / Horgan / *Grosset & Dunlap* / *Publishers New York* / [1935]

18.9 x 12.8 cm; [i-vii], viii, [1-3], 4-349, [350-360]; $0.75.

The inside front dust-jacket flap states: "The issuance of this new edition at a reduced price is made possible by (a) use of the same plates made for the original edition: (b) acceptance by the author of a reduced royalty." Pages [350-358] carry advertisements for Grosset & Dunlap books; pages [359-360] are blank. This edition uses the plates for the Harper 6th printing of 1935.

d. paperbound edition, 1961

THE FAULT / OF ANGELS / by / PAUL HORGAN / POPULAR LIBRARY • NEW YORK / [1961]

17.4 x 10.5 cm; [1-6], 7-253, [254-256]; $0.75.

The title page described above is on page [3]; the dedication as for the first edition is on page [5]; the text begins on page 7 and ends on page 253; the unnumbered pages contain advertisements for other Popular Library books. The front cover is white, with red borders and rectangles, and black type, and shows a color drawing of a couple embracing.

A6. *No Quarter Given*   1935

a. first edition, 1935

[The following set within two borders of blue-green vertical rules, each composed as follows: one thin rule, two thick rules, one thin rule, and one decorative rule] NO / QUARTER / GIVEN / *by* / Paul / Horgan / [publisher's device in blue-green] / *Harper & Brothers Publishers* / NEW YORK AND LONDON / 1935

20.6 x 13.7 cm; [i-vi], vii-viii, [ix-x], [1], 2–586, [587–590]; $2.50.

The title page described above is on page [iii]; on page [v] it states: *"This book / is for my sister / ROSEMARY / [decorative device]"*; the contents is on pages vii and viii; the text begins on page [1] and ends on page 586; pages [587–590] are blank; the book has endpapers in a blue-green design. The cover is blue-green cloth with gold and black, and black on gold, lettering and decoration on the spine. On the front cover is the publisher's device in black.

Contents: i. Mrs. Abbey—ii. Horizon—iii. David—iv. Wife-errant—v. Encounter—vi. Kind of Happiness—vii. David's Land—viii. An Early Storm—ix. Resources—x. An die Musik—xi. The Two Parts of Life—xii. Routine—xiii. The Poet—xiv. His Works—xv. To David—xvi. The Righteous—xvii. Edmund and Maggie—xviii. Return of the Widow—xix. Death and the Children—xx. Treaty—xxi. In the Open—xxii. Farewell to Morals—xxiii. The Gain and the Loss—xxiv. Mountain Summer—xxv. The Son—xxvi. The Lover—xxvii. At Mrs. Mannering's—xxviii. The Realists—xxix. Romantic Malady—xxx. Band Concert and Party—xxxi. The Slow Waltz—xxxii. War and Peace—xxxiii. The Rolands in Private—xxxiv. Courage or Folly—xxxv. One Womankind—xxxvi. Sustenance—xxxvii. Down the Land—xxxviii. The Marriage Mass—xxxix. Prelude—xl. The Dance—xli. The Arroyo—xlii. In the Cars—xliii. Lillian—xliv. Maggie and Georgia—xlv. Edmund Strong—xlvi. The Word—xlvii. Welcome—xlviii. Done with Lamentation—xlix. No Quarter Given—l. Departures—li. The Longest Way Home—lii. The Way it Ends—liii. Georgia's Abschied—liv. David on the Uptake—lv. Money—lvi. Smooth Sailing Again—lvii. Down to the River—lviii. Between the Lines—lix. A Visitor from the Past—lx. Evening and Night—lxi. News Gets Around—lxii. End of Uncertainty—lxiii. Bridal Day—lxiv. Correspondence—lxv. A Broken Chain—lxvi. What Have I Done to You—lxvii. Stopover—lxviii. David Free—lxix. Weather—lxx. Vigil—lxxi. Death Song—lxxii. The Eastbound Limited—lxxiii. Homecoming—lxxiv. Their Afterwards—lxxv. Survival.

Two sections appeared in periodicals: Chapter 19 was published under the same title, "Death and the Children," in *Harpers Magazine* (December, 1934), C85; and Chapter 8, entitled "An Early Storm," was published in an edited version as "Slow Curtain" in *Harpers Magazine* (February, 1935),

C87. The publisher put out a 16-page pamphlet of Paul Horgan's drawings of characters in the novel; see E7.

b. English edition, 1935

[the following set within a black rectangular frame composed of one thin rule, one thick rule, and one thin rule] NO QUARTER / GIVEN / *by* / Paul Horgan / Constable & Co Ltd / London / [1935]

The above description is taken from a Xerox copy of the English text that was published in 1935 for 8s, 6d. No copy of the English edition has been examined.

c. reissue, 1937

An edition was published and sold for $0.75 by Grosset & Dunlap in 1937. No copy has been examined.

d. English edition, 1940

A second English edition, or reissue, by Constable & Co Ltd was published in 1940 for 4s, 6d. No copy has been examined.

A7. *Main Line West*   1936

a. first edition, 1936

[the following set within two borders of maroon vertical rules, each composed as follows: one thin rule, one thick rule, one thick broken rule, one thin rule, one decorative rule] [title in black outline type] MAIN / LINE / WEST / *by* / Paul / Horgan / [publisher's device in maroon] / *Harper & Brothers Publishers* / NEW YORK AND LONDON / 1936

20.6 x 13.7 cm; [i-vi], vii-ix, [x], [1-2], 3-306, [307-310]; $2.50.

The title page described above is on page [iii]; the dedication, with a letter, is "FOR MY BROTHER / *EDWARD HORGAN,*" on page [v], and is dated *"Roswell,* August, 1935"; the contents is on pages vii-ix; the text begins on page 3 and ends on page 306; the printer's imprint is on page [307]; pages [308-310] are blank. The endpapers are light orange. The cover is brown cloth with gold and black, and black on gold, lettering and decoration on the spine. On the front cover is the publisher's device in black. The book was published in March.

Contents: Book I THE FATHER—i. New Time—ii. Through the Rain—iii. The Place—iv. Irma—v. The Happy Evening—vi. From the Heart—vii. The Temptress—viii. Heading Back—ix. Love and Vanity—x. The Promise—xi. The Troth—xii. The Past—xiii. Hotel Bedrooms—xiv. Someone She Knew— xv. Mind Made Up—xvi. Look Around—xvii. The Sower. Book II THE MOTHER—xviii. The Living—xix. Danny—xx. The Lasting Mark—xxi. Dance of Dust—xxii. The Cane—xxiii. Food—xxiv. The Inheritance—xxv. The World—xxvi. Love and Play—xxvii. What Life Brought—xxviii. Good and

Evil—xxix. In the Grove—xxx. The Thief—xxxi. The Dutiful—xxxii. Wilderness—xxxiii. Times Start Over—xxxiv. To Pray—xxxv. They Call—xxxvi. The Bullies—xxxvii. "Time'll Come"—xxxviii. Dedication—xxxix. "And I Will Listen!"—xl. The Deal—xli. Children to the Future. Book III THE SPIRIT—xlii. The Travellers—xliii. Not Homeward—xliv. Alien Return—xlv. Brooding Heat—xlvi. Time as Enemy—xlvii. One Fortune Prospers—xlviii. The Forwarded Letter—xlix. They Go Again—l. The Forgotten Word—li. Hope—lii. Bird and Snake—liii. Brother Trainor—liv. Flight and Return—lv. The Posters on Sunday Afternoon. Book IV THE POWER—lvi. The Heat; the Drums—lvii. The Silence—lviii. The Lover; the Beloved—lix. After Dark—lx. The Broken Night—lxi. The Conductor—lxii. On the Main Line West—lxiii. The Mexican. Book V THE SON—lxiv. Driscoll, Arizona—lxv. Hovering Idea—lxvi. Under the Sun—lxvii. Good Night—lxviii. The Kindly —lxix. Roll Along.

This book was later reprinted as part of *Mountain Standard Time* (1962), A28, which is composed of three previously and separately published novels: *Main Line West* (1936), A7; *Far From Cibola* (1938), A12; and *The Common Heart* (1942), A15. In its paper edition *Mountain Standard Time* is called *The Common Heart,* with the other two titles as a subtitle. It is listed as the paper edition of *Mountain Standard Time* (1962), A28c.

b. English edition, 1936

[the following set within a black rectangular frame composed of one thin rule, one thick rule, and one thin rule] MAIN LINE / WEST / *by* / Paul Horgan / Constable & Co Ltd / London / [1936]

19.7 x 12.8 cm; [i-xii], [1-2], 3-305, [306-308]; 7s, 6d.

The title page described above is on page [v]; the dedication as in the first edition is on pages [vii-viii]; the table of contents is on pages [ix-xi]; the text begins on page 3 and ends on page 305; page [306] contains the printer's imprint; pages [307-308] are blank. The cover is blue cloth with black on gold lettering on the spine; the dust jacket has blue and yellow type superimposed on an image of a railroad track, additional colors in black and red.

A8. *From the Royal City* 1936

first edition, limited

[page headed by a horizontal black floral rule] / *From* THE ROYAL CITY / *of the* / HOLY FAITH of *St. FRANCIS* of *ASSISI* / [second floral rule identical to one above] / Being five accounts of Life in that / place: The Captain General, 1690; / The Evening Air, 1730; Triumph— / al Entry, 1780; Bittersweet Waltz, / 1846; and Frock Coats & the Law, / 1878. / PAUL HORGAN / [black pen and ink sketch of head of Captain Gaspar de Villagra, flanked by scalloped winglike objects and an unfurled paper scroll; the whole framed by a thin black line] / [third floral rule identical to two above] / *Printed by* The Rydal Press *in* 1936 *for* / Villagra Book-shop, Santa Fe, New Mexico

23.5 x 15.7 cm; [i-ii], [1–2], 3–27, [28–30]; $2.25 and $1.50 for the hard-bound and paperbound editions.

Pages [i-ii] are blank; the title page described above is on page [1]; the text begins on page 3 and ends on page 27; pages [28–30] are blank. The illustration on the title page and the pen and ink sketches are by the author. These sketches appear at the five chapter headings: pages 3, 7, 12, 18, and 23. The book is designed by Walter Goodwin. The hardbound and paperbound editions are identical except for the bindings. The hardbound edition has a rust cloth binding with the author's name and the title of book in gold on the cover, set inside a gold floral rectangle. The paperbound edition has a gray paper cover with a rust overall design of printer's flowers and the title and the author's name in the same rust color. The publication was subsidized by Clifford McCarthy. The entire work appeared in *The Yale Review* (December, 1932), C67, without the illustrations, and was reprinted in *America in the Southwest* (1933), F25.

The exact publication date is not known, but the author's copy has an in-scription dated May 17, 1936, which is close to the publication date. The Library of Congress copy has a hand accession date of July.

A9. *The Return of the Weed* 1936

a. first edition, limited, 1936

[in green on left page] THE RETU [on right page] RN OF / THE WEED / [original lithograph tipped on left page] / [on right page] *By* Paul Hor-gan / [publisher's device in green] / [below lithograph on left page] *Il-lustrated with Original Lithographs* / *By* Peter Hurd / [on right page] *Harper & Brothers Publishers* / *New York and London* [in green] 1936

24.2 x 18.3 cm; [i-vi], [1–2], 3–97, [98].

On page [98] is stated: "This limited edition in which the original litho-/ graphs are bound is published for Edward Nicholas / Jr by Harper and Brothers, in Baskerville type, / printed on Strathmore Highway Book paper, the / whole designed by Arthur W. Rushmore, and signed / by the author and the artist. There are 350 numbered / copies, of which only the first 250 are for sale. / This copy is numbered [signed in black ink] 144. [signed in black ink] Paul Horgan   Peter Hurd."

The title page described above is on pages [ii-iii] and its design follows an idea suggested by Paul Horgan; on page [v] the book is dedicated (in out-line type): "FOR / HENRIETTE [Wyeth Hurd] / FROM / PAUL / & PETER"; the contents is on page [1]; the text begins on page 3 and ends on page 97. The cover is green cloth with the title, author's name, and pub-lisher printed on a label pasted on the spine. The slipcase is green cardboard with a label pasted on the front that includes the title, the author's name, the book's number, and the publisher's name. The original lithographs printed directly from the stone are bound in as unnumbered leaves between pages [4]–5, [14]–15, [28]–29, [42]–43, [66]–67, [82]–83, in addition to the lithograph tipped in on the title page. The book was published in November.

Contents: Argument—The Mission—The Brothers—The Mansion—The Tank —The Hacienda—The Star—Resolution. "The Hacienda" was originally published in *The Yale Review* (March, 1936), C92; it was reprinted in *The Peach Stone* (1967), A36.

b. trade edition, 1936

[lithograph by Peter Hurd appears opposite the title page] *Paul Horgan* / [thin, short horizontal rule] / [in green in outline type] THE / RETURN OF / THE WEED / [thin, short horizontal rule] / *Lithographs by Peter Hurd* / [publishers device in green] / HARPER & BROTHERS PUBLISH-ERS / *New York and London* / [in green] 1936

20.6 x 13.8 cm; [i-ii], [insert of lithograph], [iii-vi], [1–2], 3–97, [98]; $2.00.

The title page described above is on page [iii]; the dedication as for the limited edition is on page [v]; the contents is on page [1]; the text begins on page 3 and ends on page 97; the printer's imprint is on page [98]. Reproductions of lithographs appear on unnumbered pages opposite the title page and pages 5, 15, 29, 43, 67, and 83. The cover is cream cloth with the title and author's name on the front cover and on the spine in green and gold. Also on the spine in green is "Harpers."

c. English edition, 1936

An English edition by Constable & Co Ltd was published in 1936 with the title *Lingering Walls*. The price was 7s, 6d. No copy has been examined.

A10. *A Lamp on the Plains*   1937

a. first edition, 1937

[the following is set within two borders of blue vertical rules, each composed as follows: one thin rule, one thick rule, one decorative rule, two thin rules, one decorative rule] [the four lines of the title are in outline type] A / LAMP / ON THE / PLAINS / *by* / Paul / Horgan / [publisher's device] / *Harper & Brothers Publishers* / NEW YORK AND LONDON / 1937

20.5 x 14 cm; [i-vi], vii-x, [1–2], 3–373, [374]; $2.50.

The title page described above is on page [iii]; on page [v] the book is dedicated *"To* / PETER HURD"; on page [vi] is a quotation from Henry David Thoreau; the contents is on pages vii-x; the text begins on page 3 and ends on page 373; the publisher's imprint appears on page [374]. The endpapers have a white-on-white design. The cover is maroon cloth with gold and black, and black on gold, lettering and decoration on the spine.

On the front cover is the publisher's device in black. The book was published in March.

Contents: Book One: THE ANIMAL—i. War Summer, 1918—ii. The Fugitive—iii. Familiar Life—iv. The Animal—v. Something to Bear—vi. The Dogs—vii. The Great Children—viii. Pity—ix. Above the Town—x. In the Wilderness—xi. Hunt and Quarry—xii. Work—xiii. Good Works—xiv. The Temper of Money—xv. Security—xvi. Crusade—xvii. The People of Two Worlds—xviii. Resolve—xix. The School—xx. After School—xxi. Yow-ee—xxii. The Teacher and the Big Boy—xxiii. The Whistles in the Morning—xxiv. The Celebrant. Book Two: THE LAMP—xxv. Dealings with People—xxvi. The Intellectuals—xxvii. In Safety—xxviii. The Cost of Growth—xxix. Sacrifice—xxx. Winter's Reminder—xxxi. The Livelihood—xxxii. The Secret Mime—xxxiii. The Shelter—xxxiv. The Purpose and the Betrayal—xxxv. In the Church, Midweek—xxxvi. The Day of Children—xxxvii. The Lost, the Bitter, the Innocent—xxxviii. Door After Door—xxxix. Allies—xl. Firebrand—xli. "If I *Never* Saw Her Again!"—xlii. Wizard and Spell—xliii. Manhood—xliv. Windy-rumor—xlv. The New Enemy—xlvi. Verdict of the Elders—xlvii. Verdict of Mrs. Hopeman—xlviii. Taken—xlix. Carnival and Aftermath—l. Conspiratress and Others—li. In the Night Watch—lii. Repentance—liii. The Key; the Accomplice—liv. Sure Is Cold—lv. The Dirt and the Seed—lvi. A Landmaster. Book Three: THE GIVERS—lvii. A Widowed World—lviii. The Ranch—lix. Africa—lx. The Old Heart Like a Mirror—lxi. The Innocent Elders—lxii. For Newt—lxiii. Animal Care—lxiv. The Brothers—lxv. The Hot Summer—lxvi. Stephen Despoiled—lxvii. Branding—lxviii. Of the Family—lxix. End of the Marauder—lxx. Another Clay—lxxi. A New League—lxxii. In Tribute—lxxiii. Discord—lxxiv. Drouth—lxxv. Laocoön—lxxvi. The Long Rain—lxxvii. There Are No Secrets—lxxviii. Festival and Fate—lxxix. The Mourner—lxxx. The Africans—lxxxi. Betrayal and Goodbye—lxxxii. Better Get Goin'—lxxxiii. In Perpetuity—lxxxiv. The Humble Dynast. Book Four: THE HEROES—lxxxv. New Streams Released—lxxxvi. The Rebellion: Forces of Challenge—lxxxvii. The Rebellion: Mobilization—lxxxviii. The Rebellion: Battle—lxxxix. The Rebellion: No Victor—xc. The Rebellion: A Result—xci. Ghostly Dominion—xcii. Factotum—xciii. The News—xciv. Clear Premises—xcv. The Responses—xcvi. "What Are We Going To Do!"—xcvii. Everything Different—xcviii. The Dawn—xcix. Stephen's Legacy—c. Memory of Africa—ci. The Quality of Survival—cii. Toward Saturday Night—ciii. The Buoyant Past—civ. Siege and Relief—cv. The Engine and the Heart—cvi. The Seeker—cvii. The Proper Smoke—cviii. The *Frind*—cix. Confidences—cx. Weathers—cxi. The Heroes.

b. English edition, 1937

[the following set within a black rectangular frame composed of one thin rule, one thick rule, one thin rule] A Lamp on / the Plains / *by* / Paul Horgan / Constable & Co Ltd / London / [1937]

19.8 x 12.9 cm; [i-xii], [1-2], 3-495, [496]; 8s, 6d.

The title page described above is on page [v]; the dedication as in the first edition is on page [vii]; the quotation from Thoreau is on page [viii]; the contents is on pages [ix-xii]; the text begins on page 3 and ends on page [496]. The cover is green cloth with black on gold lettering on the spine; the dust jacket has red type with a design of a lantern against a stylized black landscape.

c. paper edition, 1964

PAUL HORGAN / [author's name underscored with black horizontal rule] / A LAMP / ON THE PLAINS / POPULAR LIBRARY • NEW YORK / [1964]

17.4 x 10.5 cm; [1–8], 9–319, [320]; $0.75.

The title page described above is on page [3]; the dedication as in the first edition is on page [5]; the quotation from Thoreau is on page [6]; the text begins on page 9 and ends on page 319; page [320] carries an advertisement for Popular Library books. The cover is white with black type and shows a color drawing of the heads of a man and a woman and a view of a Southwestern town.

A11. *New Mexico's Own Chronicle*   1937

first edition, 1937

[first four lines of title printed in brown] NEW / MEXICO'S / OWN / CHRONICLE / [the following set below a double horizontal black rule composed of one thick and one thin rule] THREE RACES IN THE WRITINGS / OF FOUR HUNDRED YEARS / *Adapted and Edited by* / MAURICE GARLAND FULTON / and / PAUL HORGAN / [here follows a double horizontal black rule composed of one thin and one thick rule] / DALLAS / BANKS UPSHAW AND COMPANY / [1937]

22.2 x 14.7 cm; [i-ix], x-xiii, [xiv-xvii], xviii-xxviii, [1–2], 3–[156], [24 Roman-numbered pages], [157]–372; $3.50.

The title page described above is on page [v]; the dedication is on page [vii] and states: *"To / these three frontiersmen / of / New Mexico /* [black horizontal decorative rule composed of one thick and one thin rule] / JOSIAH GREGG / (1806–1850) / *The Chronicler* / • / ARCHBISHOP LAMY / (1814–1888) / *The Priest* / • / SENATOR CUTTING / (1888–1935) / *The Statesman* / [black horizontal rule composed of one thin and one thick rule]"; the introduction is on pages [ix]-xiii; acknowledgments on page [xv]; contents on pages [xvii]-xxviii; the text begins on page 3 and ends on page 350; notes are on pages 351–364; index on pages 367–372. There are 24 Roman-numbered pages of illustrations between pages [156] and [157] of the text. The design of the cover, the drawings of New Mexico scenes on it, and the typography are by Paul Horgan.

All copies examined have page xxviii numbered as "xviii." The copy at Yale is misbound: pages [i-iv] and pages xiii-[xvi] are bound between pages [viii] and [ix]; the pages after page 356 are missing.

One section from this book is by Paul Horgan and is entitled "The Three Southwestern Peoples." The index and notes say it appeared with that title in *Southwest Review*. Actually, the article included in that periodical is entitled "About the Southwest: A Panorama of Nueva Granada" (July, 1933), C73, and the short extract in this book is an adaptation from this longer article.

A12. *Far From Cibola*   1938

a. first edition, 1938

[the following set within two borders of maroon vertical rules, each composed as follows: one thin rule, two thick rules, one thin rule, one decorative rule] FAR / FROM / CIBOLA / by / Paul / Horgan / [publisher's device in maroon] / *Harper & Brothers Publishers* / NEW YORK AND LONDON / 1938

20.5 x 13.5 cm; [i-vi], vii, [viii-x], 1-163, [164-166]; $1.75.

The title page described above is on page [iii]; the book is dedicated *"To / PHILIP STEVENSON /* [short vertical rule of one thick and one thin rule]" on page [v]; the contents is on page vii; the text begins on page 1 and ends on page 163; the printer's imprint appears on page [165]; pages [164] and [166] are blank. The endpapers have a maroon design. The cover is black cloth with maroon and gold, and maroon on gold, lettering and decoration on the spine. On the front cover is the publisher's device in maroon.

Contents: i. Until Sundown—ii. Skyward—iii. To Understand—iv. The Three Sons—v. Intentions—vi. Cowards—vii. Under the Wind—viii. Sundown and After—ix. Solace—x. Survival—xi. Fallen Image—xii. Convictions—xiii. Conviviality—xiv. To California.

The entire work first appeared in *The New Caravan* (1936), B6. It was later reprinted as part of *Mountain Standard Time* (1962), A28, which is composed of three previously and separately published novels: *Main Line West* (1936), A7; *Far From Cibola* (1938), A12; and *The Common Heart* (1942), A15. In its paper edition, *Mountain Standard Time* is called *The Common Heart,* with the other two titles as a sub-title. It appeared in paper in 1966 and is listed as the paper edition of *Mountain Standard Time* (1962), A28c.

Books for Libraries Press (Freeport, New York) reprinted the novel in 1971 in its Short Story Index Reprint Series.

b. English edition, 1938

[the following set within two borders of maroon vertical rules, each composed as follows: one thin rule, two thick rules, one thin rule, one decorative rule] FAR / FROM / CIBOLA / *by* / Paul / Horgan / LONDON / *Constable & Company Ltd* / 1938

20.4 x 12.8 cm; [i-vi], vii, [viii-x], 1–163, [164]; 6s.

The English edition used sheets printed in the United States, and was published in England on March 1, 1938. There is no printer's imprint, no extra blank page, and the endpapers are white. The cover is light blue cloth with red on gold lettering on the spine; the dust jacket is gray with black type, the whole framed in green swelled rules.

A13. *The Habit of Empire* 1939

a. first edition, 1939

[initial T in green with decorative floral design] THE / HABIT / of / EMPIRE / [the following line in green] *by PAUL HORGAN* / THE RYDAL PRESS—SANTA FE NEW MEXICO / [1939]

21 x 15.4 cm; [i-xii], [1–2], 3–114, [115–116]; $3.50.

The title page described above is on page [iii]; on page [v] appears: "[initial L in green with decorative floral design] LAND— / SCAPES / [the following line in green] *by PETER HURD";* on page [vii] the book is dedicated *"To / Vernon Knapp";* the contents is on page [ix]; a list of titles of the landscapes is on page [xi]; the text begins on page [1] and ends on page 114; page [115] is blank; a colophon is on page [116], with a stylized sketch of a monk.

Decorative initials designed by Willard Clark appear on page [iii], on page [v], and with the initial letter, set in green, at the start of each of the 14 chapters. There are eight double-page illustrations of landscapes by Peter Hurd that appear between pages [16]–17, 22–23, [26]–27, 38–39, 46–47, 68–69, [102]–103, and 108–109. The cover is gray cloth with a format similar to the title page: "[initial T in green with decorative floral design] THE / HABIT / of / EMPIRE / [the following line in green] *by PAUL HORGAN."* The title and author's name appear in black on the spine.

Contents: 1598—i The Blood of His Time—ii The Possession—iii The Summer Waters—iv The Capital—v A Shot From an Harquebus—vi Marching Orders—vii A Winter Morning—viii Man, Horse and Dog—ix Death and Transfiguration—x A Winter Afternoon—xi Storm Toward Heaven—xii The Old Men—xiii St. James—xiv A Flight of Arrows.

The landscapes by Peter Hurd, in india ink line, charcoal, and wash, have these titles: The Ford at El Paso—The Salt Lakes—The Land of the Teguas —The Rock of Acoma—The Buffalo Plains—The Puddle—The Ruined Pueblo—The Vision.

The book appeared in serial form in *The New Mexico Sentinel* (1938), C104; it also appeared, at the same time and in serial form, in Spanish in

El Nuevo Mexicano (1938), D9. Chapter VII, "A Winter Morning," was reprinted in *The Southwest in Life and Literature* (1962), F42.

b. trade edition, 1939

[initial T in gray with decorative floral design] THE / HABIT / of / EMPIRE / [the following line in gray] *by PAUL HORGAN* / HARPER & BROTHERS, NEW YORK AND LONDON / [1939]

21 x 15.7 cm; [i-xii], [1-2], 3-114, [115-116]; $2.50.

The trade edition is similar to the first, but uses gray as a second color instead of green, has page [116] blank, and has the reproductions of the Hurd landscapes between pages 10-11, 22-23, 34-35, 46-47, [58]-59, 70-71, 98-99, 110-111; however, the table of contents for the reproductions incorrectly lists pages 17, 22, 27, 39, 47, 69, 103, and 109, the pages listed in the first edition. The front cover is as for the first edition, as is the spine, with the addition of the word "Harper" in black. The only copy examined is at Hayden Library, Arizona State University.

A14.   *Figures in a Landscape*   1940

first edition, 1940

[the following is set within two borders of pale green vertical rules, each composed as follows: one thin rule, one thick rule, one decorative rule, two thin rules, and one decorative rule] FIGURES / IN / A / LANDSCAPE / *by* / Paul / Horgan / [Publisher's device in pale green] / *Harper & Brothers Publishers* / NEW YORK AND LONDON / [1940]

20.6 x 13.5 cm; [i-vi], vii-viii, [ix-xii], 1-284, [285-292]; $2.50.

The title page described above is on page [iii]; the book is dedicated *"This book is for* / EDWARD *and* MARY NICHOLAS / [floral design]" on page [v]; the contents is on pages vii-viii; and on page [ix] it states: "Various parts of this book have appeared in *The / Atlantic Monthly, The Southwest Review, The Yale / Review, Harper's Bazaar, Folksay: A Regional Miscel- / lany,* and *Scribner's Magazine.*" The text begins on page 1 and ends on page 284; on page [285] is the printer's imprint; the rest of the pages are blank. The book is bound in gray cloth with gold, and black on gold, lettering and decoration on the spine; on the front cover is the publisher's device in black; the jacket design and drawing are by Paul Horgan. The second edition (a copy is at Yale) has the title page all in black and omits pages [291-292].

Contents: I The Landscape—II Panorama—III The Heroic Triad—IV The Invader—V To the Mountains—VI The Traders—VII The Captain's Watch—VIII For Security—IX The Candy Colonel—X Belief—XI Relatives Out West—XII Two Energies—XIII The Surgeon and the Nun—XIV "Wahrheit und Dichtung"—XV A Castle in New Spain—XVI The Fire of the Eye—XVII The Tularosa Bobcat—XVIII Law 'n' Order—XIX The Captain—XX Sprite of the Machine—XXI Tribute—XXII Fun with a Mirror—XXIII For the Flowering—XXIV In Summer's Name—XXV The End of an Occupation—XXVI Hot St'ff—XXVII The Transient—XXVIII To Quiet the Bugles—XXIX Avowal—XXX The Listeners.

"The Landscape": first published in *Folk-Say: A Regional Miscellany, 1931,* under the general title "Figures in a Landscape," B3; reprinted in *America in the Southwest* (1933), F49. "The Heroic Triad": first appeared as a section of "About the Southwest," *Southwest Review* (July, 1933), C73. "To the Mountains": *The Atlantic Monthly* (January, 1938), C103; reprinted in *The Peach Stone* (1967), A36; see C194; D22 and 23; F98–107. "The Candy Colonel": reprinted in *The Peach Stone* (1967), A36. "Relatives Out West": *The Yale Review* (December, 1938), C106. "The Surgeon and the Nun": *Harper's Bazaar* (December, 1936), C97; reprinted in *The Peach Stone* (1967), A36; see F76–86. "The Tularosa Bobcat": first published in *Folk-Say: A Regional Miscellany, 1931,* B3. "The Captain": first published in *Folk-Say: A Regional Miscellany, 1931,* B3. "Tribute": *Scribner's Magazine* (October, 1935), C90; reprinted in *The Peach Stone* (1967), A36. "In Summer's Name": reprinted in *The Peach Stone* (1967), A36. "Hot St'ff": first published in *Folk-Say: A Regional Miscellany, 1931,* B3. "To Quiet the Bugles": *The Yale Review* (March, 1937), C98. "The Listeners": first published as "The Last Words of Mrs. McDonny" in *Folk-Say: A Regional Miscellany, 1931,* B3.

A15. *The Common Heart*   1942

The / Common / Heart / *by* Paul Horgan / [single horizontal rule] / . . . *what was character but the* / *world's own material of magic* . . . / [single horizontal rule] / Harper & Brothers *Publishers* New York *and* London / [1942]

20.5 x 14 cm; [i-vi], vii-viii, [1–2], 3–398, [399–400]; $2.50.

The title page described above is on page [iii]; the book is dedicated "TO / Peg and Barry Duffield" on page [v]; the author's note is on page [vi]; the contents is on pages vii-viii; the text begins on page 3 and ends on page 398; the printer's imprint is on page [399]; page [400] is blank. The book is bound in black cloth with gold and black, and black on gold, lettering and decoration on the spine. On the front cover is the publisher's device in blind.

Contents: Book One: The Family Story—I. Peter and the Country—II. The Family Story—III. The Newcomers—Book Two: The Ages of Man—IV. The Boys—V. Firelight—VI. Other Americas—VII. The Widow—VIII. Rifletime—IX. Another Country—X. The Birthday—XI. Personages—Book Three: Adam's Own Land—XII. Wandering Barks—XIII. The Destroyers—XIV. The Emperor's New Clothes—XV. The Kiss—XVI. Half Was Learned and Half Was Divined—XVII. An Old Endurance—XVIII. Hear About Love—XIX. The Poets—XX. The Cleansing River—XXI. The Program—XXII. Forgiven—XXIII. On the Moonlit Mesa—XXIV. The Strong Tide—XXV. The Trip to Hano—XXVI. Martha and Noonie—XXVII. The Return of Noonie—

XXVIII. Farewell to Molly—Book Four: The Earth's Heart Beating—XXIX. Growing Up—XXX. High Feelings from Long Ago—XXXI. Business: A Skirmish—XXXII. Peter's Own Early West—XXXIII. "Hush!"—XXXIV. The Farewell—XXXV. "Inscrutable"—XXXVI. The Train—XXXVII. Mail from Albion—Book Five: The Tributaries—XXXVIII. Dr. McGinnis—XXXIX. The Tributary.

"A Try for the Island," *Harpers Magazine* (June, 1942), C115, is Chapter 32, Sections 4–12 from this book; this same chapter under the same title was published in *Senior Scholastic* (March 29–April 3, 1943), C117. *The Common Heart* was later reprinted in *Mountain Standard Time* (1962), A28, which is composed of three previously and separately published novels: *Main Line West* (1936), A7; *Far From Cibola* (1938), A12; and *The Common Heart* (1942), A15. In its paper edition *Mountain Standard Time* is called *The Common Heart,* with the other two titles as a subtitle. This paper edition appeared in 1966 and is listed as the paper edition of *Mountain Standard Time* (1962), A28c.

A16. *You Don't Think . . .*   1944

WAR DEPARTMENT PAMPHLET NO. 21–15 / [in red open-face] YOU / [in brown open-face] DON'T / [in black open-face] THINK . . . / [June 13, 1944]

13.4 x 10.7 cm; [1–68].

This pamphlet was written and illustrated by Paul Horgan during his service as Chief of Army Information Branch, War Department, and printed in red, brown, and black. It was issued "By order of the Secretary of War," and signed "G. C. MARSHALL, / *Chief of Staff.*" This statement appears on page [68]. On that same page the order for issuing states: "One to each male officer and / enlisted man in the continental U.S." The pamphlet, which had the largest circulation of any of Paul Horgan's works—literally millions of copies were distributed free to the Army—is on the subject of venereal disease. It explains how such diseases are contracted and what can be done to cure them.

A17. *The Devil in the Desert*   1952

The / Devil / in the / Desert / by / PAUL HORGAN / Longmans, Green and Co. / New York • London • Toronto / 1952

18.7 x 12.5 cm; [1–10], 11–63, [64]; $1.50.

The title page described above is on page [3]; the dedication (see below) on page [5]; the contents on page [7]; the text begins on page 11 and ends on page 63; page [64] is blank. The cover is black cloth with gold lettering and decoration on the spine. The book was published in March.

Contents: 1. A Pair of Green Sun-Glasses—2, A Hard Journey—3. The Tri-angle—4. The Secret—5. The Cicadas—6. The Sleepers—7. In Crystal Depths —8. The Door—9. An Old Weakness and an Old Strength.

The Devil in the Desert was originally published in *The Saturday Evening Post* (May 6, 1950), C130. It is one of the three stories in the volume *Humble Powers* (1954), A20, and it was reprinted in a collection of stories, *The Peach Stone* (1967), A36. It has been translated into French (1952), D3, and twice into German (for three separate editions: 1957, 1958, and 1963), D4, 5, and 6; as part of *Humble Powers* it was translated into Italian (1956), D10, and into Spanish (1956), D11; and as part of *The Peach Stone* into Pak-Bengali (1969), D17. It has frequently been anthologized, F12–18.

This story is dedicated, page [5], "FOR / VIRGINIA RICE," who has been since April, 1928, Paul Horgan's extraordinarily able literary agent.

A18. *One Red Rose for Christmas*   1952

PAUL HORGAN / [O has decorative floral motif] *One* / RED ROSE / *for* / CHRISTMAS / LONGMANS, GREEN AND CO. / NEW YORK • LONDON • TORONTO / 1952

18.7 x 12.6 cm; [1–8], 9–96; $1.75.

The title page described above is on page [3]; the dedication: "TO / *Marie Louise Rohr* / TO WHOM—MY MOTHER'S YOUNGEST SISTER— / I OWE THANKS FOR MANY EARLY JOYS OF THE / IMAGINATION" is on page [5]; the contents is on page [7]; the text begins on page 9 and ends on page 96. The cover is yellow cloth with gold lettering on the spine.

Contents: One. Mount St. Kit's—Two. Fire and Dream—Three. The League—Four. The Secret Window—Five. Kathie—Six. For a Sign—Seven. Some of the Good Things of Life—Eight. The Sign—Nine. Ceremonial Day—Ten. Enough of a Miracle—Eleven. The Death of a Rose—Twelve. Transfiguration.

First published in *Cosmopolitan* (December, 1951), C138, the story was later reprinted in *Humble Powers* (1954), A20, and made into a one-act play (1954), E20. A dramatization appeared three times on ABC television: twice with Helen Hayes and once with Paul Horgan and Ruth White, on Decem-ber 17, 1967, in a semi-dramatic reading. It has been published in French (1953), D12, and in German (1960 and 1969), the German translation ap-pearing in three editions, D13, 14, and 15; as part of *Humble Powers* it has been published in Italian and Spanish (1956), D10 and 11. It was a selection of the *Catholic Family Book Club* (1957), F 53, and appeared in the *Catholic Life Annual 1959*, F54, and *The Best in Modern Catholic Reading, Volume II* (1966), F55.

The first edition was published in October, 1952, and with the November 1952 printing the price had increased to $2.

A19. *Great River* 1954

a. first edition, volume one, 1954

[in brown on left page] GREAT [in brown on right page] RIVER / [on left page] *The Rio* [on right page] *Grande* / in / North American / History / [on left] VOLUME ONE [on right] by PAUL HORGAN / [on left page] *Indians and Spain* / [on right page] RINEHART & COMPANY, INC. *New York* / *1954 Toronto*

22.9 x 15 cm; [i-vi], vii-xv, [xvi], [1-2], 3-447, [448]; $10 for set of two.

The title page described above is on pages [ii-iii] and was designed by Paul Horgan; the book contains on pages vii-xii: *"to Charles Arthur Henderson / a letter of dedication to serve as a preface"*; the contents is on pages xiii-xv; the text begins on page 3 and ends on page 440; there are maps by Rafael Palacios on pages 10-11 and on page 82; and "Sources for / Volume One, by Chapters" on pages [441]-447; page [448] is blank.

The first volume of two which constitute the first edition has pale blue endpapers, is bound in black cloth with gold lettering and decoration on the spine, and is boxed with volume two in a cardboard slipcase that has on its front cover the title, the author's name, and a reproduction of a painting of the river by the author. This picture runs around onto the spine where the title and author are repeated. On the back of the slipcase are comments on the work by various historians, a biographical note on Paul Horgan, and the title, author, and publisher.

Contents: VOLUME ONE: *Indians and Spain*—Prologue: *Riverscape*—1. Creation—2. Gazetteer—3. Cycle—Book One: *The Indian Rio Grande*—1. The Ancients—2. The Cliffs—3. To the River—4. The Stuff of Life—i. Creation and Prayer—ii. Forms—iii. Community—iv. Dwelling—v. Garments—vi. Man, Woman and Child—vii. Farmer and Hunter—viii. Travel and Trade—ix. Personality and Death—5. On the Edge of Change—Book Two: *The Spanish Rio Grande*—1. The River of Palms—2. Rivals—3. Upland River—4. The Travellers' Tales—5. Destiny and the Future—6. Faith and Bad Faith—7. Facing Battle—8. Battle Piece—9. The Garrison—10. Siege—11. The Eastern Plains—12. Prophecy and Retreat—13. Lords and Victims—14. The River of May—15. Four Enterprises—16. Possession—17. The River Capital—18. Collective Memory—i. Sources—ii. Belief—iii. The Ocean Masters—iv. The King and Father—v. Arts—vi. Style and Hunger—vii. The Swords—viii. Soul and Body—19. Duties—20. A Dark Day in Winter—21. The Battle of Acoma—22. Afterthoughts—23. Exchange—24. The Promises—25. The Desert Fathers—26. The Two Majesties—27. The Hungry—28. "This Miserable Kingdom"—29. The Terror—30. Limit of Vision—31. A Way to the *Texas*—32. The Great Captain—33. Fort St. John Baptist—34. Early Towns—35. Colonial Texas—36. Mexico Bay—37. Forgotten Lessons—38. Hacienda and Village—i. Land and House—ii. Fashion—iii. Family and Work—iv. Mischance—v. Feast Days—vi. Wedding Feast—vii. Mortality—viii. The Saints—ix. Provincials—39. The World Intrudes—40. The Shout—41. The Broken Grasp of Spain—Appendix A: Sources for Volume One, by chapters—Maps—1. Pueblos and Early Settlements—2. Spanish Expeditions.

first edition, volume two, 1954

[the title page is the same as for volume one, except that for "VOLUME ONE / *Indians and Spain*" is substituted] VOLUME TWO / *Mexico and the United States*

22.9 x 15 cm; [i-iv], v-vii, [viii], [449–452], 453–1020, [1021–1024].

The title page described above is on pages [ii-iii]; the contents is on pages v-vii; the text begins on page 453 and ends on page 945; maps by Rafael Palacios are on pages [450–451] and [614–615]; "Sources for / Volume Two, by Chapters" are listed on pages [947]–953; a "General Bibliography" is on pages [955]–977; "The Names of the Rio Grande" are on pages [979]–981; the index for both volumes is on pages [983]–1020; pages [1021–1924] are blank.

Contents: VOLUME TWO: *Mexico and the United States*—Book Three: *The Mexican Rio Grande*—1. A Colony for Mexico—2. A Wild Strain—3. The Twin Sisters—4. Last Return—5. The Spark—6. The *Ariel*—7. Slavery—8. Bad Blood—9. The Mexico Trade—10. Tormented Loyalties—11. "God and Texas" —12. From Mexico's Point of View—13. Fortunes of New Mexico—i. Peoples and Towns—ii. Politics—iii. Defense—iv. Church and School—v. Foreigners— 14. Revolt Up River—15. The River Republic—16. The Santa Fe Pioneers— 17. Border Smoke—18. To Mier and Beyond—19. Diplomacies—20. The United States to the River—Book Four: *The United States Rio Grande*—1. "Way, You Rio"—2. Collective Prophecy—i. New Man and New Principles—ii. Frontier Attitudes—iii. Woman and Home—iv. Community Expression—v. Language —vi. Arts and Utility—vii. Light in the Clearing—viii. Sons of Harmony—ix. Knacks and Crafts—x. First Interpreters—xi. The American Art—3. Bivouac— 4. The Army of the Rio Grande—5. The Cannonade—6. Fort Texas—7. The Listeners—8. Palo Alto—9. Resaca de la Palma—10. The River Dead—11. The Nation's War—12. Invasion Summer—13. Recurrent Frontier—14. Upstream and Inland—15. The Army of the West—16. The Secret Agent—17. Bloodless Possession—18. The Army of Chihuahua—19. The Free Missiourians—20. Brazito and the Pass—21. Counterdance—22. The Avengers—23. Massacre at Taos—24. Chihuahua—25. Trial at Taos—26. All on the Plains of Mexico—27. El Dorado—28. Contraband—29. A Thread of Spirit—30. Boundaries—31. Flag and Lamplight—32. The Rio Grande Divided—33. The Desolate—34. Confederate Border—35. The Second Mexican Empire—36. The Mexico Moon —37. Bad Men and Good—38. The Last Wagons—39. The Last Frontiersman —40. Treasure—41. The Last Earth Secrets—42. Revolution and Reflex—43. Utility and Vision—i. Utility—ii. Vision—Appendix B: Sources for Volume Two, by chapters—Appendix C: General Bibliography—Appendix D: The Names of the Rio Grande—Index—Maps—1. Texas and Mexico—2. New Mexico.

[263]

The book was published in October. Several selections appeared prior to or at the time of publication, C145, 148, 149, and 151; and many selections have been anthologized, F27-41. *The Heroic Triad* (1970), A39, includes extensive sections. Certain working notes for the book were published in 1955 as "Pages from a Rio Grande Notebook," C155, and as "Mountain to Sea: Rio Grande Notes," C165. The work was awarded the Bancroft and Pulitzer Prizes for History in May, 1955.

A symphonic work inspired by the book and entitled *Great River: The Rio Grande,* with a score by Ernst Bacon and narrative passages from the book, was commissioned by the Dallas Symphony Orchestra and first performed by them in February, 1957; see E22.

b. limited edition, volume one, 1954

[title page identical to that of first edition, volume one]

22.9 x 15 cm; [1-4], i-vi], vii-xv, [xvi], xvii-xviii, [8 unnumbered pages of illustrations], [1-2], 3-447, [448]; $25.00 for set of two.

The limited edition of volume one is similar to the first edition of volume one, with certain additions: there are four unnumbered pages [1-4] added at the start; pages [1] and [2] are blank; on page [3] appears (all in caps): "Great River / This limited edition of one thousand copies, of which / nine hundred and fifty are for sale, has been / especially illustrated and signed by the author. / [signed in ink] Paul Horgan." Page [4] is blank. An explanation of the illustrations appears on pages xvii-xviii, and eight unnumbered pages of reproductions of watercolor sketches by Paul Horgan appear between page xviii and page [1]. The endpapers contain a color reproduction of a watercolor of the river by Paul Horgan. The books are bound in a pale tan buckram and lettered in gold on the spine; they are boxed in a green cardboard slipcase with a cream label that contains the title [in green], subtitle [in black], author's name [in green], [black horizontal rule], general title of each volume [in black], floral design [in green], and publisher [in black].

limited edition, volume two, 1954

[title page identical to that of first edition, volume two]

22.9 x 15 cm; [i-iv], v-vii, [viii], ix, [x], [8 unnumbered pages of illustrations], [449-452], 453-1020, [1021-1024].

The 8 pages of reproductions of water colors by Paul Horgan are between pages [x] and [449], and the explanation of them on page ix. The limited edition of volume two has the same endpapers and binding as volume one of the limited edition. Otherwise, the limited edition of volume two is like volume two of the first edition.

Paul Horgan has a specially bound copy of the limited edition: the volumes are bound in red leather with a gold outline on the cover and gold lettering on the spine. Folded into the author's copy is a letter from Andrew Wyeth, and clipped in a card from Rinehart & Co. that states the books were sent as the compliments of Stanley M. Rinehart, Jr., and Frederick R. Rinehart.

c. English edition, 1955

An English edition was published by Macmillan & Co Ltd in 1955 that imported sheets of the U.S. two-volume first edition. The price was 50s. No copy of the English edition has been examined.

d. single-volume edition, 1960

[on the left page] GREAT [on the right page] RIVER / [on the left page] *The Rio* [on the right page] *Grande* / in / North American / History / by PAUL HORGAN / HOLT, RINEHART AND WINSTON / *New York* / [1960] / [the following four lines on the bottom half of the left page] VOLUME ONE / *Indians and Spain* / VOLUME TWO / *Mexico and the United States*

21 x 14 cm; [i-vi], vii-xviii, [1-2], 3-1020, [1021-1022]; $9.00.

The title page described above is on pages [ii-iii]; the dedicatory material similar to the first edition, volume one, appears on pages vii-xii; the contents for volume one appears on pages xiii-xv, and for volume two on pages xvi-xviii; the text begins on page 3 and ends on page 945. The division of pages is as for the two volumes of the first edition, and all the appendixes, maps, and the index of the two-volume edition are included. The binding is black cloth with gold lettering and decoration on the spine; the endpapers are white; the front dust jacket has an illustration like the one on the slipcase of the first edition: both reproduce one of Paul Horgan's watercolor sketches of the river.

The single-volume edition is considered the second edition and there are scattered emendations. This volume has no date except for the 1954 copyright date, but the stamped and hand notations in the Library of Congress copy all refer to July, 1960. This edition has gone through several printings and is still in print.

Paul Horgan has a specially bound copy in blue leather with gold decorations and lettering, and green marbled endpapers. The copy contains a card from "Mr. Stanley Marshall Rinehart, Jr."

e. paperbound edition, volume one, 1968

GREAT RIVER / *The Rio Grande* / IN / NORTH AMERICAN / HISTORY / *by* Paul Horgan / VOLUME ONE / *Indians and Spain* / MINERVA PRESS / [1968]

20.3 x 13.2 cm; [i-vi], vii-xv, [xvi], [1-2], 3-447, [448]; $2.95/volume.

The title page described above appears on page [iii]. On page xii there is a "Preface to the Third Edition," which is dated February 18, 1968, that states that "various scattered corrections" have been made "throughout the text." The basic page pattern for the two paper volumes is the same as for the two volumes of the first edition. The cover of both volumes has a reproduction of a watercolor sketch of the double bend in the river north of El Paso, Texas, by Paul Horgan.

paper edition, volume two, 1968

GREAT RIVER / *The Rio Grande* / IN / NORTH AMERICAN / HISTORY / *by* Paul Horgan / VOLUME TWO / *Mexico and* / *the United States* / MINERVA PRESS / [1968]

20.3 x 13.2 cm; [i-iv], v-vii, [viii], [449-452], 453-1020, [1021-1024]; $2.95./ volume.

The title page described above is on page [iii]; the rest of the edition is the same as the second volume of the first edition.

A20. *Humble Powers*   1954

a. first edition, 1954

HUMBLE / POWERS / BY / PAUL HORGAN / LONDON / MACMILLAN & CO LTD / 1954

19.7 x 13.1 cm; [i-vi], vii-viii, [ix-x], [1-2], 3-226, [227-230]; 4s.

The title page described above is on page [iii]; the dedication on page [v] states [all in caps]: "These stories are dedicated / separately / the first to Virginia Rice / the second to Marie Louise Rohr / the third to Dwight Starr"; the preface appears on pages vii-viii; the contents is on page [ix]; the text begins on page 3 and is divided as follows: "The Devil in the Desert," [1]-55; "One Red Rose for Christmas," [57]-135; "To the Castle," [137]-[227]; the printer's imprint is on page [227]; pages [228-230] are blank. The cover is red cloth with blue and gold lettering and decoration on the spine; the dust jacket is black with white lettering set against a design of a red rose with green leaves, with three illustrative medallions drawn in black ink. The book was published November 19, 1954.

"The Devil in the Desert" first appeared in *The Saturday Evening Post* (May 6, 1950), C130; "One Red Rose for Christmas" first appeared in *Cosmopolitan* (December, 1951), C138; and "To the Castle" first appeared in *The Saturday Evening Post* (October 13, 1951), with the title "The Soldier Who Had No Gun," C136. A brief excerpt (from "To the Castle") appeared in *The Shield* (April-May, 1966), C190. *Humble Powers* was translated into Italian and Spanish in 1956, D10 and 11. The first edition was English; the only U.S. edition was the paper edition. See *The Devil in the Desert* (1952), A17, and *One Red Rose for Christmas* (1952), A18.

b. paperbound edition, 1955

HUMBLE POWERS / PAUL HORGAN / [publisher's device] / Image Books / A division of Doubleday & Company, Inc., / Garden City, New York / [1955]

18 x 10.5 cm; [1-6], 7-8, [9-12], 13-196, [197-200]; 1st printing, $0.65, 2nd and 3rd printings $0.75.

A biography of the author is on pages [1-2]; the title page is page [5]; the preface is on pages 7-8; the contents is on page [9]; "The Devil in the Desert" on pages [11]-55; "One Red Rose for Christmas" on pages [57]-121; "To the Castle" on pages [123]-196; page [197] is blank; pages [198-199] carry advertisements for Image Books; and page [200] has a statement about Image Books. The Image Book edition was published February, 1956; first printing, December, 1955; second printing, August, 1958; and third printing, November, 1960. The cover is by Margot Tomes; the typography by Edward Gorey. The type on the front cover is black and white and the drawing is in blue, green, and gold and shows three scenes from the stories, set within three arches. The 2nd and 3rd printings have advertisements for Image Books on page [197] as well as pages [198-199].

A21. *The Saintmaker's Christmas Eve*   1955

a. first edition, 1955

[four lines of title in outline type] THE / SAINTMAKER'S / CHRIST-MAS / EVE / BY / PAUL / HORGAN / FARRAR, STRAUS AND CUDAHY / NEW YORK / [1955]

22 x 15.8 cm; [1-8], 9-112; $3.00.

The title page described above is on page [3]; the dedication "for / Constance Parry Knapp" on page [5]; the text begins on page 9 and ends on page 112. There are tan endpapers. The illustration on the dust jacket shows the back of a shepherd kneeling before an image and is reproduced in the book. It and four other full-page illustrations, and the decorations at the start of each chapter, are by Paul Horgan. There are two German editions, one in 1956, D18, and one that is undated that is published with *One Red Rose for Christmas,* D19; there is also a Spanish translation (1958), D20. The story was included in the *Catholic Family Book Club* (1956), F72. The cover has blue paper boards and a yellow cloth spine, with gold lettering on the spine.

Paul Horgan has a specially bound copy in brown leather with gold lettering, and green marbled endpapers.

b. English edition, 1956

THE SAINTMAKER'S / CHRISTMAS EVE / BY / PAUL HORGAN / *Illustrated by Fritz Wegner* / LONDON / MACMILLAN & CO LTD / 1956

22.8 x 13.8 cm; [i-vi], 1-87, [88-90]; 8s, 6d.

The title page described above is on page [iii]; the dedication, the same as for the first edition, is on page [v]; the text begins on page 1 and ends on page [88]; page [89] has the printer's imprint; and page [90] is blank.

This describes the copy now in Paul Horgan's library. The copy at Yale measures 21.8 x 13.8 cm and is priced 10s, 6d. The cover on each is red cloth with blue and gold lettering and decoration on the spine; the drawing on the

English dust jacket is not by Paul Horgan: it shows a shepherd kneeling before an image, with a burro in the background; the colors are green, white, and black, and the lettering yellow and black.

A22. *The Centuries of Santa Fe* 1956

a. first edition, 1956

[the following framed by a thin black rule] THE CENTURIES of / *SANTA FE* / BY / PAUL HORGAN / [short horizontal decorative rule] / *NEW YORK* / *E. P. DUTTON & COMPANY, INC.* / *1956*

21 x 14 cm; [i-x], xi-xiii, [xiv-xviii], [1-2], 3-363, [364-366]; $5.00.

The title page described above is on page [v]; the dedication "*TO* / DON BERKE" on page [vii]; the contents is on page [ix]; the preface is on pages xi-xiii; the quotation from Peter Heylin is on page [xv]; the text begins on page 3 and ends on page 340; the bibliography and index are on pages [341]-363; pages [364-366] are blank. The cover is black cloth with gold, and black on gold, lettering and decoration on the spine; the front dust jacket type is yellow on black and shows a color drawing of an adobe house and landscape by Paul Horgan (the chapter decorations are also by Paul Horgan); the end-papers contain maps of the far West and New Mexico by Rafael Palacios.

Contents: Preface—Book One: Under Spain—I. The Royal Notary: 1620—II. The Father President: 1635—III. The Bannerman: 1680—IV. The Alderman: 1691—V. The Matriarch: 1710—Book Two: Under Mexico—VI. The Missouri Trader: 1821—Book Three: Under the United States—VII. The United States Lieutenant: 1846—VIII. The German Bride: 1870—IX. The Doctor of Medicine: 1883—X. The Chronicler: 1915 and After—Epilogue: Past and Present—XI. The Survivals—Bibliography—Index.

The first printing was October, 1956; the second, November, 1956; and the third, December, 1963. The price of the third printing was $6.50. One chapter, "The Royal Notary: 1620," was reprinted in *Today and Tradition* (1960), F5; and an excerpt was published in *Under the Mask* (1972), F6.

b. limited edition, 1956

[the following framed by a thin black rule] THE CENTURIES OF / *SANTA FE* / BY / PAUL HORGAN / [short horizontal decorative rule] *NEW YORK* / *E. P. DUTTON & COMPANY, INC.* / *1956*

21 x 14 cm; [1-2], [i-x], xi-xiii, [xiv-xviii], [1-2], 3-363, [364-366]; $10.00.

On page [1] of the inserted page appears: "This special edition of 'The Centuries of Santa Fe' / is limited to 375 numbered and signed copies / of which this is number [in ink] 2 / [signed in ink on a thin horizontal rule] Paul Horgan." The reproduction of a half-page watercolor sketch by the author, of an adobe house, is tipped in opposite the title page. The pagination is, otherwise, as in the first edition. The whole is bound in brown leather and beige canvas with gold, and brown on gold, lettering and decoration on the spine. It is boxed in a brown and black cardboard slipcase with a white label that includes the title, author's name, edition number, and publisher.

c. English edition, 1957

THE CENTURIES / OF SANTA FE / BY / PAUL HORGAN / LONDON / MACMILLAN & CO LTD / 1957

21.8 x 14 cm; [i-ii], [unnumbered page with photograph], [iii-vi], vii-ix, [x], xi, [xii], 1–233, [234–236]; 21s.

The title page described above is on page [iii]; the dedication as in the first edition is on page [v]; the quotation as in the first edition is on page [vi]; the preface is on page vii; acknowledgments are on page viii; the contents is on page ix; illustrations are listed on page xi; the text begins on page 1 and ends on page 228; the index is omitted, but the bibliography is included on pages 229–233; a printer's imprint appears on page 233; pages [234–236] are blank. The cover is orange cloth with blue and gold lettering and decoration on the spine; the dust jacket is black with white type, with a color drawing by the author of an adobe house.

The English edition contains photographic illustrations of artistic and historic material on unnumbered leaves facing pages 28, 52, 68, 116, 172, 197, 226, and opposite the title page. A map of New Mexico is on page [xii]. The English edition has a different preface and map, no decorations by the author, and it omits Chapters VIII, IX, and X. There is a special prologue: "I. Prologue: The Place," pages 1–5; and a special epilogue: "IX. Epilogue: The Last Conquerors," pages 226–228. Chapter III's title is changed from "The Bannerman: 1680" to "The Colour-Sergeant: 1680."

d. paperbound edition, 1956

THE CENTURIES OF / SANTA FE / *by* / PAUL HORGAN / *A Dutton* [here follows the publisher's device] *Paperback* / NEW YORK / E. P. DUTTON & CO., INC. / 1965

18.5 x 10.9 cm; [i-x], xi-xiii, [xiv-xx], [1–2], 3–363, [364]; $1.75.

The title page described above is on page [v]; the dedication as in the first edition is on page [vii]; a brief biography of Paul Horgan is on page [viii]; the contents is on page [ix]; the preface is on pages xi-xiii; the quotation as in the first edition is on page [xv]; maps by Rafael Palacios are on pages [xvi-xvii]; the text begins on page 3 and ends on page 340; the bibliography is on page [341]–350; the index is on pages [351]–363; page [364] is blank.

The paperbound edition includes the same maps as the first edition (there as endpapers), on pages [xvi-xvii], and the same decorations by Paul Horgan at the chapter headings. The cover color painting of an Indian is by Paul Davis, with the type black.

A23. *Give Me Possession* 1957

a. first edition, 1957

PAUL HORGAN / GIVE ME / POSSESSION / *New York* / FARRAR, STRAUS AND CUDAHY / [1957]

20.2 x 13.5 cm; [i-x], [1-2], 3-267, [268-270]; $3.50.

The title page described above is on page [iii]; the dedication "to / Mary Katherine Cheney Henderson" is on page [v]; a quotation from Gabriel Harvey is on page [vii]; the contents is on page [ix]; the text begins on page 3 and ends on page 267; pages [268-270] are blank. The endpapers are gray. The cover is black cloth with gold, and black on gold, lettering and decoration on the spine; the top edge of the pages is stained green.

Contents: Book One: Tribal Customs—Book Two: The Young Warrior—Book Three: Maturity Rites.

Book Two was published in *Cosmopolitan* (September, 1948), C126, as "Give Me Possession." Invincible Press, Sydney, devoted pages 1-48 of issue #42 of *Invincible Love Stories* to some excerpt from the novel, but this reference has not been verified. A German translation appeared in 1959, D8.

b. English edition, 1958

GIVE ME POSSESSION / BY / PAUL HORGAN / LONDON / MAC-MILLAN & CO LTD / 1958

19 x 12.7 cm; [i-vi], vii, [viii], [1-2], 3-247, [248]; 13s, 6d.

The title page described above is on page [iii]; the dedication as in the first edition is on page [v]; the quotation from Gabriel Harvey is on page [vi]; the contents is on page vii; the text begins on page 3 and ends on page [248]; a printer's imprint appears on page [248]. The cover is red cloth with blue and gold lettering and design on the spine; the front dust jacket has white and blue type and several color drawings, with a man and a woman in black charcoal sketched over these drawings.

c. paperbound edition, 1958

[each of the three lines of the title is enclosed by a black rectangle] GIVE / ME / POSSESSION / PAUL HORGAN / [publisher's device] PERMA-BOOKS • NEW YORK / [1958]

16.3 x 10.5 cm; [i-x], 1-214; $0.35.

The title page described above is on page [iii]; the dedication as for the first edition is on page [v]; the quotation from Gabriel Harvey is on page [vii]; the contents is on page [ix]; the text begins on page 1 and ends on page 214. The first printing was September, 1958; the book was published November, 1968. The front cover is pink, blue, red, yellow, and purple and shows a soldier with a rifle and a woman standing before him; the edges are stained yellow.

d. paperbound edition, 1971

PAUL HORGAN / GIVE ME POSSESSION / PAPERBACK LIBRARY / New York / [1971]

17.8 x 10.5 cm; [1–8], 9–205, [206–208]; $0.95.

The title page described above is on page [3]; the dedication as in the first edition is on page [4], with the copyright; the contents is on page [5]; the quotation from Gabriel Harvey is on page [6]; the text begins on page 9 and ends on page 205; on page [206] is an advertisement for *The Peach Stone;* on page [207] an advertisement for *Things As They Are;* and on page [208] one for *A Distant Trumpet,* with an order blank for Paperback Library books. The cover is yellow with black type and shows a couple embracing in a wooded area; the edges are stained yellow.

A24. *Rome Eternal*   1959

a. first edition, 1959

ROME / ETERNAL / PAUL HORGAN / *Photography by Joseph Vadala* / FARRAR, STRAUS AND CUDAHY • / *New York* / [1959]

22.8 x 15 cm; [i-vi], vii-viii, [ix-x], [1–2], 3–196, [197–198]; $4.50.

The title page described above is on page [iii]; the contents is on page [v]; the dedication "TO / THE / GREATER / GLORY / OF / GOD" is on page [vi]; the preface is on pages vii-viii; the text and photos begin on page 3 and end on page 196; pages [197–198] are blank.

The first edition is bound in black cloth with gold lettering on the spine; the dust jacket is black with the title in gold and the other lettering in white. There are white endpapers. The book is designed by Stefan Salter.

The book is based upon a four-part film series entitled *Rome Eternal,* produced jointly by the National Council of Catholic Men and NBC. The contents of the book is divided into four chapters, each with the title of one of these four films: "The City of Peter," "The City of Faith," "Renaissance Rome," and "Our Moment of Time." The book contains 255 photographic stills from these four films and the text of the spoken narration used for the series. Paul Horgan discusses the television series in *Catholic Digest* (January, 1958), C166.

b. limited edition, 1959

This edition is like the first. A page is added at the start on which appears: "The limited edition of ROME ETERNAL / consists of ten signed copies, *hors commerce,* / and lettered A through J, and three hundred and fifty /

[271]

signed and numbered copies, of which this is / copy [in ink] 206 / [signed in ink] Paul Horgan." The price is $12.50.

The ten copies lettered A through J have purple endpapers and are bound in white cloth with a simulated watered silk pattern and gold lettering on the spine; the 350 numbered copies have purple endpapers and are bound in purple cloth with gold lettering on the spine; each is boxed in a white-on-white cardboard slipcase; the top edge of the pages in both editions is gold.

Copy A was presented to Pope John XXIII.

A25. *A Distant Trumpet*   1960

a. first edition, 1960

PAUL HORGAN / [3 lines of title in red] A / DISTANT / TRUMPET / FARRAR, STRAUS AND CUDAHY / NEW YORK / [1960]

21 x 14 cm; [i-viii], [1–2], 3–629, [630–632]; $5.75.

The title page is on page [iii]; the dedication on page [v] reads (in italics): "Dedicated / with affectionate thanks / to / Colonel and Mrs. Livingston Watrous / of the Army / who told me at dinner in Washington / on the eve of my separation from the / service in 1946 the family anecdote / from which this whole story took form."; the contents is on page [vii]; the text begins on page 3 and ends on page 629; page [630] is blank; pages [631–632] contain a "Postscript," signed "P.H." The cover is black cloth with the lettering in gold, and in black on gold, on the spine. The front dust jacket has white lettering and shows in color a bugle suspended over a desert; the top edge of the pages is stained red.

Contents: Book One: Scenes from Early Times—Book Two: Love and Duty—Book Three: Trial at Arms—Book Four: Recessional.

In the second printing the title is printed in black and the publisher's name changes to Farrar, Straus and Giroux. The second printing was 1965 and the third 1967. The price for the third is $6.95.

The book was published in April. There are several copyright dates that refer to earlier publication of sections: C133, 140–144, 146, and 171–172. A Spanish translation was published in Barcelona (1964), D7. "Father Abraham and the Recruit," a ballad written for the novel, was reprinted in *Songs After Lincoln* (1965), A33. The book was selected by the Literary Guild (May, 1960), the Catholic Digest Book Club (October, 1960), and the Doubleday Dollar Book Club (February, 1961). See F4, 22–23, and 110.

b. English edition, 1960

PAUL HORGAN / A / DISTANT / TRUMPET / LONDON / MACMILLAN & CO LTD / 1960

19.5 x 13 cm; [i-viii], [1–2], 3–629, [630–632]; 21s.

The sheets of the English edition were imported from the U.S. and the English edition is identical to the first. The book is bound in red cloth with gold and blue lettering and decoration on the spine. The front dust jacket is identical to that of the first edition.

c. paperbound edition, American, 1961

A / DISTANT / TRUMPET / BY PAUL HORGAN / A CREST RE-PRINT / [publisher's device] / FAWCETT PUBLICATIONS, INC., GREENWICH, CONN. / MEMBER OF AMERICAN BOOK PUBLISHERS COUNCIL, INC. / [1961]

18 x 10.5 cm; [1–4], 5–623, [624]; $0.95.

On page [1] is a quotation about the book from Lon Tinkle's *Dallas Morning News* review; the title page described above is on page [3]; the dedication as in the first edition is on page [4], the copyright page; the text begins on page 5 and ends on page 621; the postscript appears on pages 622–623; on page [624] is an advertisement for Premier Civil War Classics. The first three paper editions are the same, with different covers. The first Crest printing, October, 1961, has a brown cover, type in white and orange, and the picture of a small gold trumpet. The second Crest printing was November, 1962, and the cover is blue with white and yellow lettering and a pattern of trumpets. The third Crest edition was May, 1964, and the cover shows a photographic still of the U.S. Cavalry, from the film of the book. The edges are stained red in each printing.

d. paperbound edition, English, 1961

PAUL HORGAN / [publisher's device] / [single horizontal rule extending over two pages] / [on left page] A DISTANT [on right page] TRUMPET / [single horizontal rule extending over two pages] / TRANSWORLD PUBLISHERS • LONDON / [1961] [an illustration of three flags appears on the left page, extending above and below the two horizontal rules]

18 x 11 cm; [1–12], 13–699, [700–704]; 7s, 6p.

Pages [1–3] carry comments from the reviews of the book and on page [1] is included the title of the book and a reduced version of the three flags as on the title page; the title page described above is on pages [4–5]; the dedication as in the first edition is on page [7]; the contents is on page [9]; the text begins on page 13 and ends on page 697; the postscript is on pages 698–699; advertisements for other Corgi Books are on pages [700–704]. The cover is scarlet and gold with white and black lettering. A reissue appeared in 1970 with the following title page and basic format:

Paul Horgan / A Distant Trumpet / [publisher's device] / CORGI BOOKS / TRANSWORLD PUBLISHERS LTD / A National General Company / [1970]

17.8 x 11 cm; [1–12], 13–699, [700–704]; 50p.

Pages [1–3] carry comments on the book slightly different from those in the first issue of the paper edition; page [4] is blank; the title page described above is on page [5]; the dedication as in the first edition is on page [7]; the contents is on page [9]; the text begins on page 13 and ends on page 697; the postscript is on pages 698–699; other advertisements than in first issue of this edition appear on pages [700–704]. The cover is white with a drawing in color of a charging cavalry; the type is red, blue, and black.

e. paperbound edition, American, 1971

[a single horizontal rule] / PAUL HORGAN / [a single horizontal rule] / A DISTANT TRUMPET / PAPERBACK LIBRARY / New York / [1971] 17.8 x 10.5 cm; [1–4], 5–640; $1.25.

The title page described above is on page [3]; the dedication as in the first edition is on page [4], the copyright page; the text begins on page 5 and ends on page 639; the postscript is on pages 639–640. The cover is white with a color drawing of an Indian, a cavalry officer, and his cavalry; the type is black; the edges are stained yellow.

A26. *One of the Quietest Things* 1960

One of the / Quietest Things / By PAUL HORGAN / LOS ANGELES / SCHOOL OF LIBRARY SERVICE / UNIVERSITY OF CALIFORNIA / 1960

23 x 15 cm; [i-vi], 1–16, [17–18].

The title page described above is on page [iii]; the foreword by Lawrence Clark Powell is on page [v]; the text begins on page 1 and ends on page 16; pages [17–18] are blank. The cover is maroon with the title in white on the front cover.

This is the reprint of an address given at the inaugural meeting of the UCLA School of Library Services, September 18, 1960. A selection was reprinted as "The Language of Professionalism," *Library Journal* (December 15, 1962), C179.

A27. *Citizen of New Salem* 1961

a. first edition, 1961

[the following surrounded by double-page illustration of young Lincoln, a tree, a squirrel, and the forest] *Paul Horgan /* [on the left page] CITIZEN / [on right page] OF NEW SALEM / ILLUSTRATIONS BY / *Douglas Gorsline /* [on left page] New York [on right page] FARRAR, STRAUS AND CUDAHY / [1961]

23.4 x 15.7 cm; [1–8], 9–89, [90–96]; $3.75.

A list of works by Paul Horgan is on page [3]; the title page described above is on pages [4–5]; the dedication "to / ALLAN NEVINS" is on page [7];

the text begins on page 9 and ends on page [90]; acknowledgments are on page [93]; a colophon appears on page [95]; page [96] is blank. The pencil and wash illustrations appear throughout the book. The book has gray endpapers and is bound in blue and brown cloth; there is an apple tree in bloom on the cover, in gold and brown, and gold lettering on the spine. There was a limited edition of 75 copies bound in dark red leather with the same small tree in gold and brown on the cover and gold lettering on the spine. These copies are numbered and signed by the author on page [95]. There was a Book-of-the-Month Club edition (May, 1961) that omits the colophon and has buff endpapers. The children's edition is the same as the Book-of-the-Month Club edition, but with a dust jacket different from the one that is on the first and the book club editions. The front dust jacket for the first and BOMC editions is printed with an overall tone of mottled sand color with the title in open face white capital letters shaded in blue, the author's name in black italic, cap and lower case, and a drawing in pen and ink by Douglas Gorsline of a one-half full length figure of Lincoln as a youth, shaded in pale violet gray. The children's edition front dust jacket shows a three-color sketch in yellow, blue, and black of Lincoln as the steersman of a river raft.

The story first appeared in *The Saturday Evening Post* (March 4, 1961) and was commissioned by The Editors, C175; a condensed version was published in *The Reader's Digest* (February, 1964), C183.

b. English edition, 1961

[the following surrounded by double-page illustration of young Lincoln, a tree, a squirrel, and the forest] *Paul Horgan* / ABRAHAM / LINCOLN / CITIZEN OF NEW SALEM / ILLUSTRATIONS BY / *Douglas Gorsline* / LONDON • MACMILLAN & CO LTD • 1961

23.5 x 15 cm; [1–8], 9–89, [90–96]; 16s.

The English edition is like the first edition, but does not have the list of works on page [3], which is blank; has a different title page; and carries its own printer's imprint on page [94]; pages [95–96] are blank. The endpapers are white and the book is bound in red cloth with gold and blue lettering and decoration on the spine. The front dust jacket is similar to the first edition's, but adds in black caps at the top "Abraham Lincoln," which are the words added to the English title.

c. paperbound edition, 1962

[the following surrounded by double-page illustration of young Lincoln, a tree, a squirrel, and the forest] Citzen / of / New Salem / [following three lines on facing page] *Fully illustrated* / *Including the original drawings* / *by Douglas Gorsline* / [on right page] Paul Horgan / *A Crest Reprint* / [publisher's device] / FAWCETT PUBLICATIONS, INC., GREENWICH, CONN. / MEMBER OF AMERICAN BOOK PUBLISHERS COUNCIL, INC. / [1962]

18 x 10.5 cm; [1–14], 15–160; $0.50.

The title appears on page [1]; a line drawing of Lincoln and some text is on page [3]; a poem by Lincoln is on page [5]; the title page described above is on pages [6–7]; the dedication as in first edition is on page [9]; the title is on page [11]; Chapter 1 title page and a drawing are on pages [12–13]; page [14] is blank; the text begins on page 15 and ends on page [156]; on page [157] is a drawing of an apple tree in bloom. There is a footnote in the acknowledgments not in the original edition, on page 158; and also two pages "About the Illustrations," pages 159–160, that discuss the additional illustrations in this edition. The cover is blue with yellow and white lettering, and with a line drawing of Lincoln seated against a tree, reading, with horses, wagons, and people behind him; the edges are stained red.

d. paperbound edition, 1968

Paul Horgan / CITIZEN OF / NEW SALEM / ILLUSTRATIONS BY / [thin short horizontal rule] *Douglas Gorsline* / [publisher's device] / AN AVON CAMELOT BOOK / [1968]

18 x 10.5 cm; [1–8], 9–121, [122–128]; $0.60.

The inside front cover and page [1] have drawings of an apple tree in bloom; page [2] has a biography of Paul Horgan and the statement: "The cover art and illustrations for this edition are by / Douglas Gorsline"; the title page described above is on page [3]; the dedication "to / ALLAN NEVINS" is on page [5]; the text begins on page 9 and ends on page 121; the acknowledgments appear on page [125], but do not carry the footnote that is found in the Fawcett 1962 paper edition; pages [126–127] carry advertisements for Avon Books; page [128] and the inside back cover have the same drawing of an apple tree in bloom. The cover illustration shows a cameo of the young and the old Lincoln, in blue, brown, and orange; the edges are stained red.

A28. *Mountain Standard Time* 1962

a. first edition, 1962

[two lines of main title in outline type] Mountain / Standard Time / MAIN LINE WEST / FAR FROM CIBOLA / THE COMMON HEART / [the following line in outline type] by Paul Horgan / INTRODUCTION BY D. W. BROGAN / FARRAR, STRAUS AND CUDAHY • NEW YORK / [1962]

21 x 13.7 cm; [i-vii], viii-x, [xi], xii, [1–3], 4–5, [6–7], 8–595, [596]; $5.95.

The title page described above is on page [iii]; the contents for the entire volume is on page [v]; the introduction is on pages [vii]-x; the foreword is on pages [xi]-xii; the title page for *Main Line West* is on page [1]; the dedication "TO MY BROTHER EDWARD HORGAN" is on page [2]; the contents for this novel is on pages [3]–5; the text begins on page [7] and ends on page 199; the afterword is on pages [200]–201; the title page for *Far From Cibola* is on page [203]; the dedication "TO PHILIP STEVENSON" is on page [204]; the contents for this novel is on page [205]; the text begins on page [207] and ends on page 276; the afterword is on pages [277]–278; the title page for *The Common Heart* is on page [279]; the dedication "TO PEG AND BARRY DUFFIELD" is on page [280]; the contents for this novel is on pages [281]–282; the text begins on page [283] and ends on page 592; the afterword is on pages [593]–595; page [596] is blank.

The cover is black cloth with Paul Horgan's signature in gold on the front and the lettering and decoration in gold on the spine; the top edge of the pages is stained blue.

See *Main Line West* (1936), A7; *Far From Cibola* (1938), A12; and *The Common Heart* (1942), A15.

b. English edition, 1962

An English edition by Macmillan & Co Ltd was published in 1962 for 21s. No copy has been examined.

c. paperbound edition, 1966

The Common Heart / MAIN LINE WEST—FAR FROM CIBOLA / [single horizontal rule] / [four stars] PAUL HORGAN [four stars] / POPULAR LIBRARY • NEW YORK / [n.d.]

17.5 x 10.5 cm; [1–6], 7–589, [590–592]; $1.25.

An advertisement for the book appears on page [1]; a brief biography of Paul Horgan is on page [2]; the title page described above is on page [3]; the title page for *The Common Heart* is on page [5] and its dedication on page [6]; the text begins on page 7 and ends on page 319; the title page for *Main Line West* is on page [321] and its dedication is on page [322]; the text begins on page 323 and ends on page 513; the title page for *Far From Cibola* is on page [515] and its dedication is on page [516]; the text begins on page 517 and ends on page 589; page [590] is blank; pages [591–592] carry advertisements for other Popular Library books and on page [592] is an order blank. The cover has a gold border with the type in white, and shows, in color, a couple embracing in a dark woods.

There is no date given anywhere in the book; *Cumulative Book Index* lists 1966.

A29. *Conquistadors in North American History*   1963

a. first edition, 1963

CONQUISTADORS / IN / NORTH AMERICAN / HISTORY / Paul Horgan / FARRAR, STRAUS AND COMPANY / *NEW YORK* / [1963]

20.8 x 14 cm; [i-viii], ix-xi, [xii], xiii-xv, [xvi], [1–2], 3–303, [304]; $5.50.

The title page described above is on page [iii]; the dedication "To / Witter Bynner" is on page [v]; the quotations by Bernal Díaz del Castillo and Juan Ponce de León are on page [vii]; the preface is on pages ix-xi; the contents is on pages xiii-xv; the text begins on page 3 and ends on page 289; acknowledgments, pages 290–291; bibliography, pages 292–295; index, pages 297–303; page [304] is blank. The front endpapers show a map of "Cortés in New Spain," and the back endpapers "The Northward Explorers." The cover is black cloth with gold lettering and decoration on the spine. The front dust jacket is dark red with a black border and white and black type and shows a brown and white drawing of a Spanish Colonial retablo.

Contents: Preface—I. DISCOVERER—i. The Light—ii. The Lord Admiral—iii. The Voyage—iv. New World—II. CONQUISTADOR—i. The Captain General—ii. The New Continent—iii. Portents and Powers—iv. The Encounter—v. The Shore—vi. Island—vii. To Mexico—viii. The Meeting—ix. The Use of History—x. The Emperor and the Gods—xi. The Captive—xii. Treasure and Retreat—xiii. More News from the Coast—xiv. The Feast of Uitzilopochtli—xv. Revolt—xvi. Return to Battle—xvii. The Conquest—III. OTHER NEW WORLDS—i. Faith and Law—ii. Fabled World—iii. Making a Kingdom—iv. Broken Trust—v. Another Mexico, Another Peru—vi. The Castaways—vii. Prisoners of Space—IV. TO THE NORTH—i. Cíbola in Fancy—ii. The General and the Marquess—iii. Cíbola in Fact—iv. Winter Quarters—v. Quivira—vi. The Undiscovered—V. FRUITS OF CONQUEST —i. The Nature of Man—ii. The Ocean Trade—iii. Colonial Ways—iv. Stations on the Way North—VI. THE NORTHERN KINGDOM—i. The Known Road—ii. The Unknown Road—iii. The Capital—iv. Trouble at Ácoma—v. Another Troy—vi. The Colony Lives—vii. The Hearing—VII. THE LAST CONQUEST—i. Harsh Realities—ii. Return to the North—iii. Pacification and Persecution—iv. The Last Conquistador—v. Tombs and Banners—Acknowledgements—Bibliography—Index.

The book was published in January. A translation was made into Spanish (1966), D2; the entire book was published in *Best-in-Books* (1963), F7; and excerpts appeared in *Ideas and Patterns in Literature III* (1970), F8, and in *Portrait of America, Volume I* (1973), F9.

b. English edition, 1963

CONQUISTADORS / IN / NORTH AMERICA / Paul Horgan / LONDON / MACMILLAN & CO LTD / 1963

21.6 x 13.6 cm; [i-viii], ix-xi, [xii], xiii-xv, [xvi], [1-2], 3-303, [304]; 25s.

The English edition is like the first edition, except that the English edition adds on page 295, all in italics: "Publisher's note: In this bibliography the author has throughout referred to American / editions of works available in North America and Britain for the sake of consistency."; and includes on page [304] a printer's imprint. This edition has the same endpapers as the first. The cover is red cloth with blue and gold lettering and decoration on the spine; the front dust jacket is orange, black, green, and white, with the author's name in white, the title in orange, green, and white, and a design of a conquistador and a ship in all four colors.

c. paperbound edition, 1965

CONQUISTADORS / in / North American / History / by Paul Horgan / [publisher's device] / A PREMIER BOOK / FAWCETT PUBLICATIONS, INC., GREENWICH, CONN. / MEMBER OF AMERICAN BOOK PUBLISHERS COUNCIL, INC. / [1965]

18 x 10.5 cm; [i-vi], vii-xi, [xii-xiii], 14–240; $0.60.

The title page described above is on page [iii]; the dedication as in the first edition is on page [v]; the contents is on pages vii-viii; the preface is on pages ix-xi; the quotations as in first edition are on page [xii]; the text begins on page 14 and ends on page 228; acknowledgments, pages 229–230; bibliography, pages 231–233; index, pages 235–240. The cover is red with black, yellow, and white lettering and a blue and gold conquistador's helmet.

A30. *Toby and the Nighttime* 1963

a. first edition, 1963

TOBY and / the NIGHTTIME / by PAUL HORGAN / *illustrated by Lawrence Beall Smith* / ARIEL BOOKS / Farrar, Straus and Company • New York / [1963]

23 x 15 cm; [i-vi], [1–2], 3–71, [72–74]; $3.25.

The title page described above is on page [iii]; the dedication, "To Chico with thanks for Chipper and Willie, / and to / F. A. O. Schwarz's, the open secret of this story," is on page [v]; the text begins on page 3 and ends on page 71; pages [72–74] are blank. The cover is red cloth with black lettering on the spine. The book was published in March.

b. English edition, 1963

An English edition was published by Macmillan & Co Ltd in 1963 for 13s, 6d. No copy has been examined.

A31. *Things As They Are* 1964

a. first edition, 1964

[the following set below a black horizontal decorative rule composed as follows: one line of foliage, one line of hollow beading, one line of foliage] THINGS AS / THEY ARE / *by Paul Horgan* / NEW YORK [one character from the line of foliage used above] FARRAR, STRAUS AND COMPANY / [1964]

21 x 13.8 cm; [i-xvi], 1–239, [240]; $4.50.

A list of works by Paul Horgan is on page [iii]; the title page described above is on page [v]; the dedication *"for D."* is on page [vii]; the author's note is on page [ix]; the contents is on page [xi]; the quotations by Edith Sitwell, Jean Guitton, and Maurice Baring are on page [xiii]; the text begins on page 1 and ends on page 239; page [240] is blank. The cover is black cloth with gold lettering and decoration on the spine; the front dust jacket shows a drawing in tan, white, and black of a boy looking out the window; the type is black; the top edge of the pages is stained tan.

Contents: Chapter I: Original Sin—Chapter II: The Dawn of Hate—Chapter III: Muzza—Chapter IV: Far Kingdoms—Chapter V: Magic—Chapter VI: Black Snowflakes—Chapter VII: Center of Interest—Chapter VIII: The Spoiled Priest—Chapter IX: A Discharge of Electricity—Chapter X: Parma Violets.

Several sections of the book were previously published: "Parma Violets" as "First Passion" in *Collier's* (December 15, 1951), C137; "Black Snowflakes" in *The Saturday Evening Post* (March 30, 1963), C180; and "The Spoiled Priest" in *The Critic* (February–March, 1964), C184. The first edition was printed in May and published in August, 1964; the second printing was in July; the third in August; the fourth in October; and the fifth, the Noonday edition, in May, 1966. The book was a Midsummer Selection of the Catholic Family Book Club, 1964. "Black Snowflakes" was published in *The Peach Stone* (1967), A36. There was a Dutch translation (1968), D21. Several sections have been anthologized: "Black Snowflakes" in *Best American Short Stories 1964*, F2; "A Discharge of Electricity" in *Decisions, Decisions* (1971), F19; "The Dawn of Hate" in *Child Development Through Literature* (1972), F10; and this story and "Parma Violets" in *Perspectives on Sexuality* (1972), F11 and F63.

b. English edition, 1965

THINGS / AS THEY ARE / [a horizontal decorative rule] / *Paul Horgan* / [publisher's device] / THE BODLEY HEAD / LONDON / [1965]

19.7 x 12.8 cm; [i-xii], 1–239, [240-244]; 18s.

A list of works by Paul Horgan is on page [ii]; the title page described above is on page [iii]; the dedication as in the first edition is on page [v]; the author's note as in the first edition is on page [vi]; the contents is on page [vii]; the quotations as in the first edition are on page [ix]; the text begins on page 1 and ends on page 239; pages [240-244] are blank. The cover is red simulated cloth with gold lettering on the spine; the front dust jacket is like the one on the first edition, except that it shows less of the picture of the boy at the window and the type is in blue.

c. paper edition, 1966

[the following set below a black horizontal decorative rule composed as follows: one line of foliage, one line of hollow beading, one line of foliage]

THINGS AS / THEY ARE / *by Paul Horgan* / THE NOONDAY PRESS,

A DIVISION OF / FARRAR, STRAUS AND GIROUX [one character from line of foliage used above] NEW YORK / [1966]

20.2 x 13.5 cm; [i-xvi], 1–239, [240]; $1.95.

This edition is similar to the first. The cover is black with the title in yellow and the author's name in white. In the bottom right corner it states, in white: "Noonday 296 $1.95."

d. paper edition, 1967

[two lines of title in outline type] THINGS AS / THEY ARE / [device] / PAUL HORGAN / A FAWCETT CREST BOOK / Fawcett Publications, Inc., Greenwich, Conn. / Member of American Book Publishers Council, Inc. / [1967]

18 x 10.5 cm; [1–12], 13–224; $0.60.

The title page described above is on page [3]; the dedication as in the first edition is on page [5]; the author's note is on page [7]; the quotations as in the first edition are on page [9]; the contents is on page [11]; the text begins on page 13 and ends on page 224. The cover is white with gold and black lettering and a drawing of a gold watch and chain; the edges are stained red.

e. paper edition, 1971

[single horizontal rule] / PAUL HORGAN / [single horizontal rule] / THINGS AS THEY ARE / PAPERBACK LIBRARY / New York / [1971]

17.8 x 10.5 cm; [1–8], 9–252, [253–256]; $0.95.

The title page described above is on page [3]; the dedication as in the first edition is on page [5]; the author's note is on page [6]; the contents is on page [7]; the quotations as in the first edition are on page [8]; the text begins on page 9 and ends on page 252; an advertisement for *A Distant Trumpet* is on page [253]; one for *The Peach Stone* on page [254]; one for *Give Me Possession* on page [255]; on page [256] is an advertisement for *My Life with Jacqueline Kennedy* and an order blank for Paperback Library books. The cover is white with black lettering and a color drawing of a small boy with a black cat; the edges are stained yellow.

A32.   *Peter Hurd: A Portrait Sketch From Life*   1965

a. first edition, 1965

[first line of the title in black crayon signature] Peter Hurd / A POR-TRAIT SKETCH FROM LIFE / By PAUL HORGAN / ON THE OC-CASION OF A RETROSPECTIVE EXHIBITION / OF THE ARTIST'S WORK AT THE AMON CARTER MU- / SEUM IN FORT WORTH AND THE CALIFORNIA PALACE / OF THE LEGION OF HONOR IN SAN FRANCISCO / PUBLISHED FOR THE AMON CARTER MU-

SEUM OF WESTERN ART, / FORT WORTH, BY THE UNIVERSITY
OF TEXAS PRESS, AUSTIN / [1964 and 1965]

28 x 21.5 cm; [1–2], [unnumbered page with reproduction of a Hurd water-
color], [3–4], 5, [6], 7, [8], 9, [10–12], 13–68; $7.50.

The title page described above is on page [3]; the contents is on page 5; the
list of illustrations is on page 7; the introduction by Mitchell A. Wilder,
Director, Amon Carter Museum, is on page 9; the text begins on page 13
and ends on page 68. The text is illustrated throughout with black-and-white
and color reproductions of Peter Hurd's work: the black-and-white on pages
14, 20, 22, 26, 28, 30, 34, 36, 38, 44, 46, 52, 54, 60, 64, and 66; the color at
the frontispiece, and facing pages 16, 32, 40, 48, and 56. The cover is ochre
yellow cloth with gold lettering on the spine. The front dust jacket shows, on
an overall yellow background, a color reproduction of Peter Hurd's painting
"La Cita," under which appears in black the artist's signature in facsimile,
and the rest of the type in black. The two copies in the Library of Congress
are bound in yellow paper boards with a pale gray simulated leather spine,
with gold lettering.

A brochure was published for the exhibition at the Amon Carter Museum
that includes on its three inside folds an excerpt from the book essay. The
excerpt is entitled "Peter Hurd: The Gate and Beyond," E28. Another excerpt from this essay appeared under a similar title, "Peter Hurd: He Looks
at the Gate and Sees Beyond" in *New Mexico* (November–December,
1970), C220.

The exhibition at the Amon Carter Museum ran from October 22, 1964
to January 3, 1965. As the brochure described above was printed in 1964
and the full-length book essay in 1965, the book contains a 1964 and 1965
copyright date. The book was published on February 22, 1965.

b. second printing, 1966

[first line of title in black crayon signature] Peter Hurd / A PORTRAIT
SKETCH FROM LIFE / By PAUL HORGAN / [publisher's device] /
PUBLISHED FOR THE AMON CARTER MUSEUM OF WESTERN
ART, / FORT WORTH, BY THE UNIVERSITY OF TEXAS PRESS,
AUSTIN / [1966]

28 x 21.5 cm; [1–2], [unnumbered page with reproduction of a Hurd
watercolor], [3–4], 5, [6], 7, [8], 9, [10–12], 13–68; $7.50.

Except for the change in the title page this second printing is like the first.
A third printing appeared in 1971 and is identical to the second.

A33. *Songs After Lincoln*   1965

a. first edition, 1965
[three lines of title in brown open-faced type filled with leaf motif] SONGS /

[282]

AFTER / LINCOLN / by *Paul Horgan* / NEW YORK / FARRAR, STRAUS AND GIROUX / [1965]

21.3 x 13.8 cm; [i-viii], ix-x, [xi-xii], xiii, [xiv], [1–2], 3–74; $3.95.

The title page described above is on page [v]; the dedication "FOR ANDY AND BETSY / *one hundred years after the death of* / *Abraham Lincoln*" is on page [vii]; the contents is on pages ix-x; "Proem: The Catafalque," is on page xiii; the text begins on page 3 and ends on page 65; notes and commentary are on pages 69–74. The pen-and-ink sketch of a Civil War cap is by Paul Horgan, after Winslow Homer, page [1]. This also appears on the black cloth cover in gold. There is gold lettering on the spine. The dust jacket is white with a brown oval-framed photograph of Lincoln and brown and black type; the top edge of the pages is stained brown.

Contents: PROEM: The Catafalque—I. THE WAR—1. Daybreak Over a Battlefield—2. Far Battle—3. Pinned Down—4. Tintype of a Private of the Fifteenth Georgia Infantry—5. Commander Death—6. A Candle in the Ward—7. Last Words in a Soldier's Diary—8. Endless Autumn—9. One Man—II. THE CASUALTY—10. The Farmer's Wife—11. The Farmer—12. The Neighbor—13. Spring Water—14. The Lost Son—15. The Enemy—16. The Fellow Soldier—17. Coursing Rivers—18. The Soldier's Sweetheart—19. The Soldier's Child—III. THE PRESIDENT—20. Respect—21. Father Abraham and the Recruit—22. Wartime Evening—The White House—23. The Schoolboy—24. Duncan and Mr Lincoln—25. The Dreaming Slave—26. Reviewing Negro Troops Going South through Washington, April 26, 1864—27. The Hill—28. Biography—29. Thought of Mary Lincoln—30. A Veteran's Memory—31. The Last Photograph, April 9, 1865—POSTLUDE: Glory—NOTES AND COMMENTS.

The book was published in April. "The Neighbor," without the second-to-last stanza, appeared as "Song in Quiet Weather," *Hound and Horn* (October–December, 1930), C55; "Father Abraham and the Recruit" first appeared in *A Distant Trumpet* (1960), A25; "The Schoolboy," written prior to *A Distant Trumpet* but not published, was the inspiration for Book One, Sections vii, viii, and ix, of *A Distant Trumpet;* three poems were reprinted in *Where Steel Winds Blow* (1968), F75.

b. limited edition, 1965

This edition is the same as the first, with an extra page bound into the front on which is stated: "This special edition / of / *Songs after Lincoln* / has been prepared / for the Author and his friends. / It is limited to fifteen copies, / *hors commerce,* specially bound, / numbered, and signed / by the Author. / This is copy / [numbered in ink] 5 / [signed in ink] Paul Horgan." The book is bound in a brown leather spine with gold lettering, and the boards covered in brown, white, and black marbled paper. It is boxed in a slipcase covered in the same marbled paper, with a beige label pasted to the front on which appears the name of the author, the title, and the drawing of the Civil War cap.

[283]

A34. *Memories of the Future* 1966

a. first edition, 1966

[the following set below a black horizontal decorative rule composed as follows: one line of foliage, one line of hollow beading, one line of foliage]

MEMORIES OF / THE FUTURE / *by Paul Horgan* / NEW YORK [one character from line of foliage used above] FARRAR, STRAUS AND GI-ROUX / [1966]

21 x 14 cm; [i-vi], 1-216, [217-218]; $4.95.

The title page described above is on page [iii]; the dedication "TO / DORO" is on page [v]; the text begins on page 1 and ends on page 216; on page [218] is a statement "AFTER THE STORY." The cover is black cloth with gold lettering and decoration on the spine. The front dust jacket is a blue/purple drawing of a night water scene; the type is white; the top edge of the pages is stained blue. The book was published in May.

b. English edition, 1966

Memories of the / Future / PAUL HORGAN / [publisher's device] / THE BODLEY HEAD / LONDON • SYDNEY / TORONTO / [1966]

19.5 x 13 cm; [i-vi], 1-216, [217-218]; 21s.

The English edition is identical to the first. The cover is blue simulated cloth with gold lettering on the spine; the dust jacket shows a night water scene in blue, black, and white with orange type, similar to the scene on the dust jacket of the first edition.

c. paperbound edition, 1968

MEMORIES / OF THE FUTURE / [decorative design] / Paul Horgan / BALLANTINE BOOKS • NEW YORK / [1968]

17.7 x 10.6 cm; [1-6], 7-220, [221-224]; $0.75.

The title page described above is on page [3]; the dedication as in the first edition is on page [5]; the text begins on page 7 and ends on page 219; "After the Story" appears on page 220; advertisements for other Ballantine Books appear on pages [221-224]. The front cover is white with black type and shows a color drawing of an officer in the Navy and of a woman; the edges are stained orange.

A35. *The Serene Severities of Typography* 1966

THE SERENE SEVERITIES / OF / TYPOGRAPHY / PAUL HORGAN / THE ART LABORATORY / WESLEYAN UNIVERSITY / MCMLXVI

24.1 x 15.8 cm; 16 unnumbered pages.

Pages [1-2] are blank; the title page described above is on page [3]; pages [4-6] are blank; the text is on pages [7-9]; page [10] is blank; the colophon is on page [11]; pages [12–16] are blank. The colophon reads (all italics]: "We are grateful to Mr Horgan for allowing this little piece / to be used for classroom mutilation. The type used was / handset in Bembo and 30 copies printed by the / hands of the following on a Washington press / Karl Furstenberg / Alan Thorndike / Bruce Hartman / Wendy Cowie / Kristine Blum / James Patrick / Jeri Cantliffe / James Ruby / [decoration] / [the number in pencil] 4." Bound in boards with brown marbled paper, with the spine in black buckram, and the title in black between two short horizontal black rules printed on a white rectangle pasted to the front cover. The endpapers are white.

According to Paul Horgan, this was a workshop project for a class at Wesleyan University and was completed at the end of the spring semester, sometime late in May, 1966.

A36. *The Peach Stone* 1967

a. first edition, 1967

[the following set below a black horizontal decorative rule composed as follows: one line of foliage, one line of hollow beading, one line of foliage]

THE PEACH STONE / [thin horizontal rule] / Stories from Four Decades / [thin horizontal rule] / *by Paul Horgan* / NEW YORK [one character from line of foliage used above] FARRAR, STRAUS AND GIROUX / [1967]

21 x 13.8 cm; [1–2], [i-vi], vii-viii, [1–2], 3–470; $5.95.

A list of the works by Paul Horgan is on page [2]; the title page described above is on page [i]; the dedication *"for / Rouben Mamoulian"* is on page [iii]; a note by the author is on page [v]; the contents is on pages vii-viii; the text begins on page 3 and ends on page 467; a chronology of stories is given on pages 469–470. The cover is black cloth with gold lettering and decoration on the spine; the front dust jacket is rose and pale blue with white type; the top edge of the pages is stained pink.

Contents: Part One: To the Mountains—The One Who Wouldn't Dance—Winners and Losers—Black Snowflakes. Part Two: A Start in Life—In Summer's Name—So Little Freedom—The Huntsmen—The Treasure—National Honeymoon. Part Three: The Surgeon and the Nun—The Other Side of the Street—Tribute—The Small Rain—The Peach Stone. Part Four: The Hacienda—Old Army—The Head of the House of Wattleman—The Devil in the Desert—The Candy Colonel. Chronology of the Stories in This Collection.

"To the Mountains": *The Atlantic Monthly* (January, 1938), C103; *Figures in a Landscape* (1940), A14; C194; D22 and 23; F98–107. "The One Who Wouldn't Dance": *Collier's* (August 18, 1951), C135. "Winners and Losers": *Collier's* (April 19, 1952), C139. "Black Snowflakes": *The Saturday Evening*

Post (March 30, 1963), C180; *Things As They Are* (1964), A31; F2. "A Start in Life": *Cosmopolitan* (April, 1947), C123. "In Summer's Name": *Figures in a Landscape* (1940), A14. "So Little Freedom": *Saturday Review* (May 16, 1942), C113; F74. "The Huntsmen: *The Saturday Evening Post* (October 29, 1949), C128, with the title "Terror at Daybreak"; anthologized, F47 and 48, and F87–95. "The Treasure": *The Saturday Evening Post* (February 28, 1959), C168, with the title "The Secret of the Tin Box"; anthologized F73 and 108. "National Honeymoon": *Collier's* (March 4, 1950), C129; F52. "The Surgeon and the Nun": *Harper's Bazaar* (December, 1936), C97; *Figures in a Landscape* (1940), A14; F76–86. "The Other Side of the Street": *The Yale Review* (December, 1930), C57; F56. "Tribute": *Scribner's Magazine* (October, 1935), C90; *Figures in a Landscape* (1940), A14. "The Small Rain": written in 1966 for *The Peach Stone*. "The Peach Stone": *The Yale Review* (June, 1942), C114; translated into Japanese (1952), D16; and anthologized F66–70. "The Hacienda": *The Yale Review* (March, 1936), C92; *The Return of the Weed* (1936), A9. "Old Army": *The Saturday Evening Post* (February 26, 1944), C119. "The Head of the House of Wattleman": *The Yale Review* (December, 1929), C46. "The Devil in the Desert": *The Saturday Evening Post* (May 6, 1950), C130; see *The Devil in the Desert* (1952), A17, for complete listing. "The Candy Colonel": *Figures in a Landscape* (1940), A14.

The collection has been translated into Pak-Bengali (1969), D17. For other publications of the individual stories, see references listed with each story.

b. English edition, 1967

[the following set below a black horizontal decorative rule composed as follows: one line of foliage, one line of hollow beading, one line of foliage]

THE PEACH STONE / [single horizontal rule] / Stories from Four Decades / [single horizontal rule] / *by Paul Horgan* / THE BODLEY HEAD / LONDON / [1967]

21 x 13.8 cm; [1–2], [i-vi], vii-viii, [1–2], 3–470; 30s.

The sheets for the English edition were imported from the U.S. and the English edition is identical to the first. The cover is pale blue simulated cloth with gold lettering on the spine; the front dust jacket is pink, and light and dark blue, with white lettering; the drawing is of a garden.

c. paperbound edition, 1971

THE PEACH STONE / *Stories from Four Decades* / by Paul Horgan / PAPERBACK LIBRARY / New York / [1971]

17.7 x 10.5 cm; [1–6], 7, [8], 9–426, [427–432]; $1.25.

The title page described above is on page [3]; the dedication as in the first edition is on page [4], the copyright page; the contents is on page [5]; the note as in the first edition is on page [6]; the text begins on page 9 and ends on page 425; page 426 carries the same chronology as in the first edition; pages [427–429] carry advertisements for Paperback Library editions of *A Distant Trumpet, Things As They Are,* and *Give Me Possession;* pages [430–432] carry advertisements for other books and page [432] includes an order blank. The cover is white with red and black type and shows four drawings of four ages in life; the edges are stained yellow. The first printing was March, 1971.

A37. *Everything To Live For*   1968

a. first edition, 1968

[the following set below a black horizontal decorative rule composed as follows: one line of foliage, one line of hollow beading, one line of foliage]

EVERYTHING / TO LIVE FOR / *by Paul Horgan* / FARRAR, STRAUS AND GIROUX [one character from line of foliage used above] NEW YORK / [1968]

21 x 13.8 cm; [i–viii], 1–215, [216]; $4.95.

The title page described above is on page [iii]; the dedication *"to / Ernst Bacon"* is on page [v]; a quotation from *Childe Harold's Pilgrimage* is on page [vii]; the text begins on page 1 and ends on page 215; page [216] is blank. The cover is black cloth with gold lettering and decoration on the spine; the front dust jacket is cream with black and brown lettering; the endpapers are light tan; the top edge of the pages is stained brown.

b. English edition, 1969

Everything / to Live / for / Paul Horgan / [publisher's device] / THE BODLEY HEAD / LONDON SYDNEY / TORONTO / [1969]

19.5 x 13 cm; [i–viii], 1–215, [216]; 25s.

The sheets for the English edition were imported from the U.S. and the English edition is identical to the first. The cover is gray simulated cloth with gold lettering and decoration on the spine; the front dust jacket is purple with white and red lettering and a decorative design of a night-blooming cereus in yellow and red.

c. paperbound edition, 1968

PAUL HORGAN / [single horizontal rule] / EVERYTHING / TO LIVE FOR / [single horizontal rule] / POPULAR LIBRARY • NEW YORK / [1968]

17.5 x 10.5 cm; [1–6], 7–189, [190–192]; $0.75.

The title page described above is on page [3]; the dedication as in the first edition is on page [4], with the copyright; the quotation as in the first edition is on page [5]; the text begins on page 7 and ends on page 189; advertisements for other Popular Library books appear on pages [190–192], with order blanks on pages [191-192]. The cover is white with black lettering and shows a color drawing of the heads of a man and a woman and of a man carrying a woman; the edges are stained green.

A38. *Maurice Baring Reconsidered*   1969

[the cover is heavy gray paper with the title in black and enclosed in a frame of two thin red rules] MONDAY EVENING PAPERS: NUMBER 17 / [a red horizontal rule] / Maurice Baring / Reconsidered / by PAUL HORGAN / [a red horizontal rule] / [emblem of Center for Advanced Studies in red] / [a red horizontal rule] / CENTER FOR ADVANCED STUDIES / WESLEYAN UNIVERSITY / [1969]

21.4 x 13.8 cm; 1-41, [42-44].

On the inside front cover is a brief biography of Paul Horgan; the text begins on page 1 and ends on page 39; "A List of Principal Books / by Maurice Baring," appears on pages 40-41; pages [42-44] are blank; on the inside back cover is a list of the first 18 Monday Evening Papers and the lecturers who had delivered these papers at Wesleyan.

This paper was delivered in the Neumann Rooms at Wesleyan University on January 8, 1968, and was an early version of the introduction that appeared in *Maurice Baring Restored* (1970), A40. See also "The Sense of the Center," B14.

A39. *The Heroic Triad*   1970

a. first edition, 1970

Essays in the / *Social Energies* / *of Three* / *Southwestern* / *Cultures* / THE / HEROIC / TRIAD / *By PAUL HORGAN* / Holt, Rinehart and *Winston* / NEW YORK / CHICAGO / SAN FRANCISCO / [1970]

22.7 x 15 cm; [i-vi], vii-ix, [x], xi-xii, [1-2], 3-256, [257-260]; $7.95.

A list of works by Paul Horgan is on page [iii]; the title page described above is on page [v]; the contents is on pages vii-ix; the preface is on pages xi-xii; the text begins on page 3 and ends on page 233; the acknowledgments, page 235; the bibliography, pages 237-248; the index, pages 249-256; pages [257-260] are blank. Endpapers are brown printed in black and reproduce three maps of the Southwest and Mexico by Rafael Palacios. The book is bound in orange cloth with a circular design in blind and gold lettering on the spine; the front dust jacket is black with bright orange, pale orange, pale blue, and white lettering, and with the same design as on the cover.

Contents: Preface—BOOK ONE. PROLOGUE / Place—PAGES FROM A RIO GRANDE NOTEBOOK, Reading from Source to Mouth—BOOK TWO. INDIAN / Rio Grande Pueblos: The Ancients—i. Creation & Prayer—ii. Forms—iii. Community—iv. Dwelling—v. Garments—vi. Man, Woman, & Child—vii. Farmer &

Hunter—viii. Travel & Trade—ix. Personality & Death—x. On the Edge of Change—BOOK THREE. LATIN / Conquering Spaniards & Their Mexican Sons—I. COLLECTIVE MEMORY—i. Sources—ii. Belief—iii. The Ocean Masters—iv. The King & Father—v. Arts—vi. Style & Hunger—vii. The Swords—viii. Soul & Body—2. THE DESERT FATHERS—3. HACIENDA & VILLAGE—i. Land & House—ii. Fashion—iii. Family & Work—iv. Mischance—v. Feast Days—vi. Wedding Feast—vii. Mortality—viii. The Saints—ix. Provincials—x. New Man & New Principles—BOOK FOUR. ANGLO-AMERICAN / Sons of Democracy—I. A WILD STRAIN: MOUNTAIN MEN—2. THE MEXICO TRADE—3. COLLECTIVE PROPHECY—i. Frontier Attitudes—ii. Woman & Home—iii. Community Expression—iv. Language—v. Arts & Utility—vi. Light in the Clearing—vii. Sons of Harmony—viii. Knacks & Crafts—ix. First Interpreters—x. The American Art—4. THE LAST FRONTIERSMAN—5. A LARGER EARTH—ACKNOWLEDGMENTS—BIBLIOGRAPHY—INDEX.

The book was published in August. Beginning with Book Two the book is composed of portions of *Great River* (1954), A19. Book One: Prologue is called "Pages from a Rio Grande Notebook" and consists of material that appeared with that title in *The New York Times Book Review* (May 15, 1955), C155; and under the title "Mountain to Sea: Rio Grande Notes," *Southwest Review* (Autumn, 1955), C156. A selection from this prologue appeared in *The Washington Post* (August 9, 1970), C212. See F57–62, and 71.

b. English edition, 1971

Essays in the / Social Energies / of Three / Southwestern / Cultures / THE / HEROIC / TRIAD / *By PAUL HORGAN* / [publisher's device] / HEINEMANN: LONDON / [1971]

22.5 x 15 cm; [i-vi], vii-ix, [x], xi-xii, [1-2], 3-256, [257-260]; £3.50.

The sheets for the English edition were imported from the U.S. and the English edition is identical to the first edition. The cover is olive-green cloth with gold lettering and decoration on the spine; the front dust jacket is white with silver and gold lettering.

c. paperbound edition, 1971

Essays in the / Social Energies / of Three / Southwestern / Cultures / THE / HEROIC / TRIAD / *By PAUL HORGAN* / A MERIDIAN BOOK / WORLD PUBLISHING / [short horizontal rule] / TIMES MIRROR / NEW YORK / [1971]

20.3 x 13.1 cm; [i-vi], vii-ix, [x], xi-xii, [1-2], 3-256, [257-260]; $3.95.

This edition is identical to the first, except that it does not have maps as endpapers. The cover is white with black type and shows a color drawing of a Spanish helmet, a raccoon cap, and an Indian headdress.

A40. *Maurice Baring Restored* 1970

a. first edition, 1970

Maurice Baring Restored / [a double horizontal black rule composed of one thick and one thin rule] / *Selections from his Work, Chosen and Edited, / with an Introductory Essay and Commentaries / by* / [a double horizontal black rule identical to first] / Paul Horgan / [publisher's device] / HEINE-MANN: LONDON / [1970]

23.5 x 15 cm; [i-vi], vii-ix, [x], 1-443, [444-446]; £4.20p.

The title page described above is on page [iii]; two references from Maurice Baring are on page [v]; the contents is on pages vii-[x]; the introduction is on pages 1-52; the text begins on page 55 and ends on page 436; *"A List of Principal Books by / Maurice Baring,"* pages [437]-440; acknowledgments, pages [441]-[444]; pages [445-446] are blank. The endpapers are yellow; the cover is green cloth with gold lettering and decoration on spine; the page tops are stained yellow; the front dust jacket is bright green with black type.

The introduction is an expanded version of *Maurice Baring Reconsidered* (1969), A38; see also "The Sense of the Center," B14. The book is listed in *The Bookseller* as published in September.

b. American edition, 1970

Maurice Baring Restored / [a double horizontal black rule composed of one thick and one thin rule] / *Selections from his Work, Chosen and Edited, / with an Introductory Essay and Commentaries / by* / [a double horizontal black rule identical to first] / Paul Horgan / [publisher's device] / FAR-RAR, STRAUS AND GIROUX / *New York* / [1970]

23.5 x 15 cm; [i-vi], vii-ix, [x], 1-443, [444-446]; $15.00.

The sheets for the U.S. edition were imported from England and the U.S. edition is identical to the first edition. The cover is black cloth with gold lettering and decoration on the spine; the front dust jacket is cream with a blue border and black and maroon type; the top edge of the pages is stained blue.

A41. *Whitewater* 1970

a. first edition, 1970

[the following set below a black horizontal decorative rule composed as follows: one line of foliage, one line of hollow beading, one line of foliage] WHITEWATER / *by Paul Horgan* / FARRAR, STRAUS AND GIROUX [one character from line of foliage used above] NEW YORK / [1970]

20.7 x 13.8 cm; [i-xii], [1-2], 3-337, [338-340]; $6.95.

A list of works by Paul Horgan is on page [iv]; the title page described above is on page [v]; the dedication *"for / Edward Bisett"* is on page [vii];

[290]

the contents is on page [ix]; the quotations from a hymn by Paul Horgan from *A Tree on the Plains,* Octavio Paz, and Mikhail Yuryevich Lermontov are on page [xi]; the text begins on page 3 and ends on page 337; pages [338–340] are blank. The cover is black cloth with gold lettering and decoration on the spine; the front dust jacket is blue, cream, green, and black horizontal bars with white and black type; the top edge of the pages is stained blue.

Contents: I: To the Islands—II: Belvedere—III: Common and Uncommon Knowledge—IV: A Show of Spirit—V: The Dust and the Rain—VI: Whitewater—VII: The Homecomings.

The book was published in October. "Hitch-hiker's Song" and "Now Evening Puts Amen to Day" are from *A Tree on the Plains,* copyright 1942, E14. A selection from the novel was published in *Polymus* (1969), C199, and in *The Cornhill Magazine* (Winter, 1970–1971), C222; a condensed version appeared in *Reader's Digest Condensed Books* (1970), F112, and in *Ladies' Home Journal* (January, 1971), C224. It has been twice printed in German in two translations (1970 and 1972), D24 and D27; once in Spanish (1971), D25; and once in Swedish (1971), D26. The 1972 German edition and the Swedish one are condensed *Reader's Digest* versions. *Whitewater* was an alternate selection of the Book-of-the-Month Club and the Literary Guild. An excerpt appeared in the *Harbrace College Handbook* (1972), F113.

Whitewater received the Texas Institute of Letters Award for Fiction for 1970.

b. English edition, 1971

Whitewater / PAUL HORGAN / [publisher's device] / THE BODLEY HEAD / LONDON SYDNEY / TORONTO / [1971]

19.5 x 13 cm; [i-xii], [1–2], 3–337, [338–340]; £1.80.

The sheets for the English edition were imported from the U.S. and the English edition is identical to the first. The cover is green simulated cloth with gold lettering and decoration on the spine; the front dust jacket is like that on the U.S. first edition.

c. paperbound edition, 1971

Whitewater / by Paul Horgan / [printed on an arching line] PAPERBACK LIBRARY / ® / [publisher's device] / A KINNEY SERVICE COMPANY / NEW YORK / [1971]

17.8 x 10.5 cm; [1–8], 9, [10–11], 12–320; $1.50.

Comments from reviews of *Whitewater* appear on pages [1–4]; the title page described above appears on page [5]; the dedication as for the first edition is on page [6], the copyright page; the contents is on page [7]; the quotations as in first edition are on page 9; the text begins on page 12 and ends on page 320. The cover is white with black type and has a drawing in color of two boys and a girl walking; the edges are stained yellow.

A42. *Words for Charles Arthur Henderson* 1972

WORDS FOR / CHARLES ARTHUR HENDERSON / [thick horizontal rule, thin horizontal rule] / Memorial Meeting / St. Bartholomew's Chapel / New York City / February 14, 1972 / [thin horizontal rule, thick horizontal rule] / Paul Horgan

20.4 x 14 cm; 1–[12].

The title page described above is on the cover; on the inside front cover it states: *"One hundred copies privately printed / for / Mary Katherine Cheney Henderson / 1972";* the text begins on page 1, with the initial "I" in a decorative rectangle and the next three words in caps; the text ends on page 10; pages [11–12] are blank; the cover is pale blue heavy paper; the pages are stapled twice.

Charles Henderson was a close friend of Paul Horgan: they first met at the New Mexico Military Institute in Roswell, and the friendship continued until Henderson's death when Paul Horgan, as he describes here, was with Henderson and his wife the night before his fatal operation. Henderson was for seven years Lyndon B. Johnson's chief secretary when Johnson was in the House and the Senate.

A43. *Encounters With Stravinsky* 1972

a. first edition, 1972

[the following set below a black horizontal decorative rule composed as follows: one line of foliage, one line of hollow beading, one line of foliage] ENCOUNTERS WITH / STRAVINSKY / [thin horizontal rule] / *A Personal Record* / [thin horizontal rule] *by Paul Horgan* / FARRAR STRAUS AND GIROUX [one character from line of foliage used above] NEW YORK / [1972]

20.8 x 13.9 cm; [i-viii], ix-x, [xi-xii], [1–2], 3–299, [300]; $7.95.

The title page described above is on page [iii]; the dedication, *"for / V. de B.S. / and / R.C."* is on page [v]; the contents is on page [vii]; the list of illustrations is on page [viii]; the foreword is on pages ix-x; the quotations by Robert Craft and Henry James are on page [xi]; the text begins on page 3˙ and ends on page 279; appendixes, pages [281–288]; index, pages [289–300]. The book is bound in black cloth with gold lettering and decoration on the spine; the front dust jacket is cream with a pale blue border, a pale blue and dark maroon abstract design, and black lettering. The book was published in June.

Contents: Foreword—Book One: Before—Book Two: Realizations—Book Three: To the End. Appendix A: The Memorials—Appendix B: A Letter—Appendix C: Acknowledgments. Index.

[292]

b. English edition, 1972

ENCOUNTERS / WITH / STRAVINSKY / *A Personal Record* / Paul Horgan / [publisher's device] / THE BODLEY HEAD / LONDON SYDNEY / TORONTO / [1972]

21.6 x 13.6 cm; [1–8], 9, [10–14], 15–224; £3.00

The title page described above is on page [3]; the dedication *"For V. de B.S. and R.C."* is on page [5]; the contents is on page [7]; the list of illustrations is on page [8]; the foreword is on pages 9–[10]; the quotations as in first edition are on page [11]; the text begins on page 15 and ends on page 210; appendices and index, pages 213–224. The cover is gray simulated cloth stamped in gold on the spine; the front dust jacket is white with red and black type and a photograph of Stravinsky in sepia.

"Book One: Before" was shortened by the author for the English edition.

A44. *Approaches To Writing*   1973

a. first edition, 1973

Portions of Part One originally appeared in *Reflection* (Winter, 1968), C197; a selection from the notes in Part Two formed the framework of an unpublished lecture given at the Aspen Institute for Humanistic Studies in 1971; portions of Part One appeared in *Intellectual Digest* prior to publication, but no copy of the magazine was available for examination and no reference is made to the article in Category C; a selection from Part Two appeared in *Prose, Number Seven* (Fall, 1973), C254.

B. CONTRIBUTIONS TO BOOKS

B1. "Episodes from the Passionate Land," *Folk-Say: A Regional Miscellany, 1929*, edited by B. A. Botkin (University of Oklahoma Press: Norman, 1929), 120–124. Under the general title are three separately titled pieces: "The Isleta Priest," "The Christmas Dance," and "Fear." These impressionistic sketches have never been reprinted.

B2. "The Witch," *Folk-Say: A Regional Miscellany, 1930*, edited by B. A. Botkin (University of Oklahoma Press: Norman, 1930), 197–211. This short story has never been reprinted.

B3. "Figures in a Landscape," *Folk-Say: A Regional Miscellany, 1931*, edited by B. A. Botkin (University of Oklahoma Press: Norman, 1931), 185–194. The selection includes the first publication of five pieces later to be included in *Figures in a Landscape* (1940), A14: "The Landscape," "The Tularosa Bobcat," "The Last Words of Mrs. McDonny" (in *Figures in a Landscape* this is called "The Listeners"), "The Captain," and "Hot St'ff." The dust jacket of the book uses a drawing by Paul Horgan.

B4. "The Burden of Summer," *Folk-Say IV: The Land Is Ours*, edited by B. A. Botkin (University of Oklahoma Press: Norman, 1932), 134–147. The story is dedicated "For N. C. Wyeth" and has never been reprinted. The dust jacket of the book uses a drawing by Paul Horgan.

B5. "Preface," *Selected Poems by Witter Bynner*, edited by Robert Hunt (Alfred A. Knopf: New York, 1936), xxiii–lxix. The preface is signed "Roswell/August 1936."

B6. "Far From Cibola," *The New Caravan*, edited by Alfred Kreymborg, Lewis Mumford, and Paul Rosenfeld (W. W. Norton & Company: New York, 1936), 1–71. This was the first printing; for reprintings see *Far From Cibola* (1938), A12, and *Mountain Standard Time* (1962), A28.

B7. "George Washington," *The American Historical Scene: As Depicted by Stanley Arthurs and Interpreted by Fifty Authors* (Carlton House: New York, 1936), 8–17. A "Committee of Publication" was responsible for the volume; the foreword is signed by one of these, A. Felix du Pont. They published a special edition with the University of Pennsylvania Press, and in this reprint edition the copyright is indicated as 1935 and as held by the University of Pennsylvania Press.

B8. "Josiah Gregg Himself: An Introduction," [Part 1] *Diary and Letters of Josiah Gregg: Southwestern Enterprises, 1840–1847*, edited by Maurice Garland Fulton (University of Oklahoma Press: Norman, 1941), 3–40; "Josiah Gregg Himself: An Introduction," [Part 2] *Diary and Letters of Josiah*

Gregg: Excursions in Mexico & California, 1847–1850, edited by Maurice Garland Fulton (University of Oklahoma Press: Norman, 1944), 3–30. The first introduction is dated "Roswell, New Mexico/March, 1941," and the second, "Roswell, New Mexico/March 23, 1944." The first introduction was published in *Southwest Review* (Winter, 1941) in a slightly different form; see C112.

B9. *Look at America: The Southwest,* by The Editors of *Look* in collaboration with Paul Horgan (Houghton Mifflin Company: Boston, 1947). The introduction by Paul Horgan appears on pages 9–10, 12, 14, 16, 18, 20, 22, 24, 26, 28, 30, 32, 34.

B10. "An Introduction," *The Face of America,* by The Editors of *The Saturday Evening Post* (Curtis Publishing Company: Philadelphia, 1957), [5–6].

B11. "Foreword," *Santa Fe: The Autobiography of a Southwestern Town,* by Oliver La Farge, with the assistance of Arthur N. Morgan (University of Oklahoma Press: Norman, 1959), v-x. The foreword is signed "Roswell, New Mexico/May 15, 1959."

B12. "The Twentieth Century," *Threshold of Tomorrow: The Great Society, The Inauguration of Lyndon Baines Johnson 36th President of the United States and Hubert Horatio Humphrey 38th Vice President of the United States, January 20, 1965,* 89–95. The book published for the inauguration in 1965 was edited by Don R. Petit.

B13. "Introduction," *New Writing: The Book-of-the-Month Club College English Association Award Anthology,* edited by Faith Sale (Washington Square Press: New York, 1968), vii-xi.

B14. "The Sense of the Center," introduction to *Monday Evening Papers, Center for Advanced Studies, Wesleyan University* (Middletown, Connecticut, 1969). These eighteen lectures delivered at the Center for Advanced Studies at Wesleyan University, Middletown, Connecticut, between May, 1963, and March, 1969, are each bound separately as a pamphlet and then collected in a slipcase with an unnumbered 8-page pamphlet by Paul Horgan (Director of the Center, 1962–1967) and Philip Paul Hallie (Acting Director of the Center, 1967–1969). The pamphlet includes a two-page introduction, "The Sense of the Center" [2–3], a list of the Fellows of the Center from 1959–1969 [4–7], and a list of the authors and titles of the 18 pamphlets [8]. One of the eighteen pamphlets included is *Maurice Baring Reconsidered* (1969), A38; see also *Maurice Baring Restored* (1970), A40.

B15. "Georges Bizet," *Atlantic Brief Lives: A Biographical Companion to the Arts,* edited by Louis Kronenberger (Little, Brown and Company: Boston, 1971), 61–64.

B16. "Introduction," *The Buffalo Head: A Century of Mercantile Pioneering in the Southwest,* by Daniel T. Kelly, with Beatrice Chauvenet (The Vergara Publishing Company: Santa Fe, 1972), [vii]-ix.

B17. "Foreword," *N. C. Wyeth: The Collected Paintings, Illustrations and Murals,* by Douglas Allen and Douglas Allen, Jr. (Crown Publishers: New York, 1972), 11–13. This is a revised version of the foreword used for the 1945 catalogue at the Wilmington Society of the Fine Arts; see E16.

B18. Introduction to *New Mexico: A Pageant of Three Peoples,* by Erna Fergusson (University of New Mexico Press: Albuquerque, 1973). This re-issue of Erna Fergusson's 1951 book, first published by Alfred A. Knopf, was not available for examination prior to the publication of *Approaches to Writing* (1973), A44.

C. CONTRIBUTIONS TO PERIODICALS

C1. "Last Flurry of June Brides Makes Exit in the Heat," *Albuquerque Morning Journal* (June 25, 1922), 2. This society-page story was written during one week of service as substitute society editor.

C2. Poems: "Exotics: The Temples and the Gongs, Litany, Winter Night," *Poetry* (June, 1924), 138–140. "The Litany" was reprinted in *The Turquoise Trail* (1928), F50, and in *Signature of the Sun* (1950), F51.

C3. Poems: "The Mask: Her Frown, Her Empty Eyes, Her Hidden Smile," *Poetry* (July, 1925), 205–207.

C4. "Aren't We All—Acting?," *Theatre Magazine* (July, 1926), 24, 58.

C5. "Ex Libris: 1. In Limbo," *The Library* (November 15, 1926), 2. For a comment on this publication, see *The Library 1–7* (1927), A2.

C6. Poem: "Antony and Cleopatra," translated from the French of José María de Heredia, *The Library* (November 15, 1926), 3.

C7. Review of *Show Boat,* by Edna Ferber, *The Library* (November 15, 1926), 3. This review is signed "Vincent O'Shaughnessy," Paul Horgan's occasional pen name at this time. For further comment on the use of this name, see the note on *The Library 1–7* (1927), A2.

C8. Review of *The Silver Spoon,* by John Galsworthy, *The Library* (November 15, 1926), 3.

C9. "Ex Libris: 2. Parodies," *The Library* (December 15, 1926), 2.

C10. Review of *Hot Saturday,* by Harvey Fergusson, *The Library* (December 15, 1926), 3–4.

C11. Review of *Lord Raingo,* by Arnold Bennett, *The Library* (January 15, 1927), 2–3.

C12. Poem: "Sonnet," *The Library* (January 15, 1927), 3.

C13. Review of *Nigger Heaven,* by Carl Van Vechten, *The Library* (January 15, 1927), 4.

C14. Poem: " 'Quest' (To Witter Bynner)," *The Library* (February 15, 1927), [1].

C15. "Ex Libris: 3. Poets," *The Library* (February 15, 1927), 2.

C16. Review of *The Charwoman's Shadow,* by Lord Dunsany, *The Library* (February 15, 1927), 3.

C17. Poem: "From the Tombs of Egypt," *The Library* (March 15, 1927), [1].

C18. Review of *Prejudices: Fifth Series,* by H. L. Mencken, *The Library* (March 15, 1927), 2–3.

C19. Review of *Great Names, Being an Anthology of English and American*

Literature from Chaucer to Francis Thompson with Introductions by Various Hands and Drawings by J. F. Horabin; the Whole Edited by Walter J. Turner, *The Library* (March 15, 1927), 3-4.

C20.   Review of *Confessions of an Actor*, by John Barrymore, *The Library* (March 15, 1927), 4. This unsigned review is by Paul Horgan.

C21.   Poem: "Amoretti: *Dismalia*, addressed to his Ladye. In 3 canzons. By V.O.'S., *Gent*. AD 1609," *The Library* (April 15, 1927), [1]. This spoof of an Elizabethan poem uses the initials for Paul Horgan's pen name, "Vincent O'Shaughnessy." For a further comment on this name, see *The Library 1-7* (1927), A2.

C22.   "Ex Libris: 4. A Note on Modern Book Design," *The Library* (April 15, 1927), 2.

C23.   Poem: "The Ballad of the Burnished Caravel: To Nicholas Slonimsky," *The Library* (April 15, 1927), 2.

C24.   Review of *Fine Clothes to the Jew*, by Langston Hughes, *The Library* (April 15, 1927), 3.

C25.   Review of *Orphée: Tragédie en un acte et un intervalle*, by Jean Cocteau, *The Library* (April 15, 1927), 3-4.

C26.   Review of *Ask Me Another! The Question Book*, compiled by Justin Spafford and Lucien Esty, *The Library* (April 15, 1927), 4. This unsigned review is by Paul Horgan.

C27.   "Notes on Carl Van Vechten," *The Library* (May 15, 1927), [1], 4.

C28.   "Ex Libris: 5. From the Concert Hall," *The Library* (May 15, 1927), 2.

C29.   Review of *Orpheus, or The Music of the Future*, by W. J. Turner, and *Terpander, or Music and the Future*, by Edward J. Dent, *The Library* (May 15, 1927), 2-3.

C30.   Review of *The Bronco: The Annual of the Regiment of Cadets of the New Mexico Military Institute*, edited by J. A. McDougall, *The Library* (May 15, 1927), 4. This unsigned review is by Paul Horgan.

C31.   "The Curtain Call as Good Theatre," *Theatre Magazine* (September, 1927), 14.

C32.   "A Note on the Princess Maimonides," *Laughing Horse* (March–July, 1928), Number 15. With the article there is a reproduction of a pen-and-ink sketch by Paul Horgan. *Laughing Horse* was subtitled *A Magazine of the Southwest*, was published in Taos, New Mexico, and was edited by Willard Johnson. The Princess Maimonides is the central figure in the unpublished novel, *The Golden Rose*, E1. The author discusses this work in Part Three of *Approaches to Writing* (1973), A44.

C33.   "Buffalo Scenes: The Harbor," *Town Tidings* (August, 1928), 22, 47. This sketch was reprinted as part of ten sketches in "American Landscapes: A Little Exhibition," *New Mexico Quarterly* (August, 1936), C96. *Town Tidings* was a magazine published in Buffalo, New York, to which Paul Horgan contributed a series of pieces in 1928, 1929, and 1930.

C34.   "Buffalo Scenes: Band Concert," *Town Tidings* (September, 1928), 20, 61-62.

C35.   "Buffalo Scenes: The Yards," *Town Tidings* (October, 1928), 38, 40.

C36. "Buffalo Scenes: The Commodore," *Town Tidings* (November, 1928), 28, 71.

C37. "Buffalo Scenes: The Cathedral," *Town Tidings* (December, 1928), 44, 47.

C38. "Buffalo Scenes: The Caliph, The Vizier and The Bailiff, January Night's Entertainment," *Town Tidings* (January, 1929), 38, 70–71.

C39. "Seagle Song Recital," *Roswell Daily Record* (March 2, 1929). A clipping of this article in Paul Horgan's scrapbook does not show the page.

C40. "Buffalo Scenes: The Hotel," *Town Tidings* (March, 1929), 25, 103–104.

C41. Review of *Moussorgsky,* by Oskar von Riesemann, *The Bookman* (April, 1929), 206–207.

C42. Review of *Modern French Painters,* by Maurice Raynal, *The Bookman* (April, 1929), 213.

C43. Review of *The Edge of the Nest,* by Philip Stevenson, *The Bookman* (October, 1929), 206–207.

C44. "Peter Hurd, Artist," *Roswell Daily Record* (December 14, 1929), 4–5.

C45. "Buffalo Scenes: Entertainment," *Town Tidings* (December, 1929), 25–26.

C46. "The Head of the House of Wattleman," *The Yale Review* (December, 1929), 341–352. Reprinted in *The Peach Stone* (1967), A36.

C47. "Eddy Brown Quartet Recital Brilliant," *Roswell Daily Record* (February 15, 1930). A clipping of this article in Paul Horgan's scrapbook does not show the page.

C48. "Over the Edge of Heaven," review of *Clash of Angels,* by Jonathan Daniels, *New York Herald Tribune Books* (April 13, 1930), 4.

C49. "These Are Buffalonians: III. Lady Buyer Deluxe," *Town Tidings* (April, 1930), 60. This piece is signed "Vincent O'Shaughnessy." For further comment on this pen name, see *The Library 1–7* (1927), A2.

C50. Review of *Bambi Le Chevreuil (Une vie dans les bois),* by Félix Salten, traduit de l'allemand par Henri Block, *Books Abroad* (July, 1930), 271.

C51. "English B-1 Convenes," *The New Yorker* (September 27, 1930), 77–79.

C52. "Who's Conducting This Course?," *The New Yorker* (October 18, 1930), 96–98.

C53. Review of *La Grande Sarah: Souvenirs,* by Reynaldo Hahn, *Books Abroad* (October, 1930), 362.

C54. Review of *Voltaire raconté par ceux qui l'ont vu,* by J-G. Prud'homme, *Books Abroad* (October, 1930), 368–369.

C55. Poem: "Song in Quiet Weather," *Hound and Horn* (October–December, 1930), 82–83. This poem appears in *Songs After Lincoln* (1965), A33, as "The Neighbor," with the next to last stanza added.

C56. "Mr. Waugh," review of *A Bachelor Abroad,* by Evelyn Waugh, *New York Herald Tribune Books* (November 23, 1930), 18.

C57. "The Other Side of the Street," *The Yale Review* (December, 1930), 366–379. Reprinted in *The Best Short Stories of 1931,* F56, and *The Peach Stone* (1967), A36.

C58. "These Are Buffalonians: V. Eagle Over Desert," *Town Tidings* (December, 1930), 30. This piece is signed "Vincent O'Shaughnessy." For further comment on this name, see *The Library 1–7* (1927), A2.

C59. Poem: "Why and Wherefore of Billy the Kid," *The Maverick* (Christmas, 1930), 5. This issue of the magazine of the New Mexico Military Institute also has a reproduction of an engraving attributed to Paul Horgan, between pages 16 and 17.

C60. "School Days," review of *The Gospel According to St. Luke's,* by Philip Stevenson, *New York Herald Tribune Books* (March 22, 1931), 18.

C61. "One Line of Defense," review of *Myself and the Theatre,* by Theodore Komisarjevsky, and *Footlights Across America,* by Kenneth MacGowan, *The Yale Review* (March, 1931), 629–630.

C62. "In a Winter Dusk," *Harpers Magazine* (August, 1931), 357–366.

C63. "Santa Fe and Taos," *Senior Scholastic* (October 17, 1931), 14–15, 31.

C64. "Bugles in the Sunrise: The Color of Life at New Mexico Military Institute," *New Mexico Highway Journal* (June, 1932), 10–12, 47–48.

C65. "Indian Arts," review of *Dancing Gods,* by Erna Fergusson, *Black Elk Speaks: Being the Life Story of a Holy Man of the Ogalala Sioux,* by John G. Neihardt, and *Old Man Coyote,* by Frank B. Linderman, *The Yale Review* (September, 1932), 205–208.

C66. "The Audition," *The New Yorker* (November 12, 1932), 69–72.

C67. "From the Royal City," *The Yale Review* (December, 1932), 354–376. The article includes the following sections: "The Captain General," "The Evening Air," "Triumphal Entry," "Bittersweet Waltz," and "Frock Coats and the Law." Reprinted in *America in the Southwest* (1933), F25, and *From the Royal City* (1936), A8.

C68. "Point of Honor," *The North American Review* (December, 1932), 524–527.

C69. Review of *Wild Pilgrimage: A Novel in Woodcuts,* by Lynd Ward, Harrison Smith, and Robert Haas, *The Daily Oklahoman* (January 8, 1933), C-7.

C70. Review of *In Tragic Life,* by Vardis Fisher, *The Daily Oklahoman* (February 26, 1933), C-7.

C71. "Parochial School," *The New Yorker* (April 1, 1933), 14–16. Reprinted in *Short Stories from The New Yorker* (1940), F64.

C72. "A Noble Conquistador," review of *The Odyssey of Cabeza de Vaca,* by Morris Bishop, *The Yale Review* (June, 1933), 851–853.

C73. "About the Southwest: A Panorama of Nueva Granada," *Southwest Review* (July, 1933), 329–359. A section of this article was reprinted as "The Three Southwestern Peoples" in *New Mexico's Own Chronicle* (1937), A11; another section called "The Heroic Triad" was reprinted with that title in *Figures in a Landscape* (1940), A14; part of the article was reprinted in *Sun-of-a-Gun Stew* (1945) with the title "A Hard Land to Win," F1 and 43; with the title "Tribute to the Land" a short section of the article served as an introduction to a special New Mexican issue of *Southwest Review* (Summer, 1946), C121; and again in part it was reprinted as a broadside in 1958 with the title "Land of the Southwest," E23.

C74. "Surgical Crisis," *The North American Review* (July, 1933), 23–26.

C75. "New Mexico," review of *Rio Grande,* by Harvey Fergusson, *The Yale Review* (September, 1933), 211–213.

C76. "Earliest American," *The Sunday Review of the Brooklyn Daily Eagle* (October 29, 1933), 8–9. "The story of Miss Wentleigh in Santa Fe, by the young American novelist whose 'Fault of Angels' was recently awarded the Harper biennial prize."

C77. "The Old Order," *Vanity Fair* (October, 1933), 23–24. Reprinted in *The Evening Standard* (London: March 23, 1935), C88.

C78. "Capriccio," *The New Yorker* (December 16, 1933), 20–22. Reprinted in *The Evening Standard* (London: April 21, 1934), C81, and in *Prose, Poetry and Drama for Oral Interpretation* (1936), F3.

C79. Poems: "Westward: The Prairie Sleepers, The Branding, Threads of Sky, Last Indian Sign," *Poetry* (December, 1933), 144–149.

C80. "The Intimate Recital," *Vanity Fair* (January, 1934), 33.

C81. "Capriccio," *The Evening Standard* (London: April 21, 1934), 15. First printed in *The New Yorker* (December 16, 1933), C78.

C82. "Tribal Union," *The New Yorker* (June 2, 1934), 30, 33.

C83. "A Distant Harbour," *Direction: A Quarterly of New Literature* (Autumn, 1934), 17–26. This was the first issue of a periodical edited by Kerker Quinn in Peoria, Illinois. Conrad Aiken, Kay Boyle, Robert Frost, Wallace Stevens, and William Carlos Williams were also published in this first issue. The story was reprinted in *The Best Short Stories 1935,* F20.

C84. Poem: "Triad," *Space* (September, 1934), [49]–50. *Space* was published at the University of Oklahoma and edited by B. A. Botkin.

C85. "Death and the Children," *Harpers Magazine* (December, 1934), 99–105. With the same title, this is Chapter 19 of *No Quarter Given* (1935), A6.

C86. "Onward and Upward with the Arts: Muses of the Frontier," *The New Yorker* (February 9, 1935), 41–44.

C87. "Slow Curtain," *Harpers Magazine* (February, 1935), 323–342. With the title "An Early Storm," and in a slightly different version, this is Chapter 8 in *No Quarter Given* (1935), A6.

C88. "The Old Order," *The Evening Standard* (London: March 23, 1935), 19. First printed in *Vanity Fair* (October, 1933), C77.

C89. "The Spirit of the Fiesta," review of *Fiesta in Mexico,* by Erna Fergusson, *The Yale Review* (March, 1935), 630–632.

C90. "Tribute," *Scribner's Magazine* (October, 1935), 216–221. Reprinted in *Figures in a Landscape* (1940), A14, and *The Peach Stone* (1967), A36.

C91. "The Trunk," *Mademoiselle* (November, 1935), 11, 57–58. Reprinted in *O. Henry Memorial Award: Prize Stories of 1936,* F109.

C92. "The Hacienda," *The Yale Review* (March, 1936), 573–583. Reprinted in *The Return of the Weed* (1936), A9, and *The Peach Stone* (1967), A36.

C93. "How Dr. Faustus Came to Rochester," *Harpers Magazine* (April, 1936), 506–515.

C94. "A Fragment of Empire," *Ladies' Home Journal* (May, 1936), 5–7, 99, 101–102, 104–105.

C95. "A Journey of Hope," *The North American Review* (June, 1936), 312–348.

C96. "American Landscapes: A Little Exhibition," *New Mexico Quarterly* (August, 1936), 163–168. Ten prose pieces titled: I. Hudson River Valley (Oil); II. Kansas (Water color); III. Into Cleveland (Woodcut); IV. Brandywine Valley (Tempera); V. The Cattle Plains (Pastel); VI. New England Lake (Oil); VII. Hell at Philadelphia (Pastel); VIII. Buffalo Harbor (Lithograph); IX. Divide in the Rockies (Tempera on gesso); X. General Pulaski Skyway (Motion picture). The sketch entitled "Buffalo Harbor" first appeared as "Buffalo Scenes: The Harbor" in *Town Tidings* (August, 1928), C33.

C97. "The Surgeon and the Nun," *Harper's Bazaar* (December, 1936), 98–99, 154, 156, 158, 160, 162. Reprinted in *Figures in a Landscape* (1940), A14, and *The Peach Stone* (1967), A36. For further reprintings, see F76–86.

C98. "To Quiet the Bugles," *The Yale Review* (March, 1937), 578–589. Reprinted in *Figures in a Landscape* (1940), A14.

C99. "Proprieties," *The New Mexico Sentinel* (July 27, 1937), 6. This article appeared in a weekly Santa Fe newspaper published by Cyrus McCormick. It was part of a page called "New Mexico Writers" edited by Haniel Long, with Witter Bynner, Erna Fergusson, Paul Horgan, and Frieda Lawrence as associates. The first issue of the page appeared July 20, 1937, and the last on January 1, 1939.

C100. Poem: "Two Epigrams With Gifts: I. With a Copy of the Shorter Oxford Dictionary; II. With the Drawings of Daumier," *The New Mexico Sentinel* (August 3, 1937), 8.

C101. "Aldous Huxley," *The New Mexico Sentinel* (October 5, 1937), 8.

C102. Poems: "American Pictures," *The New Mexico Sentinel* (December 15, 1937), 6. Seven sections are included: i. Pennsylvania, 1720; ii. Buffalo, 1830; iii. Missouri Breakdown, 1840; iv. Mississippi River Boat, 1845; v. The Yellow Wish, California, 1849; vi. California Clipper, 1850; vii. Revival Meeting, U.S., 1900.

C103. "To the Mountains," *The Atlantic Monthly* (January, 1938), 5–19. Reprinted in *Figures in a Landscape* (1940), A14, and *The Peach Stone* (1967), A36. With the title "The Flavour of Danger" the story was reprinted in *Argosy* (February, 1968), C194, published in England. Alone the story has been translated into Japanese (1950), D22, and into Spanish (1964), D23; as part of *The Peach Stone* it has been translated into Pak-Bengali (1969), D17. It has been extensively anthologized, F98–107.

C104. *The Habit of Empire, The New Mexico Sentinel* (February 2 to May 1, 1938). The work appeared in thirteen installments in this newspaper, as it was being published serially in Spanish in *El Nuevo Mexicano,* also a weekly Santa Fe newspaper published by Cyrus McCormick, D9. See *The Habit of Empire* (1939), A13.

C105. "Editorial Jottings," *The New Mexico Sentinel* (August 21, 1938), 6.

C106. "Relatives Out West," *The Yale Review* (December, 1938), 305–322. Reprinted in *Figures in a Landscape* (1940), A14.

C107. "News of Mark Twain," review of *Letters from the Sandwich Islands: Written for the Sacramento Union,* by Mark Twain, introduction and conclusion by G. Ezra Dane, and *Mark Twain's Western Years*, by Ivan Benson, *The Yale Review* (June, 1939), 846–849.

C108. Review of *The Fortunes of Victor Hugo in England*, by Kenneth Ward Hooker, *Books Abroad* (Autumn, 1939), 507–508.

C109. "Lens," *The New Republic* (November 8, 1939), 11–12.

C110. Review of *Cherokee Cavaliers: Forty Years of Cherokee History as Told in the Correspondence of the Ridge-Watie-Boudinot Family*, edited by Edward Everett Dale and Gaston Litton, *Pacific Historical Review* (June, 1941), 229–230.

C111. "Comedy on the Plains," *Harpers Magazine* (November, 1941), 640–646.

C112. "The Prairies Revisited: A Re-estimation of Josiah Gregg," *Southwest Review* (Winter, 1941), 145–166. This article is a part of Paul Horgan's introduction to the first volume of Gregg's diaries; see B8.

C113. "So Little Freedom," *Saturday Review* (May 16, 1942), 24, 26–28. This story was printed in a special issue called "The Southwest: A Cultural Inventory." It was reprinted in *Roundup Time* (1943), F74, and *The Peach Stone* (1967), A36.

C114. "The Peach Stone," *The Yale Review* (June, 1942), 783–804. Reprinted in *The Peach Stone* (1967), A36. "The Peach Stone" is translated alone into Japanese (1952), D16, and as part of *The Peach Stone* into Pak-Bengali (1969), D17. It has also been anthologized, F66–70.

C115. "A Try for the Island," *Harpers Magazine* (June, 1942), 37–46. This is Chapter 32, Sections 4–12, entitled "Peter's Own Early West," in *The Common Heart* (1942), A15. With the title "A Try for the Island" the story was reprinted in *Senior Scholastic* in two issues (March 29–April 3, 1943, and April 5–10, 1943), C117.

C116. "A Tree on the Plains: An Excerpt from the Opera," *Theatre Arts* (February, 1943), 120–127. The text represents most of Part Two of the opera and is reprinted on pages 120–126; on page 127 are "Character and Costume Sketches of the 'Neighbors' in *A Tree on the Plains*, drawn by the librettist, Paul Horgan." For full publication of the libretto, and for further information on the opera, see *Southwest Review* (Summer, 1943), C118, and the reference to the copy of the text that is in the Library of Congress, E14.

C117. "A Try for the Island," *Senior Scholastic* (March 29–April 3, 1943), 23–24, 27, 30–31; (April 5–10, 1943), 25–26, 35. This is a reprint of the story that appeared in *Harpers Magazine* (June, 1942), C115. It is also part of a chapter in *The Common Heart* (1942), A15.

C118. "A Tree on the Plains: Libretto of the Opera," *Southwest Review* (Summer, 1943), 345–376. With the complete text are Paul Horgan's illustrations for a stage setting of the opera (facing page 235), and his illustration for costume sketches (facing page 360). For publication of most of the text of Part Two of the opera, see *Theatre Arts* (February, 1943), C116. A typescript of the text was made for circulation to potential producers by Annie Laurie Williams, of which there is a carbon copy in the Library of Congress, E14. The music for the opera was written by Ernst Bacon. The work was commissioned by the League of Composers for particular use by small opera groups. Among many productions, notable ones were given at Converse College, Spartanburg, South Carolina (the first performance on May 2, 1942), Columbia University, Harvard University, and Syracuse University. The text of two songs from the opera was used in *Whitewater* (1970), A41.

C119. "Old Army," *The Saturday Evening Post* (February 26, 1944), 12–13, 42, 44, 46–47. Reprinted in *The Peach Stone* (1967), A36.

C120. "Taos Valley," *The Yale Review* (September, 1944), 36–56. The four sections are entitled: "The Fortress, 1772"; "Taos Lightning, 1831"; "The Western Attorney, 1852"; and "The Rival Prophets, 1893."

C121. "Tribute to the Land," *Southwest Review* (Summer, 1946). On the inside front cover of this issue devoted to New Mexican writers appears this brief excerpt from "About the Southwest," *Southwest Review* (July, 1933), C73.

C122. "Paris Feeling," *Good Housekeeping* (February, 1947), 28–29, 215–238, 240–246; (March, 1947), 40–41, 138–139, 141, 143, 145–148, 150, 152, 154–160, 163–164, 166, 169–178.

C123. "A Start in Life," *Cosmopolitan* (April, 1947), 23–25, 156–163, 165–170, 173. Reprinted in a revised version in *The Peach Stone* (1967), A36.

C124. "The Telling of the Swan," *Good Housekeeping* (March, 1948), 36–37, 94, 98, 101–102, 104, 106–108, 111–112, 114, 117–118, 120–126.

C125. "Nightmare," *The Saturday Evening Post* (June 12, 1948), 32–33, 157–158, 160–161.

C126. "Give Me Possession," *Cosmopolitan* (September, 1948), 167–184. Reprinted as part of the center section of *Give Me Possession* (1957), A23.

C127. "Speaking Likeness," *McCall's* (March, 1949), 16–17, 126, 130, 132–134, 136, 138–140, 142–145, 151–152, 156, 159–160.

C128. "Terror at Daybreak," *The Saturday Evening Post* (October 29, 1949), 34–35, 108, 110, 112, 114–115, 117. Reprinted in *The Peach Stone* (1967), A36, under the title "The Huntsmen." For reprinting in anthologies, see F47 and 48, and F87–95.

C129. "National Honeymoon," *Collier's* (March 4, 1950), 13, 40–41, 43. Reprinted in *Collier's Best* (1951), F52, and *The Peach Stone* (1967), A36.

C130. "The Devil in the Desert," *The Saturday Evening Post* (May 6, 1950), 24–25, 86–88, 90, 93–95, 97–98, 100–101, 103. Reprinted in *The Devil in the Desert* (1952), A17, *Humble Powers* (1954), A20, and *The Peach Stone* (1967), A36. For translations, see D3, 4, 5, 6, 10, 11, and 17. For reprinting in anthologies, see F12–18.

C131. "The Style of Peter Hurd," *New Mexico Quarterly* (Winter, 1950–1951), 420–426. The article includes several black-and-white reproductions of Peter Hurd's work. The article was reprinted in a brochure published by the Roswell Museum and Art Center on its permanent collection of Peter Hurd's work, E25.

C132. "To My Husband," *Good Housekeeping* (February, 1951), 50–51, 160–162, 165–166, 168, 171–178.

C133. "Love Among the Savages," *Collier's* (March 3, 1951), 26–27, 44, 46–

47. The story later became a part of *A Distant Trumpet* (1960), A25, Book Two, part of Sections iii-xii.

C134. "The Devil's Trill," *Good Housekeeping* (May, 1951), 60–61, 283–294, 296, 298, 300, 303–304; (June, 1951), 58–59, 247–248, 250, 253–261.

C135. "The One Who Wouldn't Dance," *Collier's* (August 18, 1951), 16–17, 44, 46. Reprinted in *The Peach Stone* (1967), A36.

C136. "The Soldier Who Had No Gun," *The Saturday Evening Post* (October 13, 1951), 22–23, 140, 142, 145, 147–150, 154, 156–163. Reprinted in *Humble Powers* (1954), A20, under the title "To the Castle," and again with this title in *Catholic Family Book Club* (1957), F97. An excerpt from this story appeared in *The Shield* (April–May, 1966), C190, with the title "The Priest in Service."

C137. "First Passion," *Collier's* (December 15, 1951), 28–29, 70–71, 73. Reprinted as "Parma Violets" in *Things As They Are* (1964), A31.

C138. "One Red Rose for Christmas," *Cosmopolitan* (December, 1951), 29–31, 82–83, 85–86, 88–94. Reprinted as *One Red Rose for Christmas* (1952), A18, and in *Humble Powers* (1954), A20; see also D10, 11, 12, 13, 14, and 15; E20; and F53, 54, and 55.

C139. "Winners and Losers," *Collier's* (April 19, 1952), 29, 74–77. Reprinted in *The Peach Stone* (1967), A36.

C140. "The Angle of a Bullet," *Collier's* (August 30, 1952), 48–53. The story later became part of *A Distant Trumpet* (1960), A25, Book Two, part of Sections xvii-xxiii.

C141. "Duty," *Collier's* (November 22, 1952), 36–38, 42–43. The story later became part of *A Distant Trumpet* (1960), A25, Book Three, part of Sections iv-xi. It was reprinted in *People in Literature* (1957), F22; and in *And Yet, Entirely Different* (1967), F23.

C142. "Water in the Wilderness," *Collier's* (January 3, 1953), 52–57. Reprinted in *In Other Days* (1956), F110. The story later became part of *A Distant Trumpet* (1960), A25, Book Two, part of Sections xl-li.

C143. "My Father's Child," *Collier's* (February 14, 1953), 54–57. The story later became part of *A Distant Trumpet* (1960), A25, Book One, Sections vii-ix.

C144. "Command," *Collier's* (July 25, 1953), 14–15, 63–69. The story later became part of *A Distant Trumpet* (1960), A25, Book Two, part of Sections xxvi-xxxvi.

C145. "Place, Form and Prayer: The Prehistoric Human Geography of the Town Indians of the Rio Grande," *Landscape: Magazine of Human Geography* (Winter, 1953-1954), 7–11. A selection from *Great River* (1954), A19, Book One. *Landscape* was published in Santa Fe and edited by J. B. Jackson.

C146. "Ordeal at Fort Reprisal," *The Saturday Evening Post* (March 20, 1954), 22–23, 48, 50, 54, 57, 59–60; and (March 27, 1954), 40–41, 127–128, 130, 132–134. The story later became part of *A Distant Trumpet* (1960), A25, Book Two, part of Sections lii-lxix.

C147. "I Came to Kill," *The Saturday Evening Post* (May 1, 1954), 20–21, 96–100.

C148. "Collective Memory: XVIth-Century Spain," *New Mexico Quarterly* (Autumn, 1954), 264–289. An excerpt from *Great River* (1954), A19, Book Two.

C149. "The Cow Boy Revisited," *Southwest Review* (Autumn, 1954), 285–297. An excerpt from *Great River* (1954), A19, Book Four, from the section called "The Last Frontiersman."

C150. "A Note on the Bynner Collection," *Bulletin* (Fall, 1954), [1–2]. This is the publication of what was then called the Roswell Museum, Roswell, New Mexico. This issue was published in connection with an exhibition of the Chinese paintings and Oriental works of art from Witter Bynner's collection given to the Roswell Museum. It also contains a brief comment by Bynner, pages [3–4], and unsigned notes on this exhibition, and on the exhibition that began October 11, 1954, of Paul Horgan's watercolors of the Rio Grande. This exhibition was in honor of the publication of *Great River* (1954), A19. The 8-page bulletin also contains tipped-in reproductions of a Henriette Wyeth painting of Bynner, a Chinese painting from his collection, and a watercolor by Paul Horgan. The institution later changed its name to the Roswell Museum and Art Center.

C151. "Great River: The Rio Grande in North American History," *American Heritage* (December, 1954), 90–113. An excerpt from *Great River* (1954), A19.

C152. "Heart Attack," *The Saturday Evening Post* (March 12, 1955), 28–29, 100, 102, 104–106. Reprinted in *The Saturday Evening Post Stories 1955*, F44.

C153. "Unexpected Hero," *The Saturday Evening Post* (March 26, 1955), 22–23, 51, 55, 59–60, 63–66.

C154. "New York Girl," *The Saturday Evening Post* (April 9, 1955), 28–29, 114, 116–117.

C155. "Pages From a Rio Grande Notebook," *The New York Times Book Review* (May 15, 1955), 3, 30. These notes, made while writing *Great River* (1954), A19, and those of C156, are combined in Book One of *The Heroic Triad* (1970), A39. This article has been frequently anthologized, F57–62 and 71.

C156. "Mountain to Sea: Rio Grande Notes," *Southwest Review* (Autumn, 1955), 325–332. These notes, made while writing *Great River* (1954), A19, and those of C155, are combined in Book One of *The Heroic Triad* (1970), A39.

C157. "A Rio Grande Legend of San Ysidro," *The New Mexico Folklore Record*, X (1955–1956), 10. This periodical was published by the New Mexico Folklore Society.

C158. "The Man Called K," *The Saturday Evening Post* (March 24, 1956), 26–27, 87, 89–90, 92, 96.

C159. "The Rio Grande," *Holiday* (October, 1956), 34–41, 91, 94–97.

C160. "The Road Turns Off," *Peace, The Chronicle of St. Pius X Monastery* (January–February, 1957), 4–6. A black-and-white reproduction of a painting by Paul Horgan appears on page 6; a reproduction of the first page of the manuscript of "The Road Turns Off" appears on page [1]. The Pius X

Monastery is in Pevely, Missouri. For another periodical publication, see C161.

C161. "The Road Turns Off," *The American Benedictine Review* (Spring, 1957), 63–64. This article was first published in *Peace* (January–February, 1957), C160.

C162. "Character and Form in Creative Writing," *America* (May 25, 1957), 260–262. The acceptance speech on receiving the Campion Award of the Catholic Book Club, May 2, 1957.

C163. "Churchman of the Desert," *American Heritage* (October, 1957), 30–35, 99–101. A biographical sketch of Archbishop Lamy of Santa Fe, New Mexico. This is a different version of material similar to that used in C164.

C164. "Jean Baptiste Lamy—I: First Archbishop of Santa Fe," *The Month* (October, 1957), 203–214; "Jean Baptiste Lamy—II: First Archbishop of Santa Fe," (November, 1957), 282–292. This is a different version of material similar to that used in C163.

C165. "Dedicatory Remarks on the Peter Hurd Mural," *The Museum Journal* (1957), 37–43. Published by the West Texas Museum Association in its issue devoted to the Peter Hurd Mural, Rotunda, West Texas Museum, at Texas Technological College, Lubbock, Texas.

C166. " 'Rome Eternal' on TV," *Catholic Digest* (January, 1958), 37–40.

C167. Review of *The Church Incarnate*, by Rudolf Schwarz, *Landscape* (Winter, 1958–1959), 34.

C168. "The Secret of the Tin Box," *The Saturday Evening Post* (February 28, 1959), 34–35, 86–88. Reprinted in *The Peach Stone* (1967), A36, as "The Treasure." The story has been reprinted as "The Secret of the Tin Box" in *The Saturday Evening Post Stories 1959*, F73 and 108.

C169. "Doomsday and Mr. Lincoln," *The Saturday Evening Post* (April 18, 1959), 22–23, 46, 50, 53–54.

C170. "Wall of Flame," *The Saturday Evening Post* (August 1, 1959), 20–21, 77–78.

C171. "The Escape of Olin Rainey," *The Saturday Evening Post* (January 23, 1960), 28–29, 58–62. The story is published as an excerpt from *A Distant Trumpet* (1960), A25, Book One, substantially Sections liii–lvii.

C172. "The Captain's Lady," *The Saturday Evening Post* (April 9, 1960), 32–33, 103, 105–106, 108–110, 112–114. The story is published as an excerpt from *A Distant Trumpet* (1960), A25, Book One, substantially Sections lxxii–lxxxii. It was reprinted in *The Saturday Evening Post Stories 1961: Selected From 1960* (1961), F4.

C173. "In the Autumn of a Poet's Life a Second Flowering," review of *New Poems 1960*, by Witter Bynner, *The New York Times Book Review* (October 16, 1960), 22.

C174. "In Search of the Archbishop," *The Catholic Historical Review* (January, 1961), 409–427. Delivered as the presidential address at the 41st annual meeting of the American Catholic Historical Association, New York City, December, 1960.

C175. "Citizen of New Salem," *The Saturday Evening Post* (March 4, 1961), 18–21, 66, 69–70, 72–74. The work was commissioned by The Editors of *The*

Saturday Evening Post to mark the centennial of the first inauguration of Lincoln. It was later published as *Citizen of New Salem* (1961), A27, and was condensed in *Reader's Digest* (February, 1964), C183.

C176. "New Mexico," *The Saturday Evening Post* (January 27, 1962), 15–21.

C177. "A Member of the Board Speaks," *ALA Bulletin* (January, 1962), 28.

C178. "A Writer's Disciplines," *The Critic* (October–November, 1962), 32–35. An address given on the 23rd anniversary of the Thomas More Association.

C179. "The Language of Professionalism," *Library Journal* (December 15, 1962), 4493. An excerpt from *One of the Quietest Things* (1960), A26.

C180. "Black Snowflakes," *The Saturday Evening Post* (March 30, 1963), 30–31, 34–36. Reprinted in *Things As They Are* (1964), A31, and *The Peach Stone* (1967), A36. It also appeared in *The Best American Short Stories 1964*, F2.

C181. "Rain in Laredo," *The Saturday Evening Post* (July 13–20, 1963), 44–45, 47–51.

C182. "Andrew Wyeth," *Ramparts* (Christmas, 1963), 69–84. Included on pages 73–80 are reproductions of works by Andrew Wyeth.

C183. "Citizen of New Salem," *The Reader's Digest* (February, 1964), 234–236, 239, 243, 245–246, 248, 251–252, 255–256, 258, 261–264. A condensed version of *Citizen of New Salem* (1961), A27. The work was first published in *The Saturday Evening Post* (March 4, 1961), C175.

C184. "The Spoiled Priest," *The Critic* (February–March, 1964), 20–29. With the same title the story is part of *Things As They Are* (1964), A31.

C185. "Evening the Score," *Horizon* (Spring, 1964), 49–51. Fifteen satirical drawings of musical characters, with titles, by Paul Horgan, selected from the originals in the collection of Rouben Mamoulian.

C186. "The Western Novel: A Symposium," *South Dakota Review* (Autumn, 1964), 3–36. The report of a symposium that included Paul Horgan, Frederick Manfred, Frank Waters, Walter Van Tilburg Clark, Vardis Fisher, Harvey Fergusson, Forrester Black, and Michael Straight. Ten questions were asked each writer and Paul Horgan's written responses appear on pages 27–32. The symposium is reprinted in *The Literature of the American West* (1971), F111.

C187. "A Writer's Creed: An Anniversary Felicitation to The Catholic World," *The Catholic World* (April, 1965), 15.

C188. "The Abdication of the Artist," *Proceedings of the American Philosophical Society* (October, 1965), 267–271. Text of a paper read before the American Philosophical Society on April 22, 1965.

C189. "An Open Letter to John Tracy Ellis," *Catholic Mind* (January, 1966), 32–35. Speech given at the presentation of the Campion Award to John Tracy Ellis at America House, New York City, November 26, 1965.

C190. "The Priest in Service," *The Shield* (April–May, 1966), 10–11, 14. A brief excerpt from the story "To the Castle" that was one of three stories in *Humble Powers* (1954), A20. The magazine was published by The Catholic Students' Mission Crusade, Cincinnati, Ohio.

C191. "The State of the Union," review of *This America*, by Lyndon B. Johnson, *The New York Times Book Review* (October 16, 1966), 69.

C192. "Thornton Wilder: A Little Drawing in Line," *Book-of-the-Month Club News* (March, 1967), 6, 16.

C193. "The Sculpture of Frederick Shrady," *The Critic* (April–May), 1967, 58–65.

C194. "The Flavour of Danger," *Argosy* (London: February, 1968), 50–69. This story first appeared in *The Atlantic Monthly* (January, 1938), C103, under its original title, "To the Mountains."

C195. "Inlitcong XIX," *Reflection, The Wesleyan Quarterly* (Spring, 1968), 11–[15]. Sixteen pen-and-ink sketches, with descriptions. The full title page reads: "Inlitcong XIX / [decorative rule] / Representative Delegates to / the Nineteenth Annual Inter- / national Literary Congress, / held this year at Isola Gatta, / Italy. / [decorative rule] / Theme of the Congress: / The Third Ear And The / Corporate Silence / [decorative rule] / by / Paul Horgan / Correspondent At Large."

C196. "Fr. D'Arcy and the Ages of Man," *The Month* (June, 1968), 341–343. A two-part article with the general title "Fr. Martin D'Arcy is 80": part one is called "Fr. D'Arcy at Oxford," and is by Robert Speaight; and part two is this piece by Paul Horgan.

C197. "Reflections on the Act of Writing," *Reflection, The Wesleyan Quarterly* (Winter, 1968), 2–6. Portions of this article appear in a different form in Part One of *Approaches to Writing* (1973), A44.

C198. Review of *Just Over the Border*, by F. D. Reeve, *Book-of-the-Month Club News* (November, 1969), 9–10.

C199. "The Mourners," *Polymus* (1969), 25–29. An excerpt from *Whitewater* (1970), A41. This was the first issue of a magazine published by the students at the Choate School, Wallingford, Connecticut.

C200. "Witter Bynner: 1881–1968," *Proceedings of the American Academy of Arts and Letters and the National Institute of Arts and Letters*, second series, number 19 (New York, 1969), 97–100.

C201. Review of *The Body Has a Head*, by Gustav Eckstein, *Book-of-the-Month Club News* (February, 1970), 2, 4–[6].

C202. "A Casebook of Academiology," *The Harvard Bulletin* (March 2, 1970), 25–27. A collection of humorous sketches of academic personalities, with descriptions, selected from originals in the collection of Dr. Clair B. Crampton.

C203. Review of *Wellington: The Years of the Sword*, by Elizabeth Longford, *Book-of-the-Month Club News* (March, 1970), 2, 4, 6.

C204. Review of *Sal Si Puedes*, by Peter Matthiessen, *Book-of-the-Month Club News* (March, 1970), 12.

C205. Review of *Zelda: A Biography*, by Nancy Milford, *Book-of-the-Month Club News* (May, 1970), [1]–[6].

C206. Review of *The Bay of Noon*, by Shirley Hazzard, *Book-of-the-Month Club News* (May, 1970), 7.

C207. "A Rage to Perceive: The Letters of Aldous Huxley," a review of *Letters of Aldous Huxley*, edited by Grover Smith, *The Middletown Press* (June 2, 1970), 10. This is the local newspaper in Middletown, Connecticut, where Paul Horgan has lived since October, 1962. It is edited by Russell G.

D'Oench, Jr. This is a different review from the one in the *Book-of-the-Month Club News* (June, 1970), C208.

C208. Review of *Letters of Aldous Huxley,* edited by Grover Smith, *Book-of-the-Month Club News* (June, 1970), 8. This is a different review from that in *The Middletown Press* (June 2, 1970), C207.

C209. Review of *Last Things: A Novel,* by C. P. Snow, *Book-of-the-Month Club News* (Midsummer, 1970), 2–4.

C210. Review of *Will They Ever Finish Bruckner Boulevard?,* by Ada Louise Huxtable, *Book-of-the-Month Club News* (Midsummer, 1970), 10.

C211. "Journey to the Past—and Return: Reflections on the Work of the Historian," *The Texas Quarterly* (Summer, 1970), 34–51. The text of the address to the Society of American Historians, given in New York City, February 28, 1969.

C212. "Rio Grande: Odyssey from a Wintry Birth," *The Washington Post* (August 9, 1970), B–5. Excerpted from "Pages from a Rio Grande Notebook" in *The Heroic Triad* (1970), A39.

C213. Review of *Play It As It Lays,* by Joan Didion, *Book-of-the-Month Club News* (September, 1970), 11.

C214. "London Letter," *The Dallas Morning News* (September 6, 1970), 4-F.

C215. "Dana: The World of Washington," review of *Dana: The Irrelevant Man,* by Douglass Cater, *The Middletown Press* (October 20, 1970), 10. This is a different review from that in the *Book-of-the-Month Club News* (October, 1970), C216.

C216. Review of *Dana: The Irrelevant Man,* by Douglass Cater, *Book-of-the-Month Club News* (October, 1970), 9. This is a different review from that in *The Middletown Press* (October 20, 1970), C215.

C217. Review of *Professional Secrets: An Autobiography of Jean Cocteau,* edited by Robert Phelps, *Book-of-the-Month Club News* (October, 1970), 11.

C218. Review of *Cocteau: A Biography,* by Francis Steegmuller, *Book-of-the-Month Club News* (Fall, 1970), 11.

C219. "Convergences Toward a Biography," *Wesleyan Library Notes* (Autumn, 1970), 1–8. An abridged version of an extemporaneous talk given before the Friends of the Library on April 11, 1970. A reproduction of a water-color sketch by the author appears on page 2. A recording of the full talk is on tape in the Davison Rare Book Room, Olin Library, Wesleyan University, Middletown, Connecticut.

C220. "Peter Hurd: He Looks at the Gate and Sees Beyond," *New Mexico* (November–December, 1970), 20–24. The article is taken from *Peter Hurd: A Portrait Sketch from Life* (1965), A32. With a slightly different title than used here, another extract appears in a museum brochure (1964), E28.

C221. "The Nature of Crime," review of *Crime in America: Observations on Its Nature, Causes, Prevention, and Control,* by Ramsey Clark, *The Middletown Press* (December 29, 1970), 7.

C222. "To the Islands," *The Cornhill Magazine* (Winter, 1970–1971), 313–326. An excerpt from *Whitewater* (1970), A41.

C223. Review of *The Honours Board,* by Pamela Hansford Johnson, *Book-of-the-Month Club News* (January, 1971), 14–15.

C224. "Whitewater," *Ladies' Home Journal* (January, 1971), 109–116, 120, 122–123. A condensed version of *Whitewater* (1970), A41.

C225. Review of *Three-Cornered Heart,* by Anne Fremantle, *Book-of-the-Month Club News* (Midwinter, 1971), 7.

C226. Review of *Ride Out the Dark,* by Christabel Bielenberg, *Book-of-the-Month Club News* (April, 1971), 6.

C227. Review of *From Caesar to the Mafia,* by Luigi Barzini, *Book-of-the-Month Club News* (June, 1971), 7.

C228. Review of *The Brother,* by F. D. Reeve, *Book-of-the-Month Club News* (June, 1971), 8.

C229. Review of *Ancestors,* by William Maxwell, *Book-of-the-Month Club News* (Midsummer, 1971), 5–6.

C230. Review of *Explorations,* by Gilbert Highet, *Book-of-the-Month Club News* (September, 1971), [22].

C231. Review of *Eleanor and Franklin,* by Joseph P. Lash, *Book-of-the-Month Club News* (October, 1971), [1–5].

C232. Review of *Thresholds,* by Dorothea Straus, *Book-of-the-Month Club News* (October, 1971), 7.

C233. Review of *The Journey of August King,* by John Ehle, *Book-of-the-Month Club News* (Fall, 1971), 7.

C234. Review of *Meet Me in the Green Glen,* by Robert Penn Warren, *Book-of-the-Month Club News* (Fall, 1971), 10.

C235. Review of *Glory: A Novel,* by Vladimir Nabokov, *Book-of-the-Month Club News* (December, 1971), [1]–3.

C236. Review of *The Night Country,* by Loren Eiseley, *Book-of-the-Month Club News* (December, 1971), 5.

C237. Review of *Up and Down and Around,* by Cass Canfield, *Book-of-the-Month Club News* (January, 1972), 6–7.

C238. Review of *Dear Scott/Dear Max,* edited by John Kuehl and Jackson Bryer, *Book-of-the-Month Club News* (January, 1972), 8.

C239. Review of *Henry James, The Master: 1901–1916,* by Leon Edel, *Book-of-the-Month Club News* (March, 1972), 7–8.

C240. Review of *The Crown of Mexico: Maximilian and His Empress Carlota,* by Joan Haslip, *Book-of-the-Month Club News* (April, 1972), [1–4].

C241. Review of *This Bright Land,* by Brooks Atkinson, *Book-of-the-Month Club News* (April, 1972), 7–8.

C242. Review of *The Boys of Summer,* by Roger Kahn, *Book-of-the-Month Club News* (Spring, 1972), 2–[5].

C243. Review of *The Wyeths,* edited by Betsy James Wyeth, *Book-of-the-Month Club News* (Spring, 1972), 7.

C244. "An Elder Novelist on Youth's Revolt," a review of *The Malcontents,* by C. P. Snow, *Life* (May 5, 1972), one of an unnumbered group of pages that appears between pages 28 and 29 in the section of *Life* that varied by region. This is a different review from that in the *Book-of-the-Month Club News* (July, 1972), C246.

C245. Review of *Felled Oaks: Conversation with de Gaulle,* by André Malraux, *Book-of-the-Month Club News* (June, 1972), 8–9.

C246. Review of *The Malcontents,* by C. P. Snow, *Book-of-the-Month Club News* (July, 1972). A four-page insert was prepared for the Canadian members of the Book-of-the-Month Club offering them *The Malcontents* as the July selection. Paul Horgan's review appears on pages [2–4]. This is a different review from that in *Life* (May 5, 1972), C244.

C247. Review of *Eleanor: The Years Alone,* By Joseph P. Lash, *Book-of-the-Month Club News* (Midsummer, 1972), 1–5.

C248. Review of *People in a Diary: A Memoir,* by S. N. Behrman, *Book-of-the-Month Club News* (Midsummer, 1972), 8.

C249. Review of *Many Lives, One Love,* by Fanny Butcher, *Book-of-the-Month Club News* (August, 1972), 9.

C250. Review of *A God Within,* by René Dubos, *Book-of-the-Month Club News* (October, 1972), 9.

C251. Review of *Waiting for the Morning Train,* by Bruce Catton, *Book-of-the-Month Club News* (January, 1973), 6.

C252. Review of *Harry S. Truman,* by Margaret Truman, *Book-of-the-Month Club News* (Midwinter, 1973), [1–4].

C253. Review of *Virginia Woolf: A Biography,* by Quentin Bell, *Book-of-the-Month Club News* (February, 1973), 11.

C254. "From 'Notebook Pages'," *Prose, Number Seven* (Fall, 1973). A selection from Part Two of *Approaches to Writing* (1973), A44. *Prose* is published by Coburn Britton twice a year, spring and fall, in New York City. This article is to appear after the publication of this book.

D. TRANSLATIONS

D1. "The Baptists," translated into Russian by "K.M." as БАПТИСТЫ and published in ЗВЕНО (Paris: June 24, 1925), 2. The first published short story by Paul Horgan appeared translated into Russian in a Russian paper published in Paris. It has never been reprinted or published in English. Mr. Horgan discusses this incident in *Approaches to Writing* (1973), A44.

D2. *Conquistadors in North American History,* translated into Spanish by Antonio Garza y Garza as *Los Conquistadores en la América del Norte* (Editorial Diana, S.A.: Mexico, D.F., 1966). See *Conquistadors in North American History* (1963), A29.

D3. "The Devil in the Desert," translated into French by Thomas de Saint Phalle as "Le Serpent au Désert," and serialized in *Ecclesia Lectures Chrétiennes* (December, 1952), [13]–21; (January, 1953), [115]–122; (February, 1953), [122]–129. Originally published in *The Saturday Evening Post* (May 6, 1950), C130; see also *The Devil in the Desert* (1952), A17, *Humble Powers* (1954), A20, and *The Peach Stone* (1967), A36.

D4. "The Devil in the Desert," translated into German by Annemarie and Heinrich Böll as "Der Teufel in der Wüste" and published in the magazine *Hochland* (April, 1957), [352–365].

D5. "The Devil in the Desert," translated into German by Annemarie and Heinrich Böll as *Der Teufel in Der Wüste* (Walter-Verlag: Olten und Freiburg im Breisgau, 1958).

D6. "The Devil in the Desert," translated into German by Arno Dohm as "Der Teufel in der Wüste," and published in *Rauch über der Prärie: Die besten Western-Stories,* edited by Richard Stafford and illustrated by Werner Kulle (Mosaik Verlag: Hamburg, 1963), 112–146.

D7. *A Distant Trumpet,* translated into Spanish by J. Ferrer Aleu as *Trompetas Lejanas* (Plaza & Janés, S.A., Editores: Barcelona, 1964). See *A Distant Trumpet* (1960), A25.

D8. *Give Me Possession,* translated into German by Roswitha Plancherel-Walter as *Die Zweite Heimkehr* (Walter-Verlag: Olten und Freiburg im Breisgau, 1959). See *Give Me Possession* (1957), A23.

D9. *The Habit of Empire,* translated into Spanish by Arthur L. Campa as *El Hábito del Imperio* and published in *El Nuevo Mexicano* (February 3 to April 28, 1938). Cyrus McCormick was owner of this Santa Fe newspaper that was published weekly. The work was appearing serially and in English at the same time in McCormick's *The New Mexico Sentinel,* also a Santa Fe newspaper, C104. See *The Habit of Empire* (1939), A13.

D10. *Humble Powers,* translated into Italian by Silvio Curto as *Potere dell'umiltà* (Frassinelli Tipografo Editore: Torino, 1956). See *Humble Powers* (1954), A20.

D11. *Humble Powers,* translated into Spanish by Marisa Ábalos as *Poderes Humildes* (Ediciones La Isla: Buenos Aires, 1956).

D12. *One Red Rose for Christmas,* translated into French by Joe Ceurvorst as "Le Miracle de la Rose Rouge," and published in the magazine *Bonnes Soirées* (December 20, 1953), 35–36, 45–61. Originally published in *Cosmopolitan* (December, 1951), C138; see also *One Red Rose for Christmas* (1952), A18, and, *Humble Powers* (1954), A20.

D13. *One Red Rose for Christmas,* translated into German by Annemarie and Heinrich Böll as *Eine Rose zur Weihnacht* (Walter-Verlag: Olten und Freiburg im Breisgau, 1960).

D14. *One Red Rose for Christmas,* translated into German by Annemarie and Heinrich Böll as *Eine Rose zur Weihnacht* (St. Benno-Verlag GMBH, Leipzig, n.d.), 5–86. In the same volume *The Saintmaker's Christmas Eve* is translated into German by Annemarie and Heinrich Böll as *Weihnachtsabend in San Cristobal* and appears on pages [87]–175. Only the German title of *One Red Rose,* the author's name, and the publisher appear on the full tittle page [3]. *Saintmaker's* has its own title page [87]. The two titles appear on the dust jacket. On the front cover is a rose in gold; on the spine in gold appears "Horgan Eine Rose zur Weihnacht." The edition is illustrated with pen-and-ink drawings. See D19.

D15. *One Red Rose for Christmas,* translated into German by Annemarie and Heinrich Böll as *Eine Rose zur Weihnacht* (Verlag Der Arche: Zürich, 1969).

D16. "The Peach Stone," translated into Japanese by Tetsuo Shinjō as "Momo Nusane" and published in the magazine *Gendai Amerika Shōsetsu Shū* (August, 1952), 164–179. Originally published in *The Yale Review* (June, 1942), C114; also see *The Peach Stone* (1967), A36.

D17. *The Peach Stone,* translated into Pak-Bengali in two volumes and published by M/S Bookvilla, Government New Market, Dacca-2, Pakistan, in June, 1969. Translations of Parts I and II of the English edition by Arzina Ali and Akhtar-ul Alam, and of Parts III and IV of the English edition by Nur-ul Alam and Mahmudul Huq. See *The Peach Stone* (1967), A36.

D18. *The Saintmaker's Christmas Eve,* translated into German by Annemarie and Heinrich Böll as *Weihnachtsabend in San Cristobal* (Walter-Verlag: Olten und Freiburg im Breisgau, 1956). See *The Saintmaker's Christmas Eve* (1955), A21.

D19. *The Saintmaker's Christmas Eve,* translated into German by Annemarie and Heinrich Böll as *Weihnachtsabend in San Cristobal* (St. Benno-Verlag GMBH, Leipzig, n.d.), [87]–175. In the same volume *One Red Rose for Christmas* is translated into German by Annemarie and Heinrich Böll as *Eine Rose zur Weihnacht* and appears on pages 5–86. Only the German title of *One Red Rose,* the author's name, and the publisher appear on the full title page [3]. *Saintmaker's* has its own title page [87]. For further information on this volume, see D14.

D20. *The Saintmaker's Christmas Eve,* translated into Spanish by J. Fons Perales as *Sucedio en San Cristobal* (Ediciones Dinor, S.L.: San Sebastian, 1958).

D21. *Things As They Are,* translated into Dutch by K.H.R. de Josselin de Jong as *Zoals De Dingen Zijn* (H. P. Leopolds Uitgeversmij N.V.: Den Haag, 1968). See *Things As They Are* (1964), A31.

D22. "To the Mountains," translated into Japanese by Toyohiko Tatsumi as "Yamaho Sasoi" and published in the magazine *Seiki* (May, 1950), 61–80. Originally published in *The Atlantic Monthly* (January, 1938), C103; see also *Figures in a Landscape* (1940), A14, and *The Peach Stone* (1967), A36.

D23. "To the Mountains," translated into Spanish by Andrés M. Mateo as "A las Montañas" and published in *Antologia de la Novela Corta Norteamericana,* Tomo II, edited by Wallace and Mary Stegner (Libreros Mexicanos Unidos: Mexico, 1964), 145–174.

D24. *Whitewater,* translated into German by Herbert Roch as *Die Leute von Whitewater* (Rainer Wunderlich Verlag Hermann Leins: Tübingen, 1970). See *Whitewater* (1970), A41.

D25. *Whitewater,* translated into Spanish by Nora Bigongiari as *Agua Blanca* (Emecé Editores: Buenos Aires, 1971).

D26. *Whitewater,* translated into Swedish by Tove Bouveng as *Whitewater, Det Bästas Bokval* (Reader's Digest Aktiebolag: Stockholm, 1971), 365–521. A condensed version.

D27. *Whitewater,* translated into German by Peter Dülberg as *Die Leute von Whitewater, Reader's Digest Auswahlbücher* (Verlag Das Beste Gmbh: Stuttgart-Zurich-Wien, 1972), 6–183. A condensed version.

E. MISCELLANEOUS

E1. *The Golden Rose,* 1928. There is a carbon of a typed copy of this early novel at Yale, bound in a cream cloth binding, with the title in gold on the cover. The endpapers are gray. The copy contains Carl Van Vechten's bookplate; the following dedication in Paul Horgan's hand: "To Carl Van Vechten / from Paul Horgan / Roswell / March 4, 1928"; and this typed dedication: "To / the memory of the / Countess Nattatorrini / and to / her intimate biographer, Carl Van Vechten." The author has signed his name on page 60, at the end of the text.
This is one of the early unpublished novels that is discussed in Part Three of *Approaches to Writing* (1973), A44. According to the author this is the only extant copy. There is a typed, signed letter at Yale from Paul Horgan to Carl Van Vechten, sent with the presentation of the book. The letter is dated March 9th.

E2. "A Note for the Catalogue," *Ten Paintings by Peter Hurd, Exhibited in The Library, N.M.M.I., From December 11 to 21, MCMXXVIII,* [3-6]. The note is dated November 30, 1928. "N.M.M.I." is New Mexico Military Institute.

E3. Program Notes for New Mexico Military Institute's concert by Oscar Seagle, Baritone (March 1, 1929), 2-4. A copy of these notes is in a scrapbook in Paul Horgan's library.

E4. "The Old Post," a New Mexico Military Institute Song. The lyrics to this school song were written by "Captain Paul Horgan" and the music by "Captain J. B. Darling," sometime around 1930. The song is also called the "Alma Mater," and the words and music are published by the Athletic Department of the New Mexico Military Institute, Roswell, New Mexico.

E5. *Brother Clementine,* 1932. This high-spirited Chaucerian spoof is subtitled: "How a monke from a monastery in ye mountains went to ye city to visit his dying tante, and how he returned in strange condicioun." The first page is hand-letter in black and reads: "This edition is limited / to one copy of which / this is number / [in green] I / designed, illustrated, made / and bound especially for / ROBERT HUNT, / and signed by the / author / [in green] Vincent O'Shaughnessy / and the / illustrator / [in green] Paul Horgan / —all with large / affection." The copy is bound in brown suede cloth, decorated in gold and blind tooling, with the title and decorations in gold in the spine. The copy is in Paul Horgan's library. The brief, typed text is 5 pages long, and is liberally illustrated with pen and watercolor sketches of the monke's adventures, five of which are full-page and entitled: "In ye mountains sate ye abbey of St. Basil," "Amount upon his asse he did go," "She smilen and upraise his homely cassock," and "To proven ye which he kick ye silly monke." As is indicated in A2, Vincent O'Shaughnessy is a pen name of Paul Horgan. Robert Hunt was a poet and a friend of Witter Bynner, then living in Santa Fe. Hunt and Paul Horgan were schoolmates at the New Mexico Military Institute in 1922–1923. "Brother Clementine" was written, according to Paul Horgan, "without revision, in thirty minutes, under the rules of a mock competition between four faculty colleagues at the New Mexico Military Institute, who met each day for four days, during the school's second quarantine in the same year for spinal meningitis. Each participant wrote a composition in the allotted half-hour, and, in imitation of *The Decameron of Boccaccio,* passed the hours of the plague with literary diversions. The four days here cited thus produced sixteen tales, collectively referred to as the 'Tetrameron of Quarantinus Secundus.' So far as is known, 'Brother Clementine' is the only one of the sixteen tales to survive."

E6. Notes for *Peter Hurd, MCMXXXIII, Designs For Mural Decorations and Fifteen Paintings Shown in the Lounge of J. Ross Thomas Memorial, New Mexico Military Institute, October, 1933,* [1]–5. Paul Horgan's notes are dated, "Roswell, October 12, 1933."

E7. "Some People / from / No / Quarter / Given / [horizontal rule] / Drawn by the Author / [horizontal rule] / 1935 / Harper & Brothers: Publishers / 49 East 33rd Street, New York." A 16-page pamphlet with 17 drawings of characters, each with its name written below it in script, from *No Quarter Given* (1935), A6. These drawings by Paul Horgan are reproduced in brown on light tan paper. The cover has the above title, all but the publisher's name and address in script and all set within a decorative rectangle. There is a copy in the Zimmerman Library at the University of New Mexico.

E8. "Introduction," *Paintings by Vernon Hunter,* 1–5. An introduction to an 8-page exhibition catalogue for the University of Colorado, circa 1938.

E9. "The Meaning of a Museum," a 2-page article in a brochure called: "Roswell / Museum / Spring River Park / Roswell, / New Mexico." The 12-page brochure has the above title page in black type with an Indian design in olive and black, both printed on a cover of heavy tan paper. The article by Paul Horgan is reprinted on pages [3–4], and is from what is referred to as the "Old Timers' Special Edition" of the *Roswell Daily Record,* October 7, 1937. The rest of the brochure is an unsigned description of the museum, with several woodcuts by Manvill Chapman. A copy is owned by Ronald F. Dickey, Socorro, New Mexico. Copies of the *Roswell Daily Record* were not available for checking and no reference is made to the original publication of this article in that paper.

E10. "Spring Snow, Roswell," *Laughing Horse* (Summer, 1938), Number 20. This is a reproduction of a painting by Paul Horgan. Some bibliographies have thought it to be a prose work.

E11. "ROSWELL / MUSEUM / [Indian design] / FEDERAL / ART CENTER / [one thick and one thin red rule] / *The First Year:* / a record & comment / by PAUL HORGAN / [one thin and one thick red rule]." A 4-page brochure that reprints on pages [2–4] an article from the "Golden Anniversary Edition" of the *Roswell Daily Record,* October 3, 1938. The heavy paper is gray. On the front cover is the above title page. The Indian design in red and black is similar to that in E9; the type is black. A copy is owned by Roland F. Dickey, Socorro, New Mexico. Copies of the *Roswell Daily Record* were not available for checking and no reference is made to the original publication of this article in that paper.

E12. "The Spanish Colonial Arts Society of New Mexico," a 4-page statement for membership, with a membership application. On the front is a reproduction of a Spanish Colonial painting; on pages [2–4] is the statement by Paul Horgan; on page [4] is an application for membership to the Spanish Colonial Arts Society, Santa Fe. The date is circa 1939–1940. A copy is owned by Roland F. Dickey, Socorro, New Mexico.

E13. Essay on Peter Hurd, *Peter Hurd: Paintings and Drawings,* [1–2]. An essay in an exhibition catalogue for a show at the gallery of Mrs. Cornelius J. Sullivan, 460 Park Avenue, New York. The date is April 11–29, 1939.

E14. *A Tree on the Plains: A Musical Play for Americans,* 1942. A carbon copy of a typescript of the libretto of the opera was submitted to the Library of Congress for copyright on April 21, 1942. This copy contains the name and address of the agent, Annie Laurie Williams, 18 East 41st Street, New York City. For publication of the full text, and for further information on the opera, see *Southwest Review* (Summer, 1943), C118; and *Theatre Arts* (February, 1943), C116. The text of two songs from the opera was used in *Whitewater* (1970), A41.

E15. *Yours, A. Lincoln,* 1942. The play has various titles: *Martyrdom in Washington; Death, Mr. President;* and *Yours, A. Lincoln.* The last was used for the performances done by the Actors' Equity and Dramatists' Guild in the Experimental Theatre at a matinee on Thursday, July 9, 1942, and at an evening performance on Sunday, July 12, 1942, both at the Shubert Theatre in New York City. Vincent Price played Lincoln. A copy of the text, a program of the performances, and possible set designs by Paul Horgan, are at Yale. The typed copy at Yale, mostly a carbon, carries the title *Martyrdom* in Washington, and Paul Horgan states in a note before the text that Otto Eisenschiml's book *Why Was Lincoln Murdered?* "touched off" his desire to write about Lincoln.

E16. "Foreword," *N. C. Wyeth, N.A. 1882–1945, Memorial Exhibition, January 7 to 27, 1946.* (The Wilmington Society of the Fine Arts, Wilmington, Delaware), [5–7], [9–11]. The foreword is signed "Washington / 24 December 1945." This piece is reprinted in the book *N. C. Wyeth* (1972), B17.

E17. "Foreword," *Peter Hurd: The Permanent Collection,* [3–4]. A foreword to an 8-page catalogue for the Roswell Museum, Roswell, New Mexico. The cover is thin tan paper and the lettering is blue. It states on the back cover: "First Edition, February, 1949. 1000 copies [design in blue]."

E18. An introduction to *Paintings: Henriette Wyeth,* [2–5]. An introduction to a 12-page catalogue for an exhibition held at the Roswell Museum from September 11–October 2, 1949. On page 12 it states: "Printed in an edition of 1000 copies [design in red] September, 1949."

E19. "Introduction," *30 Drawings: Ivan Meštrović,* 4, 6, 8, 10–11. The introduction is written with Thomas M. Messer. The exhibition was first at the

Roswell Museum, September 10–October 8, 1950, and subsequently went to the Museum of Fine Arts of Houston, the Dallas Museum of Fine Arts, the Museum at Texas Technological College, and Texas Western College. The catalogue was designed by Paul Horgan.

E20. *One Red Rose,* a dramatization in one act, by Sister Mary Olive O'Connell, S.P. (Longmans, Green and Co.: New York, 1954). See *One Red Rose for Christmas* (1952), A18.

E21. "Interview" between Paul Horgan and Fray Angélico Chavez on "The Catholic Hour," NBC-TV, August 26, 1956, and printed in *Close-Up,* pages 1–9, a publication of the programs on "The Catholic Hour," printed by the National Council of Catholic Men. The same interview was aired on the radio on the program "Christian in Action" on September 23, 1956, and printed in *Christian in Action,* pages 1–9, a publication of the discussions aired on that program.

E22. *Great River: The Rio Grande,* 1957. A musical composition for symphonic orchestra by Ernst Bacon, with narrative passages from Paul Horgan's book, *Great River* (1954), A19, was commissioned by the Dallas Symphony Orchestra, Walter Hendl, Musical Director. Mr. Hendl conducted the premiere with that orchestra in February, 1957, with Mack Harrell as the narrator. Paul Horgan has a reproduction of a hand copy of the score, given to him by the composer.

E23. "Land of the Southwest . . . Number 12 and the last of the Southwest Broadsides. Printed by the Grabhorn Press at San Francisco in 1958 for the friends of Lawrence Clark Powell." This is an excerpt from "About the Southwest," which originally appeared in the *Southwest Review* (July, 1933), C73.

E24. "An Appreciation," *Five Years Forward: The Dallas Public Library, 1955–1960,* 3–4. A 32-page pamphlet on the library's growth during 1955–1960.

E25. "The Style of Peter Hurd," in a 12-page brochure entitled *Paintings of Peter Hurd,* relating to the permanent collection of the Roswell Museum and Art Center, Roswell, New Mexico (n.d.), [4–6], [8–10]. The essay originally appeared with the same title in *New Mexico Quarterly* (Winter, 1950–1951), C131. It appears here with several reproductions of works by Peter Hurd and a comment on the paintings signed "D.G.," for the director of the museum, David Gebhard. The date is sometime late in 1960, according to information given by the Roswell Museum.

E26. "Pulitzer Prize Author Paul Horgan Tried Various Styles 'Until I Came To What Sounded Like My Own Voice'," *The New Haven Register Magazine* (January 13, 1963), 3. An unsigned interview of Paul Horgan that appeared in a New Haven, Connecticut, newspaper when he became acting director of the Center for Advanced Studies at Wesleyan University, Middletown, Connecticut.

E27. "Andrew Wyeth: Impression for a Portrait," *Andrew Wyeth: An Exhibition of Watercolors, Temperas and Drawings, March 16 through April 14. The University of Arizona Art Gallery, Tucson, Arizona* (University of Arizona Press: Tucson, 1963), 11, 13, 15, 19, 21, 27, 29, 33, 39, 41–42, 48.

E28. "Peter Hurd: The Gate and Beyond," a triangularly folded brochure to accompany the exhibition at the Amon Carter Museum of Western Art, Fort Worth, Texas, October 22, 1964 to January 3, 1965. This brochure contains on its three inside folds a sketch by Peter Hurd and an excerpt from the longer essay that was published to accompany the exhibition, *Peter Hurd: A Portrait Sketch From Life* (1965), A32, and printed by the University of Texas Press. With a title similar to the one used for this brochure, "Peter Hurd: He Looks at the Gate and Sees Beyond," a selection from the longer essay was published in *New Mexico* (November–December, 1970), C220.

E29. A letter dated June 15, 1966, written for a 14-page brochure to promote the Library Fund for the College of Santa Fe. The brochure is called "The Library: Chief Source of Knowledge" and is published by the College of Santa Fe Library Committee. The letter is on page 14.

E30. "On the Painting of Samuel Green," *Samuel M. Green, Davison Art Center, Wesleyan University, Middletown, Connecticut, February 27–March 18, 1967*, [3–4]. A brief comment in an exhibition catalogue.

E31. "Preface," *Randall Davey: 1887–1964, March 14–April 1, 1967, Findlay Galleries, New York, 11–13 East 57th Street—Second Floor*, [3–4]. A brief comment in an exhibition catalogue.

E32. Letter to the Editor, *The New York Times Book Review* (June 25, 1967), 32–33. A letter sent in reference to an article on Paul Horgan by Lawrence Clark Powell, "The Horgan File," which appeared in this same review on May 14, 1967, pages 2 and 40.

E33. "Introduction," *Selected Artists Galleries Present David McIntosh, March 5–23, 1968 at 903 Madison Avenue, New York*. A brief introduction to an announcement brochure and exhibition catalogue.

E34. Remarks at Aspen Institute Dinner in honor of Edmund Wilson, June 12, 1968. A looseleaf folder in blue bound with a blue plastic spindle and containing the typed and Xeroxed speeches of Paul Horgan, William E. Stevenson, and Edmund Wilson upon the presentation of the Aspen Award to Edmund Wilson on June 12, 1968, at the Waldorf Astoria Hotel in New York City.

E35. "Introductory Note," to *Digressions and Indiscretions,* by Richard Leighton Greene, published as a CEA Chap Book by the College English Association, Washington, D.C., and distributed as a supplement to *The CEA Critic* (June, 1968).

E36. Introduction, *The Roswell Museum and Art Center: A Guide and Description,* [2]. A brief introductory statement to a pamphlet on the museum, published in 1970.

E37. "A Letter from Paul Horgan to John Ehle about *Time of Drums*," *The New York Times Book Review* (October 11, 1970), 38. The letter is published as an advertisement for *Time of Drums* by John Ehle.

E38. "Paul Horgan Is Writing A Book. It Will Appear . . . Eventually," an interview of Paul Horgan by Robert Daseler, *The Middletown Press* (December 4, 1970), 8–9.

E39. "A Second Talent: An Exhibition of Drawings and Paintings by Writers," The Arts Club of Chicago, November 15 through December 31, 1971. Paul Horgan's watercolor, "Prospect of Mexico: Antigua, Vera Cruz," is item #76 in the exhibition. It is one of a series of field study notes made in preparation for the writing of *Conquistadors in North American History* (1963), A29, all of which are in the Beinecke Rare Book and Manuscript Library, Yale University.

F. ANTHOLOGIES

F1. "About the Southwest," *Son-of-a-Gun Stew: A Sampling of the South-west*, edited by Elizabeth Matchett Stover (New York, 1945), 1–4. The brief excerpt used here appears under the title "A Hard Land to Win"; originally the article appeared in *Southwest Review* (July, 1933), C73. Listed again under F43.

F2. "Black Snowflakes," *The Best American Short Stories 1964 and the Year-book of the American Short Story*, edited by Martha Foley and David Burnett (Boston, 1964), 137–151. First appeared in *The Saturday Evening Post* (March 30, 1963), C180; reprinted in *Things As They Are* (1964), A31, and *The Peach Stone* (1967), A36.

F3. "Capriccio," *Prose, Poetry and Drama for Oral Interpretation; Second Series*, selected and arranged by William J. Farma (New York, 1936), 275–278. First appeared in *The New Yorker* (December 16, 1933), C78.

F4. "The Captain's Lady," *The Saturday Evening Post Stories 1961: Selected From 1960* (Garden City, New York, 1961), 329–358. This story is part of *A Distant Trumpet* (1960), A25, and was first published in *The Saturday Evening Post* (April 9, 1960), C172.

F5. Excerpt from *The Centuries of Santa Fe*, "The Royal Notary: 1620," in *Today and Tradition*, edited by Riley Hughes (New York, 1960), 35–39. See *The Centuries of Santa Fe* (1956), A22.

F6. Excerpt from *The Centuries of Santa Fe*, "Comic-Strip View," in *Under the Mask: An Anthology About Prejudice in America*, edited by Karel Weiss (New York, 1972), 112–113.

F7. *Conquistadors in North American History*, Best-in-Books (Garden City, New York, 1963), 3–200. The entire book appeared with *The House at Sunset*, by Norah Lofts; *I Think Rome is Burning*, by Cynthia Seton; and *Hornblower and the Hotspur*, by C. S. Forester. See *Conquistadors in North American History* (1963), A29.

F8. Excerpt from *Conquistadors in North American History*, in *Ideas and Patterns in Literature III*, edited by Edgar H. Knapp and Ralph J. Wadsworth (New York, 1970), 234–242.

F9. Excerpt from *Conquistadors in North American History*, "The Lord Admiral," in *Portrait of America, Volume 1: From the Cliff Dwellers to the End of Reconstruction*, edited by Stephen B. Oates (Boston, 1973), 16–26. Included in the same volume is an excerpt from *Great River* (1954), A19, that is listed as F41.

F10. "The Dawn of Hate," *Child Development Through Literature*, edited by Elliott D. Landau, Sherrie Landau Epstein, and Ann Plaat Stone (Englewood Cliffs, New Jersey, 1972), 396–403. "The Dawn of Hate" is the name of Chapter II in *Things As They Are* (1964), A31.

F11. "The Dawn of Hate," *Perspectives on Sexuality: A Literary Collection,* edited by James L. Malfetti and Elizabeth M. Eidlitz (New York, 1972), 166–172. For another story in this collection, see F63.

F12. "The Devil in the Desert," *Many-Colored Fleece,* edited by Sister Mariella Gable, O.S.B. (New York, 1950), 1–33. The story first appeared in *The Saturday Evening Post* (May 6, 1950), C130. For full listing, see 1952 book publication, A17.

F13. "The Devil in the Desert," *The Saturday Evening Post Stories 1950* (New York, 1950), 246–273.

F14. "The Devil in the Desert," *The Saturday Evening Post Treasury,* selected from the complete files by Roger Butterfield and The Editors of *The Saturday Evening Post* (New York, 1954), 526–538.

F15. "The Devil in the Desert," *The Saturday Evening Post Reader of Western Stories,* edited by E. N. Brandt (Garden City, New York, 1960), 306–332. In the paper edition of this volume, published by Popular Library in 1962, this story appears on pages 300–325.

F16. "The Devil in the Desert," *Adventures in American Literature,* edited by Sister Marie Theresa, Brother Basilian Richard, Sister Anna Mercedes, and Francis X. Connolly (New York, 1961), 103–122.

F17. "The Devil in the Desert," *The Best in Modern Catholic Reading, Volume 1,* edited by John J. Delaney (Garden City, New York, 1966), 689–714.

F18. "The Devil in the Desert," *Moments of Truth,* edited by Dan Herr and Joel Wells (Garden City, New York, 1966), 168–199.

F19. "A Discharge of Electricity," *Decisions, Decisions: Styles in Writing,* by Mary E. Whitten (New York, 1971), 149–150. A brief excerpt from Chapter IX of *Things As They Are* (1964), A31.

F20. "A Distant Harbour," *The Best Short Stories 1935 and the Yearbook of the American Short Story,* edited by Edward J. O'Brien (Boston, 1935), 217–227. This story first appeared in *Direction* (Autumn, 1934), C83.

F21. *A Distant Trumpet* (1960), A25. See F4, 22–23, and 110.

F22. "Duty," *People in Literature,* edited by L. B. Cook, Walter Loban, Ruth M. Stauffer, and Robert Freier (New York, 1957), 298–310. This story first appeared in *Collier's* (November 22, 1952), C141, and later became part of *A Distant Trumpet* (1960), A25.

F23. "Duty," *And Yet, Entirely Different,* edited by Bessie A. Stuart (Dearborn, Michigan, 1967 and 1968), 641–652. Published for the Dearborn Public Schools.

F24. *Figures in a Landscape* (1940), A14. See F49, 76–86, 98–107.

F25. "From the Royal City," *America in the Southwest: A Regional Anthology,* edited by T. M. Pearce and Telfair Hendon (Albuquerque, 1933), 305–331. This anthology reprints all of the article that originally appeared in *The Yale Review* (December, 1932), C67, and in *From the Royal City* (1936), A8. For another article in this anthology, see F49.

F26. *Great River* (1954), A19. See F27–41.

F27. "The Last Frontiersman," *Literature of Adventure,* edited by J. N. Hook, Vesta M. Parsons, Blanche E. Peavey, and Frank M. Rice (Boston, 1957), 72–78.

F28. "The Desert Fathers," *A Treasury of Catholic Reading,* edited by John Chapin (New York, 1957), 550–558.

F29. "A Wild Strain," *Westward, Westward, Westward: The Long Trail West and the Men Who Followed It,* edited by Elizabeth Abell (New York, 1958), 14–21.

F30. "Riverscape: The Rio Grande," *How to Read and Write in College: A Complete Course,* by Richard H. Dodge (New York, 1962), 190–192. The copy was missing from the Library of Congress and this reference has not been verified.

F31. "The Mountain Man," *The Frontier Experience,* edited by Robert Hine and Edwin Bingham (Belmont, California, 1963), 75–80.

F32. "Knacks and Crafts," *The United States in Literature,* edited by Walter Blair, Paul Farmer, Theodore Hornberger, and Margaret Wasson (Chicago, 1963), 622–624, 627. Previous editions were issued under the title *The Literature of the United States.* The copy was missing from the Library of Congress and the reference has not been verified.

F33. "A Wild Strain," *Introduction to Literature,* by William Eller, Betty Yvonne Welch, and Edward J. Gordon (Boston, 1964), 216–224.

F34. Excerpt from *Great River* in *The European Mind and the Discovery of a New World,* by Peter Schrag (Boston, 1965), 118–119.

F35. An excerpt from the Prologue to *Great River* in *Our Natural World: The Land and Wildlife of America as Seen and Heard by Writers Since the Country's Discovery,* edited by Hal Borland (Garden City, New York, 1965), 191–195.

F36. An excerpt from *Great River* in *Just English 1,* by Merron Chorny, Michael A. Kostek, and Phyllis E. Weston (Toronto, 1966), 139–140.

F37. "Wedding Feast," *Southwest Writers Anthology,* edited by Martin Shockley (Austin, Texas, 1967), 76–79.

F38. "Never to Return," *Colorado: A Literary Chronicle,* edited by W. Storrs Lee (New York, 1970), 1–7.

F39. "The Golden Age of Spain," *History As Literature,* edited by Orville Prescott (New York, 1970), 147–153.

F40. "The Mountain Man," *The American Frontier: Readings and Documents,* edited by Robert V. Hine and Edwin R. Bingham (Boston, 1972), 115–120.

F41. Excerpt from *Great River,* "Like Figures in a Dream: The Pueblo Indians," in *Portrait of America, Volume 1: From the Cliff Dwellers to the End of Reconstruction,* edited by Stephen B. Oates (Boston, 1973), 2–15. Included in the same volume is an excerpt from *Conquistadors in North American History* (1963), A29, that is listed as F9.

F42. Excerpt from *The Habit of Empire,* "A Winter Morning," in *The Southwest in Life and Literature,* edited by C. L. Sonnichsen (New York, 1962), 56–60. See *The Habit of Empire* (1939), A13.

F43. "A Hard Land to Win," *Son-of-a-Gun Stew: A Sampling of the South-west*, edited by Elizabeth Matchett Stover (New York, 1945), 1-4. The brief excerpt used here first appeared in its complete version as "About the Southwest" in *Southwest Review* (July, 1933), C73. Listed again as F1.

F44. "Heart Attack," *The Saturday Evening Post Stories 1955* (New York, 1955), 127-145. First appeared in *The Saturday Evening Post* (March 12, 1955), C152.

F45. *The Heroic Triad* (1970), A39. See F57-62, and 71.

F46. *Humble Powers* (1954), A20. See F12-18, 53-55, 97.

F47. "The Huntsmen," *Approaches to Literature*, edited by James Berkley (New York, 1969), 158-171. Originally appeared in *The Saturday Evening Post* as "Terror at Daybreak" (October 29, 1949), C128; reprinted under the title "The Huntsmen" in *The Peach Stone* (1967), A36. See second listing under title "Terror at Daybreak," F93; a second reprinting with this title, F48 and 95; and other listings of the story with the title "Terror at Daybreak," F87-92, and 94.

F48. "The Huntsmen," *Great Short Stories of the World: Selected by the Editors of The Reader's Digest* (Pleasantville, New York, 1972), 562-579.

F49. "The Landscape," *America in the Southwest: A Regional Anthology*, edited by T. M. Pearce and Telfair Hendon (Albuquerque, 1933), 145-146. The sketch first appeared in *Folk-Say* (1931), B3, and was reprinted as part of *Figures in a Landscape* (1940), A14. For another article reprinted in this anthology, see F25.

F50. "Litany," *The Turquoise Trail: An Anthology of New Mexico Poetry*, edited by Alice Corbin Henderson (Boston, 1928), [52]. First appeared in *Poetry* (June, 1924) as one of three poems with the editorial title "Exotics," C2.

F51. "Litany," *Signature of the Sun: Southwest Verse, 1900-1950*, edited by Mabel Major and T. M. Pearce (Albuquerque, 1950), 257.

F52. "National Honeymoon," *Collier's Best*, introduction and notes by Knox Burger (New York, 1951), 2-20. First appeared in *Collier's* (March 4, 1950), C129; reprinted in *The Peach Stone* (1967), A36.

F53. *One Red Rose for Christmas, Catholic Family Book Club* (Garden City, New York, 1957), 299-336. Appears with three other works: *Dede O'Shea*, by Peggy Goodin; *Bird of Sorrow*, by John Romaniello; and *Beyond All Horizons: Jesuits and the Missions*, edited by Thomas J. M. Burke, S.J. "One Red Rose for Christmas" was first published in *Cosmopolitan* (December, 1951), C138; it was reprinted as *One Red Rose for Christmas* (1952), A18, and in *Humble Powers* (1954), A20. For full listing, see the 1952 book publication, A18.

F54. "One Red Rose for Christmas," *Catholic Life Annual 1959*, edited by Eugene P. Willging (Milwaukee, 1958), 68-85, 100.

F55. "One Red Rose for Christmas," *The Best in Modern Catholic Reading*, Volume II, edited by John J. Delaney (Garden City, New York, 1966), 593-632.

F56. "The Other Side of the Street," *The Best Short Stories of 1931 and the Yearbook of the American Short Story*, edited by Edward J. O'Brien (New

York, 1931), 189–201. First appeared in *The Yale Review* (December, 1930), C57; reprinted in *The Peach Stone* (1967), A36.

F57. "Pages from a Rio Grande Notebook," *College English: The First Year*, edited by J. Hooper Wise, J. E. Congleton, Alton C. Morris, and John C. Hodges (New York, 1956), 33–35. First appeared in *The New York Times Book Review* (May 15, 1955), C155; reprinted as part of Book One of *The Heroic Triad* (1970), A39. For a reprinting of this article under another title, see F71.

F58. "Pages from a Rio Grande Notebook," *The Meaning in Reading, Fourth Edition*, edited by J. Hooper Wise, J. E. Congleton, and Alton C. Morris (New York, 1956), 33–35.

F59. "Pages from a Rio Grande Notebook," *Words and Ideas: A Handbook for College Writing*, by Hans P. Guth (San Francisco, 1959), 191 and 318.

F60. "Pages from a Rio Grande Notebook," *Using Prose: Reading for College Composition*, edited by Donald W. Lee and William T. Moynihan (New York, 1961), 16–20. A second edition was published in 1967 and the article appeared on pages 154–158.

F61. "Pages from a Rio Grande Notebook," *The Study of Literature*, William Eller, Ruth E. Reeves, and Edward J. Gordon (Boston, 1964), 301–305.

F62. "Pages from a Rio Grande Notebook," *A Question of Choice*, by Jean E. Heywood (Belmont, California, 1970), 73–76.

F63. "Parma Violets," *Perspectives on Sexuality: A Literary Collection*, edited by James L. Malfetti and Elizabeth M. Eidlitz (New York, 1972), 13–21. First appeared as "First Passion" in *Collier's* (December 15, 1951), C137; reprinted in *Things As They Are* (1964), A31. For another story in this collection, see F11.

F64. "Parochial School," *Short Stories from The New Yorker* (New York, 1940), 318–322. First appeared in *The New Yorker* (April 1, 1933), C71.

F65. *The Peach Stone* (1967), A36. See F2, 12–18, 47–48, 52, 56, 66–70, 73, 74, 76–86, 87–95, 98–107, and 108.

F66. "The Peach Stone," *The Best American Short Stories 1943 and the Yearbook of the American Short Story*, edited by Martha Foley (Boston, 1943), 166–186. First appeared in *The Yale Review* (June, 1942), C114; reprinted in *The Peach Stone* (1967), A36.

F67. "The Peach Stone," *The Yale Review Anthology*, edited by Wilbur Cross and Helen MacAfee (New Haven, 1942), 386–405.

F68. "The Peach Stone," *The Best of the Best American Short Stories 1915–1950*, edited by Martha Foley (Boston, 1952), 162–181.

F69. "The Peach Stone," *The Fifty Best American Short Stories 1915–1965*, edited by Martha Foley (Boston, 1965), 305–322.

F70. "The Peach Stone," *The Literature of the American West*, edited by J. Golden Taylor (Boston, 1971), 331–345. Another Paul Horgan item that appears in this anthology is listed under F111.

F71. "The Rio Grande," *Adventures in Appreciation*, edited by Laurence Perrine, Robert Jameson, Rita Silveri, G. B. Harrison, A. R. Gurney, Jr., V. S. Pritchett, Walter Loban, and Thomas M. Folds (New York, 1968), 208–211. Under this title appears a selection from "Pages from a Rio Grande

Notebook," *The New York Times Book Review* (May 15, 1955), C155. See also F57–62.

F72. *The Saintmaker's Christmas Eve, Catholic Family Book Club* (Garden City, New York, 1956), [279]–317. Appears here with three other works: *The Bond and the Free,* by Charles Dunscomb; *The Wooden Statue,* by Dorothy Mackinder; and *The Priestly Heart: The Last Chapter in the Life of an Old-Young Priest,* by the Right Reverend Maurice S. Sheehy. See *The Saintmaker's Christmas Eve* (1955), A21.

F73. "The Secret of the Tin Box," *The Saturday Evening Post Stories 1959* (Garden City, New York, 1960), 9–26. First appeared with this title in *The Saturday Evening Post* (February 28, 1959), C168; reprinted with the title "The Treasure" in *The Peach Stone* (1967), A36. Listed again as F108.

F74. "So Little Freedom," *Roundup Time: A Collection of Southwestern Writing,* edited by George Sessions Perry (New York, 1943), 49–62. First appeared in *Saturday Review* (May 16, 1942), C113; reprinted in *The Peach Stone* (1967), A36.

F75. Poems from *Songs After Lincoln,* in *Where Steel Winds Blow,* edited by Robert Cromie (New York, 1968), 23, 86–87, 103–104. Contains three poems from *Songs After Lincoln* (1965), A33: "Reviewing Negro Troops Going South Through Washington, April 26, 1864," "Pinned Down," and "Commander Death."

F76. "The Surgeon and the Nun," *The Best Short Stories 1937 and the Yearbook of the American Short Story,* edited by Edward J. O'Brien (Boston, 1937), 142–159. First appeared in *Harper's Bazaar* (December, 1936), C97; reprinted in *Figures in a Landscape* (1940), A14, and *The Peach Stone* (1967), A36.

F77. "The Surgeon and the Nun," *Great Modern Catholic Short Stories,* edited by Sister Mariella Gable, O.S.B. (New York, 1942), 51–74.

F78. "The Surgeon and the Nun," *Prose Readings: An Anthology for Catholic Colleges,* edited by the Reverend Vincent Joseph Flynn (New York, 1942), 582–601.

F79. "The Surgeon and the Nun," *They Are People: Modern Short Stories of Nuns, Monks and Priests,* edited by Sister Mariella Gable, O.S.B. (New York, 1943), 51–74.

F80. "The Surgeon and the Nun," *Southwesterners Write,* edited by T. M. Pearce and A. P. Thomason (Albuquerque, 1946), 114–134.

F81. "The Surgeon and the Nun," *A Treasury of Doctor Stories,* edited by Noah D. Fabricant and Heinz Werner (New York, 1946), 425–444.

F82. "The Surgeon and the Nun," *The New Guest-Room Book,* edited by F. J. Sheed (New York, 1957), 101–120.

F83. "The Surgeon and the Nun," *The Pageant of Literature: Modern American Prose,* edited by Brother Anthony Cyril, F.S.C. (New York, 1961), 120–138.

F84. "The Surgeon and the Nun," *Favorite Doctor Stories,* compiled by A. K. Adams (New York, 1963), 94–116.

F85. "The Surgeon and the Nun," *Doctors, Doctors, Doctors,* selected by Helen Hoke (London, 1964), 124–147.

F86. "The Surgeon and the Nun," *The Chicano: From Caricature to Self-Portrait*, edited by Edward Simmen (New York, 1971), 121–138.

F87. "Terror at Daybreak," *The Saturday Evening Post Stories 1949* (New York, 1949), 219–240. First appeared in *The Saturday Evening Post* (October 29, 1949), C128; reprinted under the title "The Huntsmen" in *The Peach Stone* (1967), A36.

F88. "Terror at Daybreak," *Stories for Here and Now*, edited by Joseph Greene and Elizabeth Abell (New York, 1951), 126–150.

F89. "Terror at Daybreak," *Our Reading Heritage: Exploring Life*, edited by Harold Wagenheim, Elizabeth Voris Brattig, and Mathew Dolkey (New York, 1956), 547–561.

F90. "Terror at Daybreak," *Writing: Unit-Lessons in Composition*, by Don P. Brown, et al. (Boston, 1964), 32. A brief excerpt.

F91. "Terror at Daybreak," *Prose and Poetry for Enjoyment, Volume 1, Short Stories*, edited by Julian L. Maline and Thomas J. Steele (Syracuse, 1965), 151–175. The copy was missing from the Library of Congress and this reference has not been verified.

F92. "Terror at Daybreak," *Approaches to Literature, Volume One: Studies in the Short Story*, edited by Julian L. Maline and James Berkley (Syracuse, 1967), 294–316.

F93. "Terror at Daybreak," *Approaches to Literature*, edited by James Berkley (New York, 1969), 158–171. Printed here under the title "The Huntsmen," the title used for the story in *The Peach Stone* (1967), A36. Listed again as F47.

F94. "Terror at Daybreak," *La Version et le vocabulaire anglais*, by J. Davit and A. Giroud (Grenoble, 1969), 184. A brief excerpt.

F95. "Terror at Daybreak," *Great Short Stories of the World: Selected by the Editors of The Reader's Digest* (Pleasantville, New York, 1972), 562–579. Printed here under the title "The Huntsmen," the title used for the story in *The Peach Stone* (1967), A36. Listed again as F48.

F96. *Things As They Are* (1964), A31. See F2, 10–11, 19, and 63.

F97. "To the Castle," *Catholic Family Book Club* (Garden City, New York, 1957), 273–311. Appears with three other works: *I Was Chaplain on the Franklin*, by Father Joseph T. O'Callahan, S.J.; *The Lively Arts of Sister Gervaise*, by John L. Bonn, S.J.; and *The Happy Grotto*, by Fulton Oursler. "To the Castle" first appeared under the title "The Soldier Who Had No Gun" in *The Saturday Evening Post* (October 13, 1951), C136; it was reprinted in *Humble Powers* (1954), A20, with the title "To the Castle."

F98. "To the Mountains," *Best Short Stories 1939 and the Yearbook of the American Short Story*, edited by Edward J. O'Brien (Boston, 1939), 109–138. The story first appeared in *The Atlantic Monthly* (January, 1938), C103; it was reprinted in *Figures in a Landscape* (1940), A14, and *The Peach Stone* (1967), A36.

F99. "To the Mountains," *Rocky Mountain Stories*, edited by Ray B. West, Jr. (Albuquerque, 1941), 7–32.

F100. "To the Mountains," *Pilgrims All: Short Stories by Contemporary Catholic Authors*, edited by Mary McKenna Curtin (Milwaukee, 1943), 1–27.

F101. "To the Mountains," *Half-a-Hundred: Tales of Great American Writers,* edited by Charles Grayson (Philadelphia, 1945), 176–199.

F102. "To the Mountains," *Stories of Our Century by Catholic Writers,* edited by John Gilland Brunini and Francis X. Connolly, with the assistance of Mary K. Connolly (Philadelphia, 1949), 39–70. A Doubleday Image Books paper edition of this collection was first published in 1955, with the story on pages 37–66.

F103. "To the Mountains," *Great American Short Stories,* edited by Wallace and Mary Stegner (New York, 1957), 423–453.

F104. "To the Mountains," *Prose and Poetry of America, Volume Three: The Modern Image of Man in Fiction (1914–),* St. Thomas More Series, edited by Julian L. Maline, S.J. and Vernon Ruland, S.J. (Syracuse, 1965), 257–285.

F105. "To the Mountains," *Great Western Short Stories,* edited by J. Golden Taylor (Palo Alto, 1967), 444–472.

F106. "To the Mountains," *The Literature of America, Volume 3: Modern Fiction,* edited by Julian L. Maline and James Berkley (Syracuse, 1967), 28–55.

F107. "To the Mountains," *New Worlds of Ideas,* edited by Glenda Richter and Clarence Irving (New York, 1969), 357–378. This version is abridged.

F108. "The Treasure," *The Saturday Evening Post Stories 1959* (Garden City, New York, 1960), 9–26. First appeared in *The Saturday Evening Post* (February 28, 1959), C168, as "The Secret of the Tin Box," the title used in this anthology. When reprinted in *The Peach Stone* (1967), A36, the title "The Treasure" was used. Listed again under F73.

F109. "The Trunk," *O. Henry Memorial Award: Prize Stories of 1936,* selected and edited by Harry Hansen (Garden City, New York, 1936), 243–250. First appeared in *Mademoiselle* (November, 1935), C91.

F110. "Water in the Wilderness," *In Other Days,* edited by Frances T. Humphreville (Chicago, 1956), 212–237. First appeared in *Collier's* (January 3, 1953), C142; the story later became part of *A Distant Trumpet* (1960), A25.

F111. "The Western Novel—A Symposium," *The Literature of the American West,* edited by J. Golden Taylor (Boston, 1971), 22–46. This symposium first appeared in *South Dakota Review* (Autumn, 1964), C186. Paul Horgan's written answers to the questions appear in this anthology on pages 40–44. A story by Paul Horgan also used in this anthology is listed under F70.

F112. *Whitewater, Reader's Digest Condensed Books* (Pleasantville, New York, 1970), 317–489. There is "A Letter from the Author" on pages 488–489. See *Whitewater* (1970), A41.

F113. An excerpt from *Whitewater,* in *Harbrace College Handbook,* by John Hodges and Mary Whitten (New York, 1972), 356–357.